THE TEACHER
THE PUPIL
AND
THE WIFE

C A Rees

The Teacher, the Pupil and the Wife
Copyright © 2021 by C A Rees

All rights reserved. No part of this book may be used or reproduced in any manner whatsoever including Internet usage, without written permission of the author.

This is a work of fiction. The names, characters, places, or events used in this book are the product of the author's imagination or used fictitiously. Any resemblance to actual people, alive or deceased, events or locales is completely coincidental.

Book design by Maureen Cutajar
www.gopublished.com

Print ISBN: 978-0-6489021-1-9
E-book ISBN: 978-0-6489021-0-2

My thanks to Gaye and Maggie for getting me across the finishing line.

To my family, my gratitude for your love, patience and encouragement along the way.

1

Infidelities

As he turned off the ignition, a gust of wind picked up the leaflet and dumped it in the middle of the car windscreen. Rays of late afternoon sunlight backlit the bold type. He deciphered two words: *VIETNAM* and *OUT*.

By a mere coincidence of birth, Brad Emery had dodged the call up. If he'd been born a day earlier he'd be a conscript in the Australian Army. Couldn't imagine himself as a soldier. Teaching kids in high school was tough enough, but at least they didn't shoot at you. Johnno had lucked out, poor bastard. His birthday had come out of the draw. Two years ago now. Maybe he was back home already. Neither of them had ever written. What would you say?

It was six-fifteen as he strode to the library and scanned the congregation of bowed heads. A bit of divine intervention wouldn't go astray, he decided, particularly if this assignment was going to be on time. So far he'd been lucky. He'd made deadlines by the skin of his teeth, but how long could it go on? And for how long would Emma swallow the alibis that he kept feeding her, like morsels of food, to satisfy her appetite for an explanation of his absence? How long before she'd wake-up to what he was doing? And then what?

He laid claim to an empty desk in the middle of the room as far away from the distractions of a window as possible. Emma had warned against keeping a biro in his pocket. He'd ruined one shirt already. Nevertheless he persisted, out of habit or pig-headedness he wasn't sure. With the pen now held firmly between the index finger and thumb of his left hand, he squared off the foolscap pad and began to write.

He'd composed the opening paragraph in his head as he drove to the library so the words came easily. Buggered if they didn't overflow the tip of his pen, tumbling onto the page faster than he could get them there.

His hand began to cramp so he sat back, glanced at the clock. Forty-seven minutes. Hallelujah. It had been a while since he'd worked with such intensity and focus. Lately he'd found it hard to concentrate on anything much at all. It was as if his head had been taken over by a bunch of squatters and he couldn't evict them. They sat around all day debating if he was ever going to sort out his crap marriage.

By seven o'clock he'd filled another page. Not bad. Could have been alone in the room, the silence so complete. He arched his back, stretched his arms to the ceiling and contemplated the fluorescent lights. When he looked down again, they were still there; an afterimage of phosphorescent grubs crawling along the desk. Back to the text book for inspiration, eyes moving pendulum-like across the page. He'd sworn to work uninterrupted for three hours but be buggered if Emma wasn't pushing her way back in, head space consumed. Determined, he stared at the words and waited.

The tap, tap of his pen on the desktop got the attention of the girl in front. She turned around and shot him a black look from underneath her mop of hair. No chance now, he'd lost it completely. Would have liked to make it to half way, get in ninety minutes of solid work, but they'd both stuffed it for him. Emma and the bird in front. He dropped his gear into the open briefcase and watched for a reaction as the lock snapped shut.

His footsteps echoed in the empty stairwell. Outside, the night felt fresh after the fug of the library. Brad paused to take the air into his lungs and then let it go, along with some of his frustration and disappointment at his inability to keep a promise to himself. Maybe he'd gone at it too hard, too fast tonight? Like heavy rain after a drought. The earth's too dry to soak it up. You need a fine drizzle, not a bloody flood.

August chill was still hanging around although it was the second week of September. He wrenched a jumper out of his bag, arms in first then over his head in one go. Legs never felt the cold. Shorts and long socks all year round and why hide one of your best features?

"Brad Emery. How you doing?"

"Good mate. You?" It was Martin Tierney. Hadn't seen much of him since he married Kerry. A shit hot salesman, Brad remembered. Worked in one of the car yards on Parramatta Road.

"Yeah, okay mate. Married life and all that. Join me for a schooner?"

"Not tonight, mate. Gotta get home."

"Emma getting suspicious eh?"

"Sorry?"

"Seen you a couple of times in the pub."

Brad looked to the ground and fumbled with his car keys in his pocket.

"Hey, cool it Brad mate." Martin tapped his finger to his nose. "I get it. Man's gotta survive."

"Maybe another time," Brad mumbled "bit caught up at the moment."

"Sure, and no worries mate." Martin was still tapping his nose. "Mum's the word. Let's get together real soon."

A cursory wave of a hand, they turned and walked away in opposite directions.

Fuck. How much did he know? Could be all bluff but this was too close to home. While he sat in the car waiting for his heart rate to return to normal and his breathing to slow, he decided, *no more*.

There had been too many missed lectures and he was getting too good at it, not the study, but pulling the chicks. Too easy.

At least he'd be home early. That should put a smile on Emma's face. This morning he told her he'd be in the library till late researching his essay. It was a lie, an alibi he'd used before when he knew that he had no intention of going anywhere near the library. He could have gone home, there was no research to do, but he didn't want her snooping around while he worked, asking if he needed a cup of tea or more food. Saying it this time had been different. He could look straight at her and the words didn't falter.

As he drove to the southern exit of the university grounds, the headlights picked up the hand-pitched sandstone blocks of the buildings that he loved. The architecture of the Grand Hall never failed to inspire him – majestic and ancient. He nudged the car out onto the main road and headed towards home. As usual, King Street was chock-a-block. Would stop and start all the way to the bloody highway at this hour.

Seven minutes at the second set of lights. Green had come and gone and he still hadn't moved. Should have gone with Martin, found out what he knew. He wasn't bad company after a couple of beers. It was the sweaty, wet-fish handshake that put you off. If he stopped for a quick drink and let the traffic clear, he'd be no worse off.

Just one schooner – a pledge to himself – and the parking spot was there waiting, too easy. A cacophony of voices rose above the cloud of smoke, drinkers spilling onto the footpath. It was a fight to get to the bar, treading on feet while relishing the body heat and the softness of a breast up against his chest, or a buttock that pressed into his crotch. He was aware of being sized up by every chick he passed.

"Schooner of Toohey's thanks love," he shouted over the shoulder that blocked his way. The barmaid exchanged a dripping glass for his fiver and tossed the change onto the counter.

He eased forward then turned around, his back against the counter, one foot on the brass rail and savoured the beer, watching the flirting and the pairing off. It turned him on – the cocking of a head, tongues lingering around moistened lips, a hot breath blowing into an eager ear. He watched a hand slide down a bare arm, pause, then tentatively slide lower to fondle a firm arse cheek. No resistance, rather a subtle arching of the spine, a subtle push back into the grasping fingers.

He drained his glass and, through half-closed eyes, watched a chick making her way towards him, maybe to the bar? Nope. She stopped short and her leg pressed against his.

He could have put his empty glass down, wedged past her and walked back to the car where his wedding ring lay in the glove box. Instead he stood his ground. What do they tell the druggies? Dissociate yourself from the people and places of your past life; don't put temptation in your way. His mistake had been coming into a pub in the first place. When the craving took hold, the desire to fuck was stronger than any desire he had to be true to his wife.

"You look like you needed that," the girl said as he added his glass to a pile of empties. She was wearing a dress tied at the back of her neck, revealing bare shoulders. She saw him look and her hand moved, as if to check the knot was secure.

"I'm having another. Can I get you one?" he asked.

"Don't drink beer, sorry." She smiled coyly.

"Then what is it?"

"Red wine please."

He liked the look of her which was surprising because she wasn't his type. Boyishly short hair, a nose honed to an acute angle and her narrow mouth sat above a receding chin. Brad preferred a softer countenance and longer hair but he decided that cropped short was the only option for her. It suited the economy of her features and he gave her points for not attempting to be fashionable.

"Like your hair." he said

"Thanks, just had it cut."

"Was it long?"

"Yes, but it made my face look too thin".

He nodded in agreement. "Looks good like that. So does the

rest of you." An appreciative smile spread across her spare lips. She was so small that he imagined he could wrap his hands around the tops of her soft thighs and his fingers would touch. He'd need to be gentle with her. The way you handle delicate porcelain. They made small talk, chatted a bit about surfing. She knew the moves. They got onto education and she had a lot to say about the lousy pay for teachers in Australia. Suggested he go to Canada where they earned twice as much. Brad said he'd look into it.

It took a total of ten minutes to find out she had her own flat and two more glasses of wine to get her back there. They both knew what they were going to do but he didn't want to risk her going off the boil, so he caressed her back, his fingers running along her spine as they walked side by side up the stairwell to her front door. She handed him the key and he ushered her in.

Sometimes they liked to start away from the bedroom and he wanted to give her the option, so he slumped down on the Nite-n-Day, loosened his tie and patted the space next to him. Not this one. She hauled him up with two hands and led him down the passageway with her fingers to her lips. So easy, nearly a turn off, but not quite.

"Flatmate," she whispered pointing to a locked door. He scrutinised her body in the half light. She looked like a young boy with small breasts. Her movements, however, were fluid and feminine and he wondered if she could be a dancer. He'd read in a *Playboy*, they could do the splits standing up and maybe he could enter her from that position. Just walk right in.

She turned the brass knob of the bedroom door then reached for the light switch cord.

He reached over and pulled her hand away. "I don't think we need that."

"Can do it with your eyes closed I bet," she joked as she undid the bow at the back of her neck and let the dress drop to the floor. Her nipples gleamed like brown pennies in the soft glow from the street lights. He was right about her shape – lean and taut, not womanly.

The bed was strewn with cushions in a jumble of colours. She threw them onto the floor, then tossed back the velveteen cover. She watched as he pulled his jumper and shirt over his head in one go, and laughed as he folded them neatly alongside the pile of crumpled clothes that lay on the chair in the corner. He sat atop them to wedge his shoes off and stuffed his socks inside, placing them against the wall – rummaging under the bed, or amongst dishevelled sheets for misplaced clothing, was a bad end to a good night. As he undid his belt he turned around to allow her time to admire his body and saw her hand nestled between her legs. Now he was having trouble getting the zip over his erection.

"You want any help?" she teased.

"Think I can manage," he chuckled as he squirmed his way free.

He sat by her where she lay and began to kiss her neck, at the same time taking her left nipple between his thumb and forefinger and moulding it gently but firmly. The skin puckered and her limbs twitched and her body turned this way and that, as if he were a puppeteer pulling the strings. When he placed his full lips over her small mouth she opened wide for him. He replaced her hand with his own. She was ready, but he wasn't – not quite. He needed her to plead, to beg him, and so he lingered until she did as he asked. Their movements were at first gentle, then more urgent.

"You're good, very good," he whispered, then silence as his head reared up, his breath stilled and he saw the blinding light that came before the sweet moment of oblivion.

When he opened his eyes she was staring at him and he felt exposed, so he turned away. He watched as she fumbled in the drawer for a packet of cigarettes.

"Mind if I smoke?"

"Wouldn't mind a drag myself," he replied.

The flame cast a shadow on the walls as she held the match between her fingertips, then with a shake of her wrist tossed it into the half full ashtray. The butt was shared back and forth, intermittent sucking the only sound in the still night air. When it burned down completely, he got up. She stayed as she was, a sheet draped over her thighs, breasts bare and lit up for the second time. Almond eyes followed as he retrieved his clothes and with his back turned, began to dress. He didn't try to make conversation. Never did afterwards. It was over and there was no point and, usually, they were all right about it.

He tucked his shirt in, tightened his belt then moved to the side of the bed. Bending over, he propped her up with a second pillow before kissing her cheek. As his fingers wrapped around the door knob, he turned and saw the cigarette tip moving from side to side – a goodbye streak of amber light in the darkness.

It occurred to him as he scurried along the cramped back streets, that it might be worth trying to hook up with her once more, to see if she could, in fact, do the splits standing up. It had seemed too much to ask first time round.

As the car motor kicked over, he turned on the radio to drown out the noise in his head. The squatters were back in there, this time going full bore, mocking his inability to keep his fly done up. Carole King was singing *It's Too Late, Baby. Spot on Carole*, he thought, as he tapped out the rhythm on the steering wheel and made for home.

The garage door squealed as he hauled it open. Was supposed to oil the bloody thing weeks ago after the neighbours complained. Emma would still be awake and as usual, she wouldn't suspect a damn thing. That infuriated him. If she wanted him home more, she should have done her bit and kept tabs on him. As he put his key into the lock he heard the scramble from inside, as the door snagged on the security chain

"Coming. Hang on." He steeled himself for the pink corduroy dressing gown and the fluffy pink slippers.

"Hi, you're later than you thought."

"Yeah I am a bit. Sorry. Had a run on and kind of lost track of time. Got through a bit though." His cheek felt the brush of her lips as he passed by. "Might have a shower. I feel grotty."

The door opened as he was drying off. She handed him his pyjamas.

"Casserole's on the table. I'm going to read for a bit. See you in bed? "

'Yeah, I won't be long. Leave the tele on will you?"

As he mopped up the last of the gravy with a slice of bread he thought about the first time he couldn't get a hard-on with Emma. He'd freaked out thinking his old fellow had carked it. But he soon confirmed that wasn't the problem.

Emma missed it. He knew she did because he found a book under her side of the bed with tips about how to seduce your husband. She started showering before bed, even bought a negligee.

The bedroom light went off just as *The Late Nite Show* came on. He turned the sound down, then waited another fifteen minutes before making his way to the bedroom. As he pulled the blankets around his chin, she rolled over and laid her hand on his chest but expected nothing more. He was playing a double part in a real-life drama. Exhausted, sleep drew itself around him like a curtain at the end of the first act.

The whistle of the kettle woke him, then the sound of cupboard doors opening and closing. Every time it was like this, waves of remorse washing away the rapture of the night before. He shook his head to get rid of the shame, hauled himself upright, swung his legs onto the floor and headed for the kitchen. She was already dressed.

"Morning sleepyhead. It's late, can you eat now? Greg'll be here any minute."

"Yeah, guess so." He sat at the table and watched her break eggs into a bowl. "You look nice Emma." She was wearing the blue and white striped shift she had been working on for the last few weeks. He jumped when the toast popped. The pottery vase she had made sat in the middle of the table and held a bunch of dried grasses she had collected from the sand hills. He twirled a stalk of paspalum between his thumb and forefinger.

"You still half asleep?" She laid his eggs and toast on the table. The sound of a horn bleating.

"That's Greg. Got to go. Leave the dishes, see you tonight. Love you." She pecked him on the cheek, grabbed her bag and was out the door. He watched through the window – running, the sound of the car door shutting and she was gone.

School didn't start for another hour, so he poured himself a second cup of tea. In the V neck of her new dress Emma had been wearing the locket he had given her their first Christmas together. Been too embarrassed to take it to the engraver himself and had to get his sister to do it. *Emma, you are my life now, with all my love, Brad.* He laid his head in his hands as the loss of that love bore down on him.

He remembered himself as a child, observing his father through the glass walls of the greenhouse, big hands deep in dark, loamy soil. Brad watched as this man he hardly knew tended two sick and dying orchids that a friend had passed on, rather than abandoning them to the compost heap. His father removed the dead and decaying leaves, then mixed and prepared a new bed of soil and fertilizer. He talked tenderly to the plants as he introduced them to their new home, and slowly, over the following weeks, they had recovered.

Brad wondered if he could revive his love for Emma in the same way his father had brought new life to the orchids.

2

Conscripted

"GET A LOOK AT THIS." Steve Thompson passed the leaflet to his son then sat quietly, hands wrapped around his coffee cup, as John read one side then the other.

"Who's Bertrand Russell, Dad?"

"A British intellectual and political commentator."

John handed the pamphlet to his mother who skimmed the headlines before tossing it into the middle of the table. "If what he is saying is right, this is a bad war and we shouldn't be there at all," she said tersely.

"Well dear, John's got to register, he's nearly twenty. He could get called up. What then? You think he should be a conscientious objector? You really think Mr Russell is right? You think we can't trust our government? Is America really in it for the money?"

"I hate it when you do that Steven – just ask questions."

"Simply trying to be balanced, love." When he became 'Steven' and not 'Steve' it was time to back off.

"Balanced! Nothing balanced about a war that's all about Yankee dollars and has nothing to do with our being safe. It's hideous if we're there just to keep America's economy ticking over. All that rubbish about reds under our beds. All those young men who've been killed."

"I agree Laura, but there's still a lot of people whose opinion I admire, who support our involvement. It's a hard call, dear." Mr Thompson sipped his coffee. "What do you think son?"

John twirled the handle of the sugar spoon while his parents waited for his answer then pushed the bowl to one side and met his father's gaze.

"I agree with Dad, Mum. I don't know for sure that we *shouldn't* be there so I guess I don't have the conviction to be a conscientious objector. If I get posted to Vietnam, I'll give you the lowdown from the inside. On the spot coverage so to speak."

Mr. Thompson was quietly proud of his son's response. His own sense of duty to his country was stronger than any private doubts he had about the war.

"Well, let's hope it never comes to that," he said. No point in worrying about something we've got no control over. We'll know soon enough. Lovely dinner Laura. You've excelled once again." A kiss to the back of his wife's head as he made his way to the front verandah for a quiet smoke. *No control whatsoever*, Mr. Thompson mused to himself as he lit up. *It is literally the luck of the draw as to who gets called up, who goes to fight and who stays.* Birthdates were picked from the same barrel that had been used to draw the Tattersalls Lottery. It was three weeks later that John's number rolled out.

Mrs Thompson checked for mail at the same time each day. Often her trip to the letterbox was fruitless but she enjoyed the walk to the front gate and back. On this particular day she quickened her pace when she spied what she thought was the corner of a brown envelope. Her hands trembled as she retrieved it and saw John's name typed in capital letters on the front. On the back, there it was, plain as day, in cursive script – *Department of Labour and National Service*. She turned on her heel and walked quickly back inside. After placing the envelope on the hall table where John would see it as he came through the door, she retreated to her kitchen, made a cup of strong, sweet tea, added a dash of brandy and sat down to wait.

"Hi Mum. That for me?" John asked pointing to the envelope. His mother was standing now, at the end of the hallway, tea towel in hand.

"Yes son. You better see what's inside."

He laid his car keys down, picked it up and ripped open the seal. His eyes scanned the words:

I am writing to inform you in relation to your call-up for national service, that you are required, in accordance with the provisions of The National Service Act, to submit yourself to a medical examination, before a Medical Board.

"John, it's the army isn't it, John?" His mother was silhouetted in the rays of the sinking sun that streamed through the west-facing window, her face hidden in the darkness.

"Got to go for a medical, Mum." John forced a smile. "Think Dad'll give me the day off?"

"How can they do this?" She shook her head in disbelief. "Just order you around like that?"

"Well they can Mum and they have. What's for dinner, anything good?"

She stood her ground as he walked past and ignored the conciliatory pat on the back. "Don't we live in a democracy? You're not even old enough to vote for heaven's sake!"

"Nothing we can do, Mum."

"What else did they say?" She chased after him. "Can I have it? The letter? Please Son?"

Her hand shook as she took it from him. "The medical's in three weeks, John!" Her bottom lip trembled.

"I know Mum. Come on, it's okay. What've you cooked up for tonight?"

"I'm going to ring your father," she said flapping the paper in the air. "There must be something he can do."

"Leave off, Mum, give it here. Dad'll be home soon enough, and anyway, we've talked about this. I've got to go." He left her then, head bent, re-reading the order to report to Sydney District Employment Office, Grace Building, 77 York Street, for his medical. Up the stairs, two at a time, he hung his suit on the valet and exchanged it for a pair of jeans and T-shirt. Silent doubts had been surfacing for a while but had been easy to ignore. Not anymore. He was part of this war now. A week after the medical, he received notice that he was to undergo training at Singleton Army Base.

During the remaining days, his mother never failed to make physical contact – a rub on the arm, a touch to the base of his neck, a hand to his cheek. He put up with it for her sake. She prepared his favourite meals: Steak Dianne, Beef Wellington, chocolate mousse, pavlovas heaped with strawberries and cream. A labour of love and a diversion from her own anxieties. John didn't complain. He'd work the weight off soon enough. His father displayed his usual pragmatism and set about finding a replacement sales manager. It wouldn't be easy. John was good at his job.

The gang gave him a piss-up at the pub. He was the only bloke now without a partner. Barney was married to the voluptuous Bernadette, Tony to Michelle and Darren was engaged to Roslyn. Emma and Brad were there. He hadn't seen them since their wedding. If she'd married him instead of Brad, he wouldn't be going to Vietnam. As a married bloke, he'd be exempt. Not that he'd have needed an excuse to marry Emma, if she'd been at all interested.

The night before he left there was a dinner for the family and close friends Sam and Lee Thurgood. The Thompson and Thurgood kids had grown up together and the wives continued to find time for a get together over a cup of tea. Sam and Steve Thompson still met up at the club on Saturdays, both in and out of football season.

It was a struggle to keep the mood lively. Sensing the need to bring the evening to a close, Mr Thompson proposed a toast:

"To John. I know you will do your duty, Son and you will make us proud. I don't have to ask for that. What I do ask is that you come back to us," his voice faltered, "because you are the most precious thing in our life."

His mother broke down and was ushered into the kitchen where she was ably consoled by John's grandmother, who had lost a husband in the Korean War. There was a lot of backslapping from Sam who thought that fighting was a good way to end most conflicts.

Early the next morning John spotted his father on the verandah, cigarette in hand. He had never seen his Dad light up before breakfast. His mother worked quietly in the kitchen as her men showered and dressed. The family walked to the garage in silence. John sat in the front seat of the Falcon with his father. There were to be no long goodbyes. That was agreed. His mother was unusually restrained and sat quietly in the back. He wondered if she had taken a Valium.

"Bye Mum, bye Dad." He got out as soon as the Falcon pulled into the kerb, retrieved his suitcase from the boot, strode in the direction of the station steps and didn't look back. The trip to camp took John most of the day.

Later that afternoon he was crouched down, packing his gear into a locker when a large hand appeared in front of his face.

"G'day mate."

A bloke with a neck as wide as his head towered above him, "Pete Barker."

"John Thompson." He jumped up and offered his hand in return. "You a regular?" Looked like he could be. Khaki was his colour and John was sure that those enormous feet had never worn anything but boots.

"Nah, got pulled in the lottery mate. You too?"

"Yeah. Only bloody thing I've ever won. Want a fag?"

They squatted on the ground outside the hut, squinting into the afternoon sun.

Pete pulled a packet of tobacco and papers from his pocket. He had the rolly ready in seconds.

John lit his Winston and held out a dwindling match for Pete. "You from the country?" he asked, blowing smoke from his nostrils.

"Yeh, out West." No one knew where Hilltop was. "How'd ya guess?" Pete was tracing a pattern in the dry dust with his free hand.

"Just highly intelligent and intuitive."

"Sounds like bullshit to me," Pete said as he rose up to his full six foot two.

"Reckon, you might be right, mate." Their cigarette butts skidded under the hut as they strolled back inside.

This was the first day of their ten weeks corps training. Six weeks jungle training at Canungra would follow. They made an unlikely duo, the pretty city boy and the rough country kid, but it worked from the get-go and they stuck together for the next two years. Two of the sixteen 'Nashos' amongst the 34 members of their platoon.

John had never used a gun, but for Pete, shootin' was like shavin' and he was used to living rough. He adapted well to army life whereas John never quite got the hang of it. Not that he failed to pass muster. His unease was something that Pete sensed. John was a fish out of water when it came to fighting and killing. He was the only soldier he knew who wore a peace symbol amongst his dog tags.

"I'm buggered mate!" John said as he fell into his bunk at the end of a 10-mile pack run.

"Too much easy life Johnno. Going outside for a fag. You comin'?"

"Nah mate. Give this one a miss."

Pete didn't mind the hard yakka. But some of the instructions made no sense and they had to follow them anyway, just do what they were told. That was the worst of it – for them both.

"Jesus, mate." John said. "Does the way I fold my socks make any difference to winning the bloody war?"

But orders were orders and had to be obeyed unquestioningly. Do as you're told and you might just survive. Think like a civvy and you were dead meat. By the time they left for Vietnam, what started out as useless discipline began to make sense and the questions ceased.

There had been no visible signs of affection between the two mates in their time together – unless you could count watching each other's back for weeks on end in the pitch black of a jungle night where not even your hand is visible in front of your face. There were hours when sleep wouldn't come and John lay still and silent, sure that no one else was awake, until the glow of a cigarette approached from the direction of Pete's stretcher. They got to know what the other was thinking without speaking, because words could be heard by the Vietcong but thoughts couldn't. Card games that lasted five hours were played in silence. Pete usually won.

They celebrated their twenty-first birthdays on the same day in the jungle and began the countdown to the day of their discharge.

3

Lace Corsets and Red Ribbons

"Hey mate! Got time for that beer tonight?" Brad looked around to see Martin slouched against the entrance to the library, his arms crossed and one leg swung over the other.

"I was seriously going to study mate. Exams coming up."

"One won't hurt you. Come on, I've been waiting for twenty minutes."

Brad checked his watch. "Just one then, but I'm a bit light on at the moment. Didn't expect to be doing this."

"No problem," Martin reassured him. "I sprung it on you after all."

They walked to the Lansdowne and Martin ordered two schooners. "Cheers." Brad watched as he wiped the foam from his upper lip, then tapped his cigarette on the table top.

Martin broke the silence. "Saw you again at the pub the other night. You left with that chick."

Brad stalled with a swig of his beer and a drag on his cigarette.

"As I said, you getting a bit on the side mate. Doesn't worry me." Martin leaned in and nudged Brad with his elbow. "Don't mind a dabble myself. Feel I'm entitled, if I can't get it at home.

Same for you?"

"In a way." Brad shrugged.

"Yeah, I know how it is. Another schooner?"

"Sure. Why not." He needed to see where this was going.

Martin carried two overflowing glasses back to the table. "Listen. A tip mate: if you're going to get a bit on the side it should be the best bits."

"Only kind, I reckon."

"So, I'm right then," Martin went on, "you'd be interested in a bit of high class fun, eh?" His legs were banging together under the table.

Brad leaned back in the chair, balanced it on the two spindles and took a drag on his cigarette. "What you got in mind?" No point in upsetting the bloke.

"Well, you see mate," he said leaning in closer, "judging by what I saw the other night, you pull chicks pretty easy." He held up his hand to silence Brad's interjection. "No, you don't have to answer, just hear me out. I don't, you see."

Brad tried to see Martin from a female perspective. Of significance was his height, or lack of it. But Brad knew some short guys who pulled chicks. They weren't, however, wearing black rimmed glasses reminiscent of Clark Kent's. The lenses of Martin's spectacles were as thick as the bottom of Coke bottles. If he took them off, he would be as blind as a bat. His hair, poor bloke, ranked high in the ugly stakes. It was lank and greasy and it kept falling over his face and probably caused the acne on his forehead. He could do something about that – like wash it. But there wasn't a thing he could do about the lack of proportion in his features. His lips were full, and appeared bloated, rather than voluptuous. His nose in contrast, was so flat that Brad wondered how his Coke bottles managed to stay in place.

"Haven't got your suave good looks buddy." Martin confided as if it were a secret.

Brad squirmed. Should he agree or be generous and object? Before he had made up his mind, Martin continued.

"So, I have to think outside the square."

"You've lost me," Brad interrupted.

"Well, I found this place see. Amazing women. *Playboy* centrefolds, all of them."

Brad wondered which pub.

"The things they know, just blow your mind."

"Sounds like you found paradise mate."

"I think I have." Martin put down his empty glass and leaned forward. "You want to join me in paradise?"

"What… now you mean?"

"Yeah. Why not?"

Brad glanced at his watch.

"What time you expected home?"

"Couple of hours, but I told you, I've got to hit the books." He was clinging to his last vestige of willpower.

"Couple of hours'll do it." Martin stood up, slapped Brad on the back then hoisted up his trousers, like a man ready for work. "Follow me. We'll take my car." Without waiting for an answer, he headed out the door and along the street at a canter. Brad grabbed his bag and made chase, determined to head him off and make his apologies. Then Martin stopped in front of a new MG Midget.

"Shit mate. Like your wheels."

"Want to drive?" He tossed Brad the keys. "Straight up George Street then head for the Cross."

Brad hoisted his briefcase into the back and slid into the driver's seat. "Soft leather, eh."

"Like the inside of a woman's thigh, mate," Martin said.

He pushed the seat back four inches, turned the key and gave her a rev in neutral, savouring the rumble of the twin SU carburettors. Into first, then merge gently into the traffic. By the time he got to fourth gear he'd hit William Street, so he flattened the accelerator for the run up the hill and was doing one hundred and twenty as he approached the Coca-Cola sign.

"You need to chuck a left. Then a right," Martin called over the noise of the engine.

Brad used the gears rather than the brakes to slow into the corners.

"Now to the end of the street. Park anywhere." They listened reverently to the click, click of the motor as the metal cooled and contracted. "What d'ya think? Goes well, doesn't she?"

"Like a dream mate. Thanks for letting me give her a run. Where are we anyway?"

"Outside paradise mate. Over there." He pointed to a sandstone brick house with a shiny black door.

"That someone's house?"

"Not exactly."

What? It's a brothel?"

"Well kinda. It's more like a pleasure palace."

"Don't think so, mate. Not my scene."

"Why not? I'll pay, okay?" Martin could see he had overcome one objection so he kept pitching. "Look, you can just have a drink. Grog's free. Have a look around. No one's going to make you do anything you don't want. Just a friendly chat with the girls if that's all you're up for." He unfastened his seat belt. Brad followed his lead As they crossed the road, Martin draped his arm around his mate's shoulder.

"Wait till you eyeball these babes. Blow your mind," he said. "What they don't know about screwing isn't worth knowing. One of them's got this trick she does with a string of beads."

They reached the front door and Martin rang the bell while smiling into the peep hole.

"She puts one bead in at a time." He continued, hands in pocket, bouncing up and down on the balls of his feet. "You don't feel a thing, then just as you start to come, she pulls them out. Real quick. Never felt anything like it."

Brad nodded his head and smiled, hoping that Martin wouldn't cotton on to the fact that he had no idea what he was talking about. As the door opened, the penny dropped and Brad's sphincter muscle contracted involuntarily.

"No need to look so terrified, handsome, we're all very friendly in here." A woman of about forty stood before them, her large breasts thrusting out of a low-cut blouse. "Come in gentlemen."

Brad grinned to disguise his concern that they might be a little too friendly for his liking. He squeezed past, excusing himself. She would have been a real looker when she was young but was past it now. He presumed correctly that she ran the place. A grand archway, hung with heavy black drapes, opened into a parlour and reminded him of a scene from a movie. The lights from the chandelier glinted in the gilt-edged wall mirrors. Seated on red velvet lounges were guys, young and old, a drink in one hand and the other caressing the leg of the girl sitting next to them.

Two chicks got up from the antique chairs in the corner when the madam entered. They were both lookers. "Bridgette's missed you, Martin," she said. The blond one thrust a drink into his hand.

Brad's girl was small and her long straight hair fell over one shoulder. She wore a black lace corset, with a red ribbon trim around the plunging neckline. Her breasts were white and plump as was the skin that peeked from each side of her red suspender belt holding up the sexiest fishnet stockings he had ever seen.

"Beer or Bourbon, honey?" Her heart-shaped lips purred at him.

"Beer, I guess. Every year's a good one, eh?" He accepted the tall glass then allowed himself to be led to a chaise longue on his left. Martin was already nuzzling into Bridgette, whose legs, which went on forever, were draped over his lap.

Brad checked his girl out for beads. She wasn't wearing any so he settled back for the time being and swallowed half his beer in an open gullet. She was a good talker. They chatted a bit about the beach. She liked Avalon. He told her he was a teacher and talked about Canada, the extra money, and she said he should go. Well informed, easy going and she was classy with it. Not what he had expected. He imagined young tarts or old scrubbers. He'd certainly got that wrong.

Bridgette uncrossed her legs and took Martin's hand. Without a backward glance, he followed her up the stairs. Brad's girl took their departure as her cue.

"Shall we?" she said, focusing her violet eyes on his and cocking her head to one side as Martin disappeared around a corner at the end of a long corridor.

"Sure," he replied as he took her outstretched hand, keen to see if a bought one was any better than one he got for free.

"In here honey," she sighed pulling him in along the corridor in the opposite direction to Martin. A door opened to a small room with a big bed. "You make yourself comfortable and I'll be back in a jiffy."

He did as he was told, sat back on the black satin bedspread and took a quick gander around the room for beads, just to be sure.

"You okay?" she said coming back into the room. "I'm not going to bite. Unless you want me to, that is."

"It's just that I'm usually the one calling the shots. This is a bit different for me."

"We can do this any way you want," she said as she crawled along the bed towards him. Trouble was, he wasn't sure what he wanted. Hadn't been for a long time. What he really fancied was to sit and talk awhile, the way they had downstairs.

She started to undo the buttons on his shirt. "Let's get this show on the road, shall we?"

He lay back and let her take the lead and it was over in minutes and as far as he was concerned, not worth paying for. "Mind if I smoke?" he asked.

"Be surprised if you didn't." She handed him an ashtray.

"You wondering what I'm doing here? Married and all that." He held up his left hand and grinned. "Forgot to take off my ring, didn't I."

"None of my business, love. Anyway, we get lots of married blokes. Frigid wives and all that."

"Not my problem. She's not frigid, I mean." He took several more drags waiting for her to answer. "You taught not to ask questions?"

"Up to you if you want to talk. I'm here for whatever you want. We've got time. You were quick off the mark. Thought it might have been a while for you."

"With my wife, yeah. Can't get it up with her. You think that's normal?"

"Nothing's strange to me, honey. If that's what it is for you I'm sorry. But don't ask me what's normal."

"You reckon it might be something to do with my childhood?"

"Hey, this is a bed, not a couch. You get molested or something?"

"God no. Oldies were perfect. Never did anything wrong. Expected me to be the same but looks like I haven't made the grade."

"You can't help it if she doesn't turn you on."

"Yeah. Should never have got married. They really liked her, you see. The oldies. She and my Mum were thick as thieves. That's when we got engaged. Too late to back out after that."

"So, you going to keep pretending forever?"

"Probably, and fuck myself silly with other women. Sounds like a fun life, eh?"

A knock on the door. "You coming mate?" A snigger. "Get your arse downstairs, Brad my boy."

She leaned across the bed and kissed him for the first time that night. "For luck. Hope it works out for you."

"Yeah, thanks."

"Off you go. I've got some cleaning up to do."

Martin was in the reception, counting fifty-dollar bills into the hand of the madam. He turned to Brad as he stuffed his wallet into the back pocket of his trousers.

"What d'ya reckon? Worth every penny, eh mate?" Here was a happy man.

"You're right about that." Then again, he hadn't paid the bill. They strutted, side by side, along the road and narrowly missed being sideswiped by a passing car.

"That was close," Brad said.

"Yeah, but if you've got to go, now would be a good time, with a big smile on our faces." Martin slid into the driver's side. "What'd I tell you. Magic, aren't they. *Playboy* babes." He adjusted the seat and started the motor.

"Yeah, sure are. Thanks mate." Brad meant it. "And listen, this stays between you and me, right?"

"Are you kidding? We're in this together buddy. Listen, I'm starving, what about you. A good screw always makes me hungry. Big, juicy steak coming up."

"I don't have any coin, mate. I told you."

"Forget it. The night's on me. What d'ya reckon?"

A sandwich with some year eleven students was all Brad had eaten since breakfast and now he was running on low. He checked his watch. Might still make it home on time if they were quick.

"Yeah, why not."

"Yeeha!" Martin yelled as he did a tyre-squealing U turn and headed back into the heart of the Cross to park in the main drag. Together they strolled to the Bourbon Bar and Grill where a doorman greeted Martin like a long-lost friend.

"G'day Andy." Martin slapped him on the back. "Inside please."

"Nice joint," Brad said. His eyes were really being opened tonight. He thought the restaurant would be seedy, being in the Cross, but this place wasn't. The tablecloths were starched, waiters were in uniform, chairs were black leather and exotic drop lights lit up the well-healed diners. This was the kind of place he and Emma might go to for their anniversary. Thing is, they'd have to save up for six months to afford it. Martin just kept doling out wads of cash. He was rolling in it and he'd never studied for anything. Just a shit hot car salesman. Makes you wonder.

The waiter offered menus but Martin brushed them aside. He knew what he wanted.

"Prime rib buddy, medium rare, mushrooms, onion rings, chips and don't go light on the gravy."

"Make that two please," Brad said not wishing to hold up the proceedings. What looked like half a cow was delivered to them before the cork was out of the bottle of claret. A steak had never tasted so good. Martin proposed a toast.

"Here's to carnal pleasures, my friend."

Brad could feel the food and wine taking effect. A warm, mellow sensation snaked its way from his toes to the top of his head. Martin insisted on having his favourite dessert, Bombe Alaska, and it took half an hour to prepare. Just long enough for them to finish off a few cleansing ales. Marty wasn't such a bad guy after all. Brad was actually enjoying his company.

"Great night," he said as they stepped onto the pavement at eleven thirty-five. "Sorry it's over."

"Doesn't have to be. There's a strip joint a couple of doors up the street. Let's take a look."

"You're unreal." Brad decided he was already in deep shit. "Which way?"

Martin guided them to the entrance of the Pink Purring Pussy. The façade was covered with backlit photos of the strippers in various stages of undress. A bouncer with a face like a bulldog ushered the boys inside. They walked along a shoulder-width corridor under a halo of flashing lights. Martin slipped the concierge ten bucks and it secured them prime position with a bird's eye view of the floor show. Brad leaned back in his chair and focused his eyes. He'd never seen so much flesh up so close.

As the show progressed he was compelled to lean forward, his arms supporting his chin like the legs of a telescope. He had no idea people could do the things these girls did, in public, on a stage. A second bottle of claret stood empty in front of them and when a new girl appeared, Brad was having trouble with his eyes. Couldn't tell the big hand from the little one no matter how hard he stared at his watch.

"Fuck's sake, mate." He whispered, holding his arm under the dim table lamp. "What time is that? That can't be right?"

"We'll go as soon as this chick's finished. She's got a great arse, don't you reckon? Ten minutes tops." Martin uncrossed his legs, leaned back in his chair and took a long drag on his cigarette. He blew the smoke out the side of his mouth to allow himself an uninterrupted view. His concentration was complete. As if the show was just for him.

It was one fifteen AM when they got back to the library car park. On the way, they'd wound down the windows to sober themselves up. Brad's VW stood as a solitary reminder of his good intentions. He tried to jump out of the MG as soon as it stopped, but Martin held his arm and refused to let him go until he made a solemn pledge to do it all again, soon.

As he drove home Brad tried to remember the name of the girl in the brothel. Candy? Mandy? Or something similar? She was a real pro, knew exactly what she was doing. He couldn't fault her technique, she was good at her job. But he liked to be the one in charge, make the first move. Don't want it served up on a plate, miss the thrill of the chase. The rest was incidental and sometimes an anticlimax.

"Must be the only bloke I know," he chuckled to himself, "to have an *anti*-climax."

Ten minutes later he was feeling melancholy. The booze must be wearing off. He hadn't always found sex this complicated. Didn't in the beginning with Emma.

It was straight forward and easy back then. Emma. Yep, she'd be going crazy not knowing where he was. He'd say he had broken down. Had to wait for the service guys. That would do for an alibi tonight.

It was good that they couldn't afford to get the phone on. Better this way.

4

Freedom

"PUT YOUR CROSS HERE, MATE."

"I'd kiss your arse if it meant getting out of here sooner," Pete mumbled as he picked up the pen to sign his discharge papers. Both he and John had passed the physical exam with flying colours but no one thought to look inside their heads where the real trouble lay.

It was a clear spring day and the wattles were morphing from green to gold when they left the camp.

"Want to go home?" Pete asked as they marched towards the station.

"What do you think?"

"'Member those kids that wrote us?"

"What kids?"

"From the school, in Gilgarra, out west. Their crazy teacher got them to write to us. We wrote back, remember? She said we could go visit them any time. What d'ya think?"

"Be good to go out west for a while."

"Could do a bit of roo shooting on the way back."

"What about wheels?"

"Old man's been looking after me car. Can pick it up and be gone by tomorrow."

"Sounds good to me, mate. You're on."

"By the way," Pete said as he kicked a stone along the road, "did I tell you that you look shit-hot in your shirt with the flowers, mate."

"It's a Hawaiian shirt, you drongo." John came up from behind and wrapped his arm around Pete's head and pulled him down towards the tarmac. Pete feigned a right hook to John's solar plexus then straightened up, laughing at the relief of it all.

"Freedom!" John's fist punched the air. They walked to the station in silence, demobbed but not deprogrammed, still as primed and ready for war as when they were sent into the jungle.

"Two tickets to Central, thanks mate," Pete handed over a five-dollar bill.

"Train should be here in about twenty minutes, boys."

"Thanks, Mate."

"Seen a few Nashos come through in the last couple of years. Where you headed?"

"Dubbo."

"Home?"

Nup. Doing a bit of shooting."

"Thought you'd've had enough of that."

"Bloody roos don't shoot back, mate," Pete said. It was obviously the funniest thing that the station master had heard for a long time.

The train arrived at Central half an hour before their connection to Dubbo was due.

"Fancy a burger?" Pete asked, handing John his ticket.

"Or three. And a Coke, I reckon."

"Back in a minute."

Pete was running down the station stairs as the train pulled in, a real clunker with seats hard enough to crack an egg on.

"Could have splurged on a sleeper, mate." John said as he hauled his pack onto the luggage rack. They had the cabin to themselves. It was soon filled with the smell of fried onions and greasy meat.

As he sipped a Coke, John rested his head on the window pane and watched as the glare of the city faded and the evening cast its pallor over the suburbs of Sydney.

Pete drowsed next to him until his eyes began to close. He shook himself awake, stood up and lifted his gear down from the luggage rack. The floor space between the seats was just long enough. His pack became a pillow and within two minutes he was snoring.

Pete saw the first light of dawn seep into the cabin. He lay motionless listening to the change of rhythm as the train approached the next station. A foot nuzzled his arm.

"Wakey wakey sleeping beauty."

"I'm awake, mate. Just enjoying the five-star accommodation." He hoisted himself onto a seat and opened the window. The smell of arid, thirsty country came rushing in with the morning air.

"I'm starving!" John said, stretching his arms wide. "Those burgers didn't go far."

"Could eat the arse out of a flyblown sheep, meself. We'll get something in town." Pete checked his watch. "Not long to go. Got a fag? I'm out."

They lit up together and watched as a smattering of houses interrupted the desolation of the countryside, evidence that their stop was not too far away.

No one was around to take their tickets so they tossed the stubs into the bin and walked towards town. Pete picked up a handful of dirt that he let run through his fingers, then brushed his palm against his jeans.

A truck drove out of the loading yard as they hit the road. They chased after it, shouting as they ran.

"You boys want a lift?" the driver called as he pulled over at the intersection to the main road.

"Thanks, mate," Pete called up to the open window of the cab.

"Where ya goin'?"

"Turnoff to Hilltop."

"Get in."

John hesitated. "What about breakfast, Pete?"

"Make up your friggin minds." The truckie said. "I'm not a bloody chef."

"No problem mate, we're good." They climbed into the cabin and wedged their packs into the space behind the seats.

"Army?" The truckie asked.

"Yeah, just out."

"Regulars?"

"Nah, Nashos. Vietnam. I'm Pete, this is Johnno." The truckie nodded, then spat out the window and put his foot on the accelerator. Two hours later they pulled into a truck stop. "Fifteen minutes, or I'm going without you," he said as he hauled on the handbrake, got out of the cabin and walked into the café. "Usual, love," he called to the waitress. She acknowledged his order with a single nod of the head."

"Friendly bastard," John remarked as they strode to catch up.

"Beggars can't be choosers, mate. Let's get some tucker."

The choice was easy. *Special Breakfast with the Lot* for $1.60. Two eggs, four bacon rashers, two sausages, fried tomatoes and baked beans. As they wiped the grease off their plate with the last of the four slices of half-inch thick white toast, the truckie walked to the counter and paid his bill. Pete and John threw back what was left of their milky sweet tea and followed him out.

"Good tucker, eh." Pete attempted conversation, as they climbed into the cabin.

"Does the job."

Three hours later they were at the turnoff.

"Thanks, mate," Pete called as he hauled his pack onto his back. John gave a half-hearted salute and the horn of the truck sounded in reply as it drove off.

"How far?" John asked.

"About eight miles."

Ninety-five minutes at marching pace put them at the head of a dusty driveway, walking towards a bunch of buildings that looked like they hadn't seen paint since the First World War was declared.

Pete let out a whistle that would have woken the dead and two dogs came bounding towards him – a russet brown and a black kelpie.

"G'day Bluey, me mate. Rusty, here love. Come on. Pete's home. Good girl."

A flyscreen door slapped back on its hinges and a cry went up as Pete's Mum confirmed her suspicions. Her big, floppy arms opened wide, ready to enclose her son.

"Oh, you're home! You're home!" Mrs Barker attempted a run for the first time in many years but common sense prevailed and she stood with the dogs circling her thick ankles as she patted the space above her heart.

"Calm down, Mum. You knew I was comin'."

"Not until next week," she scolded. And your father's in town till tomorrow." They held each other, then Mrs Barker stood back to make sure her eyes weren't deceiving her and repeated the ritual once more, just to be sure.

"Johnno, mate, nearly forgot. Mum, this is John." Mrs Barker nodded, dabbed her eyes with her apron, then smoothed her hair down. *Has that effect on all women*, Pete thought as she hugged his mate. It was the blond hair and olive skin that got their attention and the turned front tooth was a boyish distraction. Made them think he needed some mothering.

"I haven't got your bed made up and nothin' baked. Haven't got a thing ready." She smoothed down her apron. "And look at me!" Pete couldn't remember seeing his Mum this flustered.

"Tell you what Mum. We'll go away and come back again so you've got time to fix things up for us."

"Don't be silly, love. I just can't believe that you're here and safe. Come inside, sit down and I'll make you a cuppa.

"Don't suppose Dad's got any beer in the fridge?" Pete asked as he opened the kitchen door.

"When did you start drinking in the mornin'?"

"The Army does funny things to you, Mum. Anyway, a cuppa will be fine. We're not hanging around. Got some business to do. Just come to pick up the car."

"What! You're going away again, straight off. And without seeing your father?" she added, to give her objection more substance.

"Only for a week or so. We're going to visit a school in Gilgirra."

Pete explained how the kids had been writing to him and John, and they'd been writing back. The school had asked them to visit when they got home.

"Well, they must be very special kids if they're more important than your family."

"Oh, Ma, let up," Pete joked as he fetched his mug from the cup hook and tossed it in the air. "I wasn't due till next week. We could have snuck in and got the car but I'd hear the old man complaining from here to there."

"You're right about that." She took the simmering kettle from the stove and filled the tea pot. "You weren't writing those kids terrible things about the war, I hope?"

"No Mum, we just told them the boring stuff about what we ate and where we slept. We left out the bits about our socks and underdaks."

John sniggered. "What underdaks?"

"You mean you went around without clean underwear and socks?" Mrs Barker chose a cup and saucer from the dresser and passed it to John.

"Mum, you reckon Dad's bad. We wore the same pair of socks until they fell apart."

"Oh goodness me." She shook her head as the swamp black tea filled his cup then passed around a tin of homemade shortbread.

"They lasted about six weeks," John added, "and we'd just chuck them away then put on new ones."

"Don't tell me you did the same with your underpants." Mrs Barker shook her head to clear the image then bit into her shortbread, indicating approval of the texture with a little nod.

"Nope, never wore any, not if you wanted to avoid being driven crazy by itch all the bloomin' time. Just smothered the good bits in white powder to keep dry – was all you could do."

"Oh, it doesn't sound very pleasant, all in all."

Pete kept his thoughts to himself, no point in scaring her. John stared into his teacup.

Pete broke the silence. "Car keys still in the same place?"

"Yes son. Now, what will I tell your father?"

Peter jangled the keys as he kissed the top of her head. "Tell him thanks for looking after me beautiful Bellett."

"Oh, what will I do with you? I guess you do deserve a bit of a holiday."

"See ya Mum. In about a week. Then I'm home for good," Pete said as he downed the dregs of his tea, spitting the stray leaves back into his mug.

"Come here. Give your Mum another hug. I'm tickled pink to have you home, Son." She turned to John. "You both stay safe now."

"Mum we've just survived a bloody war."

"No swearing, Son. You're not in the army now, remember."

"Bye Mrs. Barker. Thanks for the cuppa." John extended his hand.

"Bye, love. You two look out for each other." Mrs Barker hesitated, then pulled him to her and standing on tiptoes, planted a kiss on his cheek. "Well, I can't stand here all-day nagging. Off you two go now," she said. "I've got washing up to do." She turned her back and began to pour hot water from the kettle into the enamel wash basin in the kitchen sink.

Pete could see the Bellett had been cleaned and polished. He circled her, tenderly brushing his hand along the curve of the wheel arch then along the boot.

"Dad's been getting her ready." They got in and Pete turned the key. Foot on the accelerator, choke out, bit of a pump and she started after just two goes.

They drove all afternoon and through the night, taking turns to kip in the back seat. Sleeping in short stints was second nature to them now.

"Mate, wake up. Your turn." Pete had only to say it once, softly and John was sitting bolt upright, talking at a hundred words a minute as he tucked his shirt in.

"How far mate? Nearly there? My turn eh? No problem." Wide awake, alert and ready.

They pulled over to take a leak by the side of the road and were on their way in minutes. Neither of them was sure what the rush was, but they both felt they had to keep moving. A couple of times just on sunset, they spotted a roo feeding by the side of the road. Startled by the noise of the vehicle it raised its head, eyes shining like headlights.

"Dangerous time of day," Pete said. "Stupid bastards, just as likely to run into our lights as away from them." He usually hunted solo – preferred it that way – wandering along with nothing but his swag, billy and gun, relying on his instincts and skill to feed him and guide him home. Every couple of months he'd go bush just to experience the pleasure of his own company and to reconnect. It held him in good stead in Nam, although that bloody jungle was a lot tougher than any scrub he'd ever had to get through in outback New South Wales. Funny name. He was sure it looked nothing like Wales. The nights were blacker in Nam too, or maybe they seemed that way, not knowing what was out there. They reckoned you could smell the Cong, the stinky little bastards. So you think you'd know if a platoon of them passed by within, say, thirty feet. Thing is you didn't, until the footprints and flattened jungle were found the next morning. Neither of them slept well after that, they'd lie awake sniffing the air, listening for any noise that didn't sound right.

5

Infected

Each time he urinated the burning sensation intensified. Try as he might, Brad couldn't ignore the connection between the pain and the girl in the brothel. As he lay awake in bed that night, the consequences swirled around and around in his head. He buried his face in the pillow as the thoughts spiralled out of control and threatened to overwhelm him to the point that he thought he might cry out.

The following day, he held on for as long as he could and when the lunch bell rang, he made a bee line for the staff toilets. As the flow of urine began, the pain shot up his prick like an electric shock. It was much worse than it had been. So far, he had refused to look down in the hope that if he ignored the connection between the facts and his fears, it would all go away. Mustering up courage, he lowered his gaze and knew that he had been wise to keep his eyes averted. Without finishing what he had come for, he held his shorts closed and headed for the privacy of a cubicle.

He secured the door lock, faced the window above the toilet, took a deep breath, opened his eyes and there it was, a thick creamy discharge oozing from the tip of his penis. He felt bile rise from the pit of his stomach and eased himself onto the toilet seat. If that wasn't enough, as he adjusted his position he felt a painful tenderness in his testicles.

"Oh no, Jesus Christ, no," he whispered into the stale air of the men's toilet as he threw his head back onto the wall behind the cistern.

"Please God let this go away and I promise to stop."

A trip to the family GP was not an option but he wanted this thing gone. It would have to be the hospital. He had a Year Nine afternoon class then two free periods, so he could nick off early.

As he entered the outpatients' department, Brad scanned the faces of the people waiting in line – a couple of old blokes who looked like boozers, a mother and her kid, sucking his thumb as she rocked him back and forth. The kid looked sick. There were two women reading magazines and an older one holding onto her handbag like she had the crown jewels inside. He didn't recognise anyone, thank God.

The clerk sitting behind the glass took Brad's details, told him to take his place in the queue and wait. He lowered himself into a plastic chair next to the old woman. Forty-five minutes later, his name was called by a young doctor who led him to a cubicle. A bloke, thank God again. If a woman had come for him, he was going to ignore the call, get up and walk out. The doctor yanked the curtain and consulted his paperwork.

"What seems to be the problem?" he asked, looking up.

Brad cleared his throat, leaned forward in the chair. He outlined his symptoms so quietly that the doctor on several occasions had to ask him to repeat himself. He was told to take his pants down and lie on the bed. He did as instructed then began to count the curtain rings around the cubicle while gloved hands examined his flaccid penis and tender testicles.

It had been his ardent hope that the doctor would take the hint and keep his voice down as he delivered his diagnosis, but he was oblivious to Brad's distress. The occupants of the cubicles either side of them stopped talking when the doctor said the word

'Gonorrhoea.' Brad was sure of it. He sat on the edge of the bed with his arms crossed, trying to focus on what the doctor was saying while listening for their reaction.

"You'll need two injections for the treatment to be effective," the doctor said curtly.

"More than one, eh?" Brad tried to smile.

"You must have the first immediately and the second must be within two days."

Then came the crunch. "Anyone you have had sexual intercourse with in the last two weeks will also need to be treated, straight away. Gonorrhoea can cause infertility in women. You can make the appointments at the front desk."

Brad held out his arm. The discomfort from the injection was nothing compared to the gut wrenching realisation that Emma would have to be treated. Two nights ago, he was dreaming about the pub girl and woke up with an enormous horn. He had climbed on top of Emma and they made love in a drowsy half sleep, half wakefulness.

He couldn't stomach going straight home from the hospital. He had to think, so he drove to the beach and sat in the car, watching the wind destroy what was left of a few good waves. He thumped the steering wheel in frustration. It had been the first time for them in months. He couldn't believe his rotten luck and contemplated driving into the sea. He'd have to fess up, there was no other way to get her to the hospital. She'd put two and two together then and he'd be done for.

"Oh, hello." Emma looked up as he came through the door. "You're earlier than usual." She put the lid back on the saucepan and walked to the sink, a spoonful of bolognese sauce in one hand and the other hand cupped underneath to catch the drips.

He loosened his tie.

"Actually Emm, I'm not too well."

"Poor thing. What's wrong, then?" She said, sampling the sauce with the tip of her tongue then reaching for the salt canister.

"I've got a bit of an infection." His voice squeaked and the moisture had gone from his tongue. He felt it stick to the roof of his mouth as he spoke.

Emma measured the salt in the palm of her hand, dropped it into the pot and gave the sauce a stir. "You sound a bit croaky." She spoke above the noise of the water running over the wooden spoon. "Your throat, you think?" She placed the cleaned utensil into the spoon rest on the sink.

At this point, Brad was standing at the entrance to the kitchen, his arms crossed over his chest so that she wouldn't hear his heart thumping like breakers hitting the shore after a storm.

"Actually, I went to the doctor's on the way home, Emm."

"You *must* be feeling bad," she said as she dried her hands on the tea towel and turned to face him, her head tilted inquisitively to one side. "I can never get you to go to the doctor's."

"It's a pretty serious infection Emm and you could catch it.' He backed into the lounge room and enticed her onto the divan by patting the space next to him. Emma sensed his concern and put her hand to his head as she sat down.

"You're not hot. I don't think you've got a fever. Have you?"

He pushed on. "I've got to have an injection and you should too."

"What are you talking about? You're the one who's sick." She hated needles. "You're not getting *me* to have any stupid injection." She sat back against the wall and grabbed a pillow, hugging it to her chest.

He twisted around to face her. "Emma, you need to. You could get what I've got."

She began to pick at the skin around her thumb nail. "What is it that you've got?" She bit into a piece of loosened skin, then went back to her picking while she waited for his answer.

"I told you, an infection." He couldn't look at her.

"What about antibiotics?" She said. "They'll fix anything."

"Emm, the doctor didn't give me antibiotics because they won't work."

"Sounds like you've got the plague." She noticed she had drawn blood and began to suck at the damaged cuticle.

"No, I haven't got the plague, but the infection can have serious consequences if it isn't treated." Brad continued exactly as rehearsed. "It can interfere with the reproductive system in women." The waiting was agony. He wished she would get it over and done with.

"Affect *my* reproductive system? How can it do that?"

"Well, it's infectious and if you got it and um," he cleared his throat, "it could stop us having a family." Brad knew how desperately she wanted a child. This time, one they could keep.

Emma sat holding her throbbing thumb, pondering his words then began to rhythmically smooth out the pillow with her closed fist.

He reached out and stilled her hand. "You don't want that to happen, Emm".

"You don't either. Do you?" She looked up at him.

"Course not. That's the last thing I want."

She laid the pillow aside, stood up, walked to the kitchen, lifted the lid on the saucepan, then turned to face him.

This is it, he thought. *She's worked it out. My oldies will never speak to me again.*

And then she said it. "What do I have to do?" As easy as that.

He sat bolt upright and let out the breath that he didn't know he'd been holding. "We need to see the doctor tomorrow. I've made an appointment for the morning. I'll take you there before work."

"You're absolutely sure I can't just get some antibiotics?" She sat next to him and took hold of his arm. "You know how terrified I am of needles," she pleaded.

"We'll ask them again. But to be honest, I don't think you can."

"I'll do whatever I have to, if it could stop us having children."

He nodded his head, reassurance that he felt the same. A gullible wife was, on occasions, an asset.

They ate their spaghetti at the battered laminex table. The plastic on the chairs was cracked and brittle and scratched his thighs below his shorts. Emma was worried about her work. He tried to concentrate but couldn't remember much of what she said, something about the company being in trouble but her job was okay.

"I think it's only the workshop that might get shut down," she confirmed. "Brad, did you hear me?"

"Sorry. What did you say?"

"Don't worry. It's nothing to worry about yet."

He stood up and carried their plates to the sink. They did the dishes together, changed into their pyjamas then watched TV. He was relieved when she fell asleep.

"Come on Emm." Brad shook her gently. "Bedtime." He helped her to her feet, switched on the bathroom light, then turned down the bed.

"Sorry, I crashed," she said as she shuffled into the bedroom, still half asleep.

"I'm going to stay up for a while. Hop in and I'll put out the light." He brushed his lips against her cheek, pulled the door to half way and went into the bathroom. He couldn't put off urinating any longer but the pain wasn't nearly as bad as before. Perhaps the injection was already working.

Brad slept fitfully and woke before the alarm. While Emma was showering, he made tea and toast. She would often skip breakfast because she maintained her metabolism wasn't up and running until about ten o'clock, and the food didn't digest properly. He carried it into the bedroom so she could eat while she did her hair and make-up. Didn't want to risk her getting light-headed and fainting.

"What's this?" she said. "My last meal?"

"Don't be silly Emm. You should have something in your stomach."

The hospital car park was full but Brad found a space in a back street and together they ran up the hill and into the Outpatients. It was seven twenty and Emma's appointment was for half past. After she registered with the clerk, they took a seat in the waiting room. Emma thumbed through some old magazines but was distracted by thoughts from early that morning. What could have caused the infection? She recalled Brad had surfed at the point last week. Maybe cut himself on one of the old oyster shells that were scattered amongst the rocks at the entrance to the water? It could easily have become infected. She had tried to ask him on the way to the hospital, but they were running late and he was too stressed out to listen. As she was about to bring it up for the second time, her name was called so she laid the magazine aside, took hold of his arm, and together they followed the nurse along the corridor.

"I'm scared," Emma whispered. Brad reached across and squeezed her hand.

The doctor from the day before held back the curtain to the cubicle. Brad managed to avoid eye contact. What happened from now on was out of his control.

"Take a seat please Mrs Emery."

"My husband said I can't just have some antibiotics to swallow."

"That's correct."

"Can he stay then, please, my husband, when I get the injection?"

"Yes, that's no problem. "He looked at his notes and confirmed Emma's personal details.

On cue, a nurse appeared carrying a tray. Emma looked at the gleaming instruments and then back at Brad. She tried to still her bottom lip by biting it. Brad stepped closer when the doctor asked her to roll up her sleeve and he noticed Emma's hands shook as she fumbled with the button on her cuff.

"Want to lie down?" Brad whispered. He knew he did.

"No, I'll be all right." She didn't look it, was white as a sheet, so he stood behind her and massaged her shoulders with his fingertips, at the same time providing support for his own trembling knees.

Emma's eyes closed. A child in the cubicle opposite started crying. The mother spoke soothingly. A trolley rattled past on the other side of the curtain.

"All done," the doctor announced. "You can put your head between your legs if you feel faint."

"I'm okay," she said, with an upward intonation that supported her contention that she was in fact, 'all right'.

Brad bent down and spoke softly into her ear. "You did great Emm." The colour had come back into her face. "I'll go get the car and bring it to the front door."

"Yes. You go on." She smiled up at him. "Thanks."

"I'll be really quick," Brad said as he stole away, desperate for a cigarette.

Emma watched as the nurse put a small round bandaid over the puncture point of the needle. She adjusted her sleeve and waited for the doctor to finish writing up his notes. "Excuse me," she said, as he put his pen into the top pocket of his white coat. "Can you tell me how you get these infections?"

He caught the eye of the nurse, who stared back at him. Emma glanced from one to the other. There was an awkward silence during which she was sure that she must have said something silly.

"Oh, you know, um, our ah, promiscuous society". He looked back at the nurse for reassurance.

"Oh, right." Emma said, although she knew that he certainly was not right. She and Brad hardly ever had sex. They were definitely not promiscuous. The doctor was wrong.

Then she remembered the girl from work. When Cheryl came back from her honeymoon, she had to stop having sex with her husband because she had an infection from all the sex she had been having. The doctor probably assumed she and Brad were the same, but they had only done it once in the last couple of months. She couldn't tell the doctor that. She couldn't tell anyone. How could she admit her husband no longer wanted to make love to her? Emma fumbled on the ground for her handbag to hide the hot shame of rejection rising up her neck and into her cheeks.

"You can stay here until you feel ready," he said, "just leave the curtain open when you leave.

"I really am okay now, thank you," she called after him as he turned to go.

"Goodbye, dear," the nurse said, "all the best," and followed the doctor.

"Oh, good bye. Thank you, too," Emma replied as she stood up and brushed down her skirt. She was sure they were whispering about her as they walked away.

Brad wasn't anywhere to be seen so she found her way along the labyrinth of corridors to the pick-up bay. It was five past eight and she hoped he wouldn't be much longer. Insecurities had begun to invade her thoughts. If she had more experience with boys, things might have been different, she would know how to make Brad want her. But she was the first of her friends to go all the way and at eighteen, the first to get married. Nobody had much idea about the whole sex thing. How were you supposed to learn?

Emma didn't notice the VW pull into the pick-up bay and Brad had to sound the horn twice to get her attention. He leaned over and opened the door as she ran to the car.

"Everything all right?" he asked and she smelt the nicotine on his breath.

"Yes, all good."

"You were brave, Emm."

"I was, wasn't I?"

"You deserve a medal," he said. "Told you that needles are nothing to be afraid of."

As they drove out of the hospital grounds he turned down the radio and gave her knee a pat. "Emma, I'm having my second injection this afternoon. You need another one on Wednesday.

"You never told me that."

"Well, I'm telling you now. You've got to see it through, okay." From the corner of his eye, Brad detected a nod of her head. He glanced at his watch. "You'll be on time for work, anyway. We'll make it easily. Same routine on Wednesday. Then it's finished, Emm. Two medals. Okay?"

If she responded, he couldn't tell as her head was turned away.

"You've been great about this, you know," He wasn't sure how much she had figured out.

"Anything's better than not having children," she told him as she wound down the window and let the fresh air fill her lungs. Her hair was being blown about by the wind, but she didn't care. She tilted the seat back, shut her eyes and tried not to think about Wednesday.

6

Coming Home

AT 7AM, THE CAR DROVE into the main street of Gilgirra with the fuel gauge showing empty. Nothing much was moving except a few dogs, scratching and sniffing. Boredom seeped from every doorway as they cruised up the street, windows down, the dust settling in their nostrils.

"Keep your eyes peeled for a service station, Johnno, need to fill 'er up."

The garage attendant was a young kid who'd put his trousers and shirt on over his pyjamas. It was bloody cold in the mornings.

Pete made conversation as they stood by the pump, watching the gauge tick over. "Smells a bit like rain comin'."

"Yeah, but it never gets here."

Pete could tell from the dry scratching sounds of everything underfoot that it had been a long time since the last wet.

"Anywhere we can get something to eat this early mate?"

"Yeah, June's cafe's up the end of the road. She opens 'bout now."

"Thanks mate, keep the change."

"Jeez thanks, mister," the kid said, cradling the coins in his hand. He hadn't been tipped for a while.

"What time we expected?" John asked.

"About ten."

Pete had phoned the school and spoken to the headmistress. He wasn't sure that she'd remember their letters. It had been nearly six months since they last wrote but she knew them straight up. When Pete told her they wanted to visit the kids, she said that they would be 'most welcome' and she'd arrange for them to billet with one of the families.

"You want to stay with the kids' parents?" he asked John.

"What do you think, could be gettin' a bit up close and personal?"

"Let's check out the caravan park. Need a wash before we front up anyway. I smell like a dog's crotch."

At 9.30 after a feed at June's and a wash in the shower block of the caravan park, they set out to find the school. Locating it wouldn't be hard. You could drive from one end of town to the other in about three minutes. Pete didn't like the idea of reporting to the Principal's office – he'd made a similar trip too many times when he was young.

Mrs Fillmore was a sturdy woman, who probably looked older than she was. Could have been the way her hair was pulled back, severely, into a bun. She shook hands like a bloke.

"Pleased to meet both of you. Have you been back long?"

"No Ma'am. Not long," they chorused.

She rose from her desk and moved towards the door. "It is really most kind of you to think of the children. They're very excited. They don't get many visitors, certainly not soldiers who've been to such an exciting place as Vietnam."

"Yeah, Ma'am, it was *real* exciting," Pete agreed.

"Miss Levison is their teacher if you remember," she informed them as she marched along the corridor, the clump of her sensible shoes heralding her approach. They followed in step.

"If you come by my office when you've completed your visit, I'll fill you in on your accommodation."

"Oh, Mrs Fillmore," John spoke up. "We really appreciate your trouble, but we've already checked in to the caravan park. Needed to freshen up you see."

"Oh, right you are then, I'll let the parents know." She knocked on the door of 5A classroom.

Through the glass petitioning, they could see Miss Levison. Twenty, maybe twenty-two, John guessed. Her ebony-black pony tail brushed her shoulders as she sashayed between the desks towards the front of the room. You could see her eyelashes, thick and dark, even from this distance. She glanced up and John was sure she fluttered them for his benefit.

"She's mine, okay mate?" he said to Pete. "Bet you ten bucks."

"Not if I can help it," Pete said, grinning like a shot fox.

Mrs Fillmore held open the classroom the door. "They're ready for you now." She turned on her thick heels and was gone.

Miss Levison stepped into the corridor. "You must be...?"

"Oh, Pete, Miss." he said, wiping his palm on his trousers and extending his hand.

"And John, obviously. I'm Jane Levison. It is so good of you to come to see the children. They're so excited."

"Not half as excited as we are." John was laying it on already.

"We really appreciated getting the letters Miss Levison." Pete tried a different tack. "Gets pretty lonely out there."

"We weren't sure if you got them at first, but when we received your reply, they were so delighted. Please come in."

As Pete looked at the kids, he hoped to God that none of them would ever have to go to war. They sat wide eyed on the floor with their little skinny legs crossed in front of them.

"I thought it would be nice if you sat with the children. If you can manage these little chairs?"

"No problem," said John as his knees rose around his ear lobes.

Miss Levison had already shown the class where Vietnam was on the map that was drawing-pinned to the wall. John told them how they had flown there in the Boeing 727 jets. He explained about the Iroquois helicopters that provided transport to and from base. The kids wanted to know how they got food in the jungle, and John explained about dehydrated rations, what the jungle looked like and about the tiger they saw – but not that they blew it up thinking it was a Vietcong. Pete was concerned that he was making it sound like fun, a bit of a holiday and wondered if they weren't doing to these kids what had been done to them. No one had told them the truth.

John overbalanced on his chair when the bell for play lunch rang out. The kids got a good laugh and he didn't mind. Miss Levison seemed to think he had staged it for their benefit.

"You all right there?" she asked, offering a dainty hand up.

"Fine Miss, but I might need a bit of attention later." A few children giggled and nudged each other. Miss Levison hushed them playfully.

When the formalities concluded, she walked the boys to the front of the school and once again, offered her hand.

"Thank you both so much. If you like, I'd be happy to catch up later, if you want to, of course."

"I think the appointment book's free," John said. "We'll meet you out front after school, if you like, Miss."

"Hey, I'm not your teacher you know. Jane please." Then more earnestly, "Why don't you meet me at my place. It's number 5 Wentworth Street, opposite the cemetery. Dead easy to find. I've got a big willow out the back, makes for a lovely place to relax after work. And I've got beer in the fridge."

"You're on, Jane. What time?"

"I finish at half two. Sports day. See you there about three." She cocked her head towards the classroom. "Better get back." She crinkled her nose. "Sounds a bit rowdy."

John swaggered to the car, confident that his ten bucks was still looking good.

It was two twenty when they left June's for the second time that day and drove past the pub. "They should have left it alone," John commented. "The paint job stands out like a sore thumb now, lost its integrity."

"Poofy architect are you now, mate?" Pete joked.

"Shut up and drive."

At that moment, Jane walked around the corner.

"Slow down mate. Don't want to look too anxious."

"Johnno, I'm going to leave you to it. I'll drop you off, then I'm going back to wash the car."

"Oh, mate, you're sure? It's gunna cost you."

"Just enjoy yourself, okay?"

John didn't argue. He sat tight until Jane reached number five then stepped out of the car. She looked up to see Pete complete a U turn, then wave as he drove off.

"He's got a pressing appointment, Jane. Hope you don't mind."

"Not at all. Come on in."

John knew that the chain wire gate would squeal before she opened it. The house felt dark and cool as she ushered him into the front room. It smelt musty and he guessed that she didn't use it very often. The daylight struggled through the lace curtains. He waited, unsure if they were going out the back or staying inside. She answered his question.

"Take a seat, John. It's still a bit warm outside. How about that beer?

What a girl. "Yes thanks, that would be great."

She didn't offer him a glass, knew that it tasted better straight from the bottle, and he found himself a seat on the bottle-green Pullman lounge. She poured herself a sherry from the decanter on the sideboard.

"Cheers," she said turning to face him.

"Nice furniture." He meant it. It reminded him of the stuff his Grandma had. Thick, heavy and solid, like it would be around for ages. "You always lived here?"

"Goodness no. And the furniture isn't mine, it was here when I moved in. I'm renting. I only arrived in January, doing my country posting. Hopefully, I'll be out of here as soon as I finish the year. Not that it isn't a nice place, the kids are great too, but I'm from Sydney and I miss it."

"Oh, a city girl. I should have picked it up. What part of Sydney Jane?"

"My parents live in Drummoyne, but I flatted in Bondi when I went to teachers' college." She paused and tilted her head to one side. "I think I've seen you before."

"Yeah? Where d'ya reckon?"

"Did you used to go to Whisky?"

"Sure did. For R & R. It was our regular haunt." He took a slug of his beer. "Why don't you come and sit over here?" He stroked the spare cushion. The worst she could do was kick him out.

She sauntered over and sat with her thigh tight up against his.

"I love the colour of your hair." She wove her fingers amongst the curls that were beginning to transform his regulation haircut.

"That feels really good." He turned and kissed her neck, her lips, and then he pulled back to gauge her reaction. Just a smile.

He stood up and downed his beer. "Skoll, or whatever they say in Gilgirra." Then he held out his hand. "I can't escort you to the bedroom because I don't know where it is."

"First room to the left. Give me a minute."

Christ, that was easy, he thought. *Guess she gets lonely out here.*

John hadn't made love to a woman for nearly six months, but he restored his average back to better than respectable during that afternoon.

"You're insatiable." She stretched her arms above her head, then sighed. "And very attentive."

"Mmm, but I think I'm done for a while though." His voice was drowsy, the lack of sleep from last night catching up.

Jane rolled onto her side and propped herself on one elbow. Her free hand rested lightly on his chest as his breathing slowed. Behind the fine translucent skin, his eyes began to dart from side to side, as if they were looking out for something. His limbs twitched and his hands clenched and she wondered what his dreams were made of. She rolled over, careful not to disturb him, and her feet found the floor.

As she stepped from the tepid bath water a high-pitched wail stopped her dead. The neighbours would have heard it without doubt and the gossip would move through the town like a plague of locusts. Not that the people of Gilgirra were malicious, just bored stiff. She waited a moment to allow John time to find himself, then made her way back to the bedroom with a drink of water.

"You all right?" She asked, passing the glass. "That sounded like something big and hairy was after you." She finished buttoning her brunch coat then sat on the bed and rested her hand on his shoulder.

"Yeah, I'm good." He didn't look it, he was pale and drenched with perspiration.

"I'll get you a face washer."

John downed the water and propped an arm behind his head. "Look, I can't stay Jane," he called. "I'm sorry, but I really need to catch up with Pete. We'll call by tomorrow morning before we leave."

She stood in the doorway, leaning on the door jam, the face washer dangling from the fingers of her right hand.

"That would be nice," she said, although she never expected that he would turn up. The wet face washer landed on the bed. "The shower's in there if you want one."

"I'm good, thanks." He wiped his face. "Can't fault your welcome home, Jane." He winked at her as he straightened up.

"Country hospitality," she said as she watched him hoist up his trousers, and decided that there was much more to John Thompson than she would ever know.

"Maybe we could catch up in Sydney," he said, as he tucked in his shirt.

"I'd like that. I'll be at my parents' to start." Papers were stacked high on the dressing table. Homework for marking, John thought. She tore a corner from the top sheet. "Here's the phone number. Or maybe you'll get back here before then?"

"If I do, you'll be the first to know." He kissed her full on the mouth. "I'll let myself out. See ya Lady Jane. Take care."

"You too." She blew him another kiss as he turned to her at the door, then walked across to the bed and threw back the covers.

It was damp where he had lain and she wondered if the demons would ever let him rest. She pulled open the drawer to the bedside table, took out the photo and put it back in its place. Nearly two years had passed since Dennis had been killed. He would have been home by now. His time would have been up last April and they were to marry at the end of the year.

She touched his face behind the glass, to revive the reality of him that was fading as the months went by. Occasionally she panicked when she thought he might become merely a recollection. He deserved more than that. At those times, she would close her eyes, and imagine him bit by bit, from the top of his wiry hair, black like boot polish, to the soles of his enormous feet, twice the size of her own. Then he came alive again, as did the pain and the abyss in her heart. It was the price she was willing to pay to keep him close. His parents had sent her one of his medals. It was nice of them, something to keep. She held it in the palm of her hand until the cold metal warmed, then placed it back in the box beside her engagement ring and went to make herself some dinner.

7

Apples and Oranges

WHEN HE THOUGHT HE WAS going to be exposed, not only as a fornicator, but as a diseased fornicator, Brad felt a terror unequalled by anything experienced in the past. Facing up to a four metre swell that could bury him at the bottom of the ocean was nothing by comparison. Then he realised just how close he had come, and how lucky he was to get away with it and a sweet relief washed over him, so intense it was euphoric. His ability to relive each of these experiences, the terror and the elation, with undiminished clarity, probably accounted for his new-found enthusiasm for fidelity.

And he had not forgotten his bargain with God. The prayer offered up that day, while sitting on the toilet seat, contained a promise. *Make it well*, Brad had begged *and I'll stop*. And a deal was a deal. On their own each one of these inducements, the fear, the euphoria and his oath, would have been grounds enough for Brad to be confident he would maintain his conviction to change, but he needed more than good intentions to resist the call of the Sirens. *Smart bloke that Odysseus was, strapping himself to the mast.* The solution to his problem came from an unexpected source.

On the afternoon of his final exam, he decided to celebrate with a drink. As he pulled into the car park, he congratulated himself a second time, for making it past the city pubs and on to local territory. Even he wouldn't be stupid enough to stray at the Sports Club and for extra insurance, being a Friday, his father would be there.

"Go okay, son?" Mr Emery asked when Brad explained the reason for his visit.

"Yeah, I think I did all right."

Mr Emery passed a schooner to Brad and with his whisky glass held high said, "Well done, my boy." They toasted his success and as the glasses landed on the bar, his father looked into the amber liquid, wiped the condensation from the sides of his glass and said, "You'll have a bit of spare time now." He took another sip, then leaned an elbow on the bar and turned to his son. "Got any plans?"

"Haven't done much surfing lately, got a bit of catching up to do." Brad licked the froth from his upper lip.

"You know what they say, son, the devil finds work for idle hands." Brad knew that the remark was an attempt at humour and although it wasn't unusual for his father to spout pious maxims, the coincidence was unnerving and he couldn't convincingly laugh it off.

"You see, your mother and I have bought ourselves a modern new dining suite," his father continued.

"Good on you, Dad." *He had actually opened his wallet.*

"We thought that you and Emma would like the old one. Being a family heirloom and all that." *He's got no idea, silly bugger, that the country style furniture he's about to give away is the latest trend.*

"Would be good, I guess. Our one's had it." The backs of Brad's legs were still chafed from the split vinyl rubbing away at his skin while he sat at the table studying.

"It needs a bit of doing up, you see. Had too many coats of paint over the years. Needs a good stripping back. Perfect timing, we thought, with the holidays coming up."

"Yeah, I guess that sounds fair." He figured he'd knock it off in a couple of afternoons, keep everyone happy.

"One for the road, son?" asked Mr Emery draining his glass.

"My shout Dad."

"No, my boy, you save your money for the paint stripper and sandpaper."

"That serious eh?" Brad was going cold on the idea. He wanted something to keep him out of trouble, not a full-time job, but he kept his thoughts to himself while his father updated him on Johnno. The talk was he'd been discharged but had gone AWOL. No-one had heard from him, didn't know where he was, and his parents were upset and worried.

Around the bar it was agreed that their time in Nam screwed up a lot of those Nashos. They weren't right in the head when they got back. A few who used to spend time at the club had stopped coming. Just didn't fit in any more.

Conversation moved to the disastrous performance of the team last weekend as Mr Emery drained the last of his scotch. Brad wondered what would happen if he went AWOL, what would they say about him over a beer in the club?

"Why don't you call in on the way home, son," his father said as he pushed the empty glass away. "Your mother would like to know that the exams went well."

Brad knew this was an instruction rather than a suggestion. "Okay, I'll follow you, but I said I'd be home for tea."

"You can have a gander at the new acquisition while you're there. Not that we'll be eating off it," he chuckled. "Your mother's frightened it will get marked, would you believe." He left the bar shaking his head in wonderment.

Brad sauntered up the yard, hands in his pockets, and stood back to assess his new project. The four chairs were stacked on top of the drop-side table, their spindled legs heavily chipped and scuff-marked. He should do this for her. After all, she didn't get her medals, so maybe she'd settle for a new table and chairs. He'd let her choose the colour although he knew it'd be white.

His father came from behind. "You'll have to strip it by hand if you're going to do the job properly. Then it'll need some sanding and maybe two or three coats of paint."

Brad picked up one of the chairs and turned it over. He estimated there was a good eighth of an inch build-up of paint that would have to come off. *Bloody hell.* He thought again of Odysseus. *I'll be tied to this job for most of the holidays. May as well complete the picture and put some wax in my ears to shut the old man up.*

"No worries Dad," Brad reassured his father as they walked to the car. "Thanks for thinking of us."

As he headed for home, he tuned the radio to the 7 o'clock weather forecast. The announcer informed him that a low-pressure system was moving up the coast, bringing with it strong winds and big swells. There'd be no surfing tomorrow, so he pulled over at the phone box on the corner of his street and rang his father to tell him that he had decided to start straight away.

"Good decision, son. Get stuck right into it. I hear the weather forecast's not too good, anyway." As usual, his old man was one step ahead of him. "You can have the garage to work in. Just remember to leave it the way you find it, when you're finished. I'll park the car in the driveway when I'm not at work".

"Thanks Dad." *Next, he'll be installing a bundy clock.*

"And I've got some left-over paint stripper that should get you started. No need to spend money unnecessarily. I'll leave it out for you on the bench at the back. And the tools you'll need will be next to it."

"Thanks, Dad." *And then he'll be telling me when to stop for lunch.*

"Your Mum and I are very, very pleased that you're doing this, Brad. Let me know if you need help."

"I'm sure I'll be okay. It's not nuclear physics, is it, Dad?" *Still thinks I can't do a thing right.*

"No, it's not. But you've not done a lot with your hands. See how you go, Son."

You've got no idea what I can do with my hands, Dad.

THE TEACHER, THE PUPIL AND THE WIFE

Monday morning, Brad left the flat early and passed Greg on his way to pick up Emma. Funny bloke, Greg. Never said much and always looked like he'd fallen out of bed. A real untidy bugger. But he was good for a lift to work for Emma and saved him the trouble.

It had been a few years since he'd been in the old man's garage but nothing much had changed. The rear wall was lined with two shelves of recycled jars filled with screws, nails and washers. On the right-hand side, as you walked through the door, a backing board had been mounted to the wall. On it hung a range of screwdrivers, hammers, wrenches, pliers, saws, jigsaws, levels and three tools that he couldn't identify. Each item was silhouetted in white paint so it could be restored to its rightful position after use. *A place for everything and everything in its place.* The words echoed in Brad's ears. Mr Emery had moved the drip tray that sat under his own V-Dub, to clear a space for his son to work. Brad gazed in wonder. You could have eaten off the floor.

Before he got started, Brad spread several editions of the afternoon *Sun* over his work area. His father had already removed the table legs to make sure the job was done properly. Brad decided to work first on the centre leaf and balanced it on a milk crate. The paper was open at the photo of the bikini clad weather girl and he could feel the beginning of a boner as he admired her enormous tits sticking out at him. He touched the bulge in his pants and his prick let him know it needed some attention. A good few years had passed since he'd wanked off in the old man's garage. As a teenager, it was the only place that he felt private. Never knew when his mother was going to poke her head around the bedroom door to make sure he wasn't doing anything dirty. Brad stood with his legs astride blonde Tracy on page three and unzipped his jeans. She looked really nice and he was sure she wouldn't mind.

A great way to start the day he decided as he looked through the tools his father had left for him. With the screwdriver lying on top of the can of paint stripper, he opened the lid, and with the brush his father had assigned for the job he began applying the viscous fluid to the table top. The pungent fumes made him gag after a few applications and he remembered that he had closed the door. He wedged it open along with a rear window to get a cross breeze.

It took him a while to know at what point he should begin to remove the paint stripper. If he left it too long it would dry out, and the old paint would be become brittle and he would have to repeat the process. If he was too eager, the chemicals wouldn't have time to do their job. It soon became apparent that timing was critical as was the amount of stripper he applied.

In addition, it was necessary to fine-tune the pressure he used on the scraper. Too much and he would gouge out a piece of the table, and too little left bits of paint behind. By the time the tin donated by his father was empty, Brad had mastered the simple combination of tasks.

Hunger pangs prompted him to check his watch. It was twelve forty-five. The morning had gone quickly. He'd been at it for over three hours and finished half of the centre leaf of the table. He straightened up, stretched, then brushed his hand over the surface to remove the larger scrapings. He bent down and blew away the finer curlicues of old paint.

After lunch, he paused to admire his work and noticed that the scraping had left behind tiny flecks of ingrained paint. The purpose of the sandpaper became clear. With a circular movement he began rubbing away at the stubborn specks to reveal the pale yellowish brown of the Moreton Bay Pine.

At the end of the first day, the floor was littered with a kaleidoscope of paint residue. Vivid lime green had been overpainted with a sombre mission brown. Going further back in time, Brad uncovered a pastel yellow and sky blue. He imagined his grandfather applying these colours under instructions from Nana Emery.

During the weeks that followed, there were numerous days when the surf conditions were favourable yet he found himself driving towards the garage, keen to tackle another leg, or the seat of a chair. The pile of discarded sandpaper grew in height and he had to fork out for another three cans of stripper.

The work allowed him mental space and time for reflection, and he thought often of Emma and what had become of them. Fixing up a marriage wasn't as easy as renovating the table. Scraping away the years of wear and tear, going back to the way it was in the beginning. Not that simple.

Brad took respite from the work over Christmas and took Emma camping up the North Coast. He managed to make love to her twice. At least she was happy. When he looked back at the excitement of last year, it was like comparing apples and oranges. Occasionally he convinced himself that he didn't miss that life, preferred the oranges but suspected his state of mind was like that of an alcoholic who was off the grog to prove a point, and still hanging out for the next drink.

A week before school resumed, the table and chairs were ready. Brad gathered up the rubbish, swept the floor, and made sure that everything was restored to its rightful position and the garage was spotless. Only then did he place the table in the centre of the floor with a chair on each of the four sides. He was pleased with the job he had done. It had served its purpose, kept him out of trouble, but enough was enough. The shine had gradually worn off the repetitive and solitary task, and for most of the holidays he'd been inside the four walls of his father's garage.

On Saturday morning, he took Emma to pick up the table.

"Great job, son," his father commented and his mother agreed.

"The colour is perfect, dear. White gloss will give the flat a lift Emma, with all those dull browns you have in there at the moment."

"It looks great, Darling." Emma kissed her husband's cheek and accepted the truth in her mother-in-law's back-handed compliment. Brown was a sombre colour for such a small unit. Mrs Emery never did hold back but Emma never took offence. It was Brad who couldn't come to terms with her tactless jibes.

A joint effort got the table onto the roof racks with its legs in the air and Emma thought it looked like an albino bug that had rolled onto its back and died. The chairs wouldn't fit.

"Why don't you both stay for a barbecue when you come back for the chairs," Mrs Emery suggested.

Emma looked to Brad. "Sure, Mum," he said, wondering what the chances were that his Dad would break open one of his good reds.

As he backed down the driveway Brad saw his father walking towards the garage to do a final inspection. He knew he'd find something not quite right and he'd hear about it over lunch.

When they reached the bottom of the street, Emma laid her hand on her husband's thigh.

"I know you gave up some good surf time to get the job finished. But it's worth it, you know. It will look fantastic. Brighten up the unit."

"I didn't mind. Like I said before, actually got to enjoy it."

"And I have a special dinner planned."

"Might not need it after one of Mum's barbecues."

"S'pose not. We can have it tomorrow night. Celebrate your going back to school."

"You're kidding aren't you?"

"It's a big thing having a year twelve class. You nervous?"

"Yeah, kind of. First time and all that."

The car slowed and Emma jumped out to open the garage door. Brad accelerated past her as she ushered the him through with a wave of her hand.

At first she was confused and pressed her palms to her ears to block out the deafening noise. It took only seconds for her to realise it was the sound of splitting timber, echoing around the bare walls of the garage.

Brad's foot hit the brake and the car shuddered to a standstill. His hands left the steering wheel and flew to his head as the clamour of falling timber died away.

Emma's eyes darted from the ground to the roof of the car then back again and she began to giggle.

The bitch.

She knew it was stupid to laugh, but sometimes you get it wrong. Especially when you're not sure what to do.

He was looking, not at the floor, where the table lay in pieces, but at her, gripping the steering wheel, seemingly lost for words, clenching his jaw and staring, eyes wide open, fixated and piercing.

She has no idea how much I hate her right now.

"I'm sorry, I'm so sorry," she said, staring at the pieces of table, then raised her head and saw his eyes. "I'm not laughing at you," she said, trying to explain what she didn't understand.

No answer.

"Brad? I know it's my fault. I should have called out, warned you."

Still he ignored her, so she sat down on the spare tyre that was leaning against the wall to prevent herself falling between the gaping chasm that had opened up between them.

Still nothing. She could hear the creaking of the motor as it cooled and see the dust from the floor dancing in the sunlight that streamed in through the doorway. He sat motionless in the driver's seat, holding the steering wheel, then slowly he let go and dropped his head into his hands.

Emma knew then that this wasn't just a little setback, a difficulty that they could overcome, a predicament that would simply pass them by and leave them untouched. This wasn't a glitch in their marriage that could be fixed, glued together like the broken legs of the table. The air was thick with an acute awareness that the imprint of this day would not leave them unscathed. She perceived that there had been too many times like this, too many broken bits left unmended. Too much to repair.

His voice echoed around the concrete walls. "No, it's both our faults."

Emma knew he wasn't referring to the table. "I know," she said, "but it's happened."

She walked towards the car, opened the passenger door, leaned in and placed a hand on his arm. "Why don't we just go back to your oldies, get the chairs and have lunch. We don't have to tell them."

Brad snatched his arm away and now it was his turn to laugh, there was no humour in it, it was a cackle that had a ring of hysteria. Then it stopped as quickly as it had started and he threw open the driver's door, jumped out and tore away the ropes that held the remains of the table, letting everything drop to the cement floor. He kicked the pile of timber with his foot, climbed back in and started the motor.

Emma chased after him as he backed out of the garage, the passenger door swinging wildly. She beat the bonnet with one hand and tried to hold onto it with the other.

"What are you doing? What's happening? Answer me!" she screamed.

The car fishtailed as he reversed onto the road, then he spun the bonnet around and out of Emma's grasp, and ripped through the gears as he tore up the street.

Her solitary figure saw him turn the corner and heard the rumble of the motor die away. When a car drove into the street, she retreated to the footpath then made her way to the garage. The table legs that were scattered over the floor disappeared in the shadow of the closing door.

Overcome by an extreme exhaustion she hauled herself up the stairway. Had she taken their love for granted? In a way, she had. Her love was like the ocean or the sky, a permanent presence, a vital part of her existence. It would always be there and she thought it would be the same for him. Maybe their love had simply seeped away. That's how osmosis works. You can't see it happening and then suddenly, everything is changed.

She opened the door to her home, walked to the fridge and stared inside. Where was he now? Probably at the beach. He'd be hungry when he got home so she took out a packet of cheese slices and a tomato and began to butter the bread. They were supposed to be at lunch. She should ring them. Not now. Later. First, she needed to sit down. How tired she felt, barely enough strength to push the plate away. Her limbs were so heavy. She pushed herself into a standing position and moved to the divan, curled onto her side and reached for a cushion. Something to hold on to.

A knocking woke her. He was back. She jumped off the couch and felt the room spin but continued to stumble towards the door, desperate to tell him again that she was sorry, that it could all be made better.

"Dad." Mr Emery was standing in the doorway. His eyes travelled from her bare feet to her red eyes and dishevelled hair.

"Sorry to disturb you, Emma, but Mum and I were worried, you didn't come back for lunch."

"It's my fault, I should have called you."

"Where's Brad?"

"We had a bit of an accident."

He frowned. "Are you hurt?"

"No, we're all right."

Emma went on to explain the morning as best she could as they stood on the landing. A neighbour's door opened and closed.

Mr Emery placed a guiding hand under Emma's elbow. "Let's go have a look, honey." He escorted her to the garage. "Needs oiling," he said as he raised the door.

They stood side by side, their eyes adjusting to the poor light. The table top was upturned with one leg hanging at an angle. The other three were no longer attached and lay on the floor. Two had snapped off at the dovetail joints but one had broken neatly in half.

"Such a shame," Mr Emery said as he bent down on his haunches. He carefully examined each broken piece then used a table leg to lever himself upright. Tears were running down Emma's cheeks. "Oh honey, I didn't mean to upset you." He handed over a clean handkerchief. "I can fix it. You'll have your lovely table back in no time."

"Thanks, Dad," she wiped her eyes.

Mr Emery reached out to gently touch her arm then cleared his throat. "I'll tidy up here. You go on up and make yourself a nice cup of tea." As she turned to go he asked, "Where's Brad, Emma?"

"At the beach I guess. His surfboard's gone."

He nodded to himself. "I'll take it home and get started this afternoon. Is that all right? Will you be okay?"

She wanted to say, *I've got no idea*, but held her tongue.

"Do you want to come home with me?"

"No, I'll stay. I'll be fine."

"You sure, honey?" He surprised her by patting her shoulder.

"Yes. Thanks Dad. I might lie down for a bit."

"I'll walk you up the stairs."

As they reached her front door, she turned to him. "It was my fault, Dad. I should have been watching. I should have seen what would happen."

"Emma," he said firmly, "it wasn't your fault. Brad might try to make you think that. But he has always tried to blame other people for things that happen in his life."

"I didn't mean to imply...."

"Emma, I know he thinks we were too strict with him and I suppose compared to some people we were. But it wasn't an unhappy home. There was lots of love, but he forgets that. His distance hurts his mother a lot. But you know, there comes a time in life when you have to accept responsibility for who you are and not blame other people. Off you go now and get some rest."

"Yes, I'm really tired. Thank you."

She leaned against the door as it closed. This was the most her father-in-law had ever said to her and the first time he sounded like a real person. Without question she had believed Brad, that they were cold, that they pushed him to study, deprived him of things other kids had. But maybe they weren't all that bad after all.

8

Broadened Horizons

Pete heard John's footsteps well before the knock on the caravan door.

"It's open. You back already, Mate? Jane give you the boot?" He was lying on the bed, arms above his head, watching the tele.

"Nah, all good. Very content in fact." John rubbed his hands together. "Worked up a bit of a thirst though. It's your shout, Mate."

Pete stood up and slapped him on the back. "Grub looks okay at the pub. Let's go."

The last rays of the setting sun warmed their backs as they walked the two blocks to the hotel and took a seat at the bar.

"Two roast beef dinners, love. And two schooners of old."

They were onto their second round as the food arrived.

"Good, eh?" Pete confirmed, mopping up the roast beef gravy with his last slice of bread and butter."

"Anything beats bloody army rations."

"You used to dream about your Mum's lamb roasts, remember. Moaned out loud. At least that's what you told us it was about."

"Yeah, couldn't convince you bastards that I missed Mum's cooking more than the sheilas."

He glanced up at the TV in the corner as he slid his empty plate across the bar. The six o'clock news was on.

"Get a look at this," he said with a nudge to Pete's arm.

A big crowd was backed up along Elizabeth Street, into Hyde Park. Placards were held high for the benefit of the cameras. *DID WE HAVE TO KILL THEM TO SAVE THEM? GET THE HELL OUT OF VIETNAM? MURDERERS NOT SOLDIERS!* There had been rumblings before they left, but nothing like this.

"Looks like we're not too popular. What d'ya reckon?" John asked.

"A bit bloody late with their complaining."

A protester stepped forward and thrust a placard at the TV camera. *OUT OF VIETNAM NOW.*

"Reckon we can forget the ticker tape parade," Pete said as he threw ten dollars on the counter. "Finish your beer mate, we'll get out of here and put some miles under us. Bed down by the side of the road tonight and get off early tomorrow." He took a backward glance at the TV as they made for the door.

"Got to get some salt before we go."

"What for?"

"To preserve the skins till I get home."

They drove until late afternoon, picked up a dirt track and followed it as far as the Bellett would allow, then walked on. At dusk they picked out a spot to set up their hoochies.

The first afternoon Pete killed a big buck. John left the skinning to Pete and sat nearby smoking, to keep the smell of blood out of his nostrils. They ate the stringy meat with tins of baked beans, washed down by a warm beer.

It was rabbits for the next two nights. While Pete prepared them John collected firewood, his contribution to the fire-lighting. He like to stay close, to watch Pete as he laid out the leaves, twigs, sticks and logs along the ground, then carefully calibrate each piece into a towering nest. One match was all it took and John watched as the flames hungrily consumed the parched kindling, then the larger pieces of dry timber, until they began to glow orange red.

On their last night, they sat by the embers, finishing the last of the beer, their kidneys feeling the chill from the dark that had fallen behind them. Pete threw a cigarette butt into the fire and watched the sparks fly as it was devoured by the coals. He leaned back on his elbows and turned the soles of his shoes to the warmth of the fire.

"You're a bit of a dark horse, mate," he said as he kicked a fallen log back into place, "didn't know you had a girl at home."

"Don't have, Pete."

"Then who's Emma"

"My mate's wife. What's it to you?

"You've been calling out her name in your sleep."

John stood up, crushed the empty beer can in his hand and hurled it into the bush. He walked to the edge of the campsite, stopped at a scraggy mulga and unzipped his fly. With his legs astride, he leaned one hand on the tree trunk and watched as the steam rose into the chill of the night air. "Same time in the morning?" he said turning around as he zipped up.

"I'll have my eggs sunny side up, okay."

"Get nicked," John said as crawled under the hoochie.

They left at sunrise and headed towards Orange where John could catch a train back to Sydney. Pete planned to stay out for a few more days.

"Catch up soon, eh mate?" John said as the car pulled alongside the station steps. "Come and see the surf sometime."

"Yeah, sure. Just need a bit of time back home." Pete got out to open the boot. "It's been hard on my old man with me gone."

"Thought he'd enjoy the peace and quiet," John quipped as he retrieved his pack.

"Bloody smart arse." Pete let the boot lid drop shut.

"What about your oldies."

"Yeah. Bit pissed off that I didn't come straight home. But dinner's on tonight." He threw his pack over his shoulder. "See ya buddy."

"Yeah, see ya."

A handshake seemed inadequate but it was all there was on offer. They stood for a moment longer than was comfortable.

"Now piss off, you bastard." Pete walked to the driver's door and got in. The motor started and the wheels spun in the dirt.

"Bloody hoon!" John called out as the Bellett tore up the road, leaving him standing, in a cloud of dust.

Two weeks later he was back working, selling bumper bars. Pete was driving tractors. Getting home and back to normal life was what they had both looked forward to, so neither of them could understand why they felt so lousy.

Pete found himself doing things that he knew didn't make sense. He couldn't sit with his back to a door. He knew it was stupid, but he just couldn't do it.

Three months later he was still checking the rear-view mirror while he was driving, constantly vigilant, fearful, watching. He wasn't sure what for, but he couldn't stop himself, just in case. Jumpy all the time.

"What's wrong, love?" his mother kept asking. Over and over. Again and again.

"For Christ's sake Mum, just lay off, will you. Nothin's wrong." The kitchen door slammed as he strode towards the moonlit dam, hands in his pockets and head bent. Mrs Barker glanced across the table at her husband who shrugged his shoulders and went on stirring his tea.

"He needs to find a nice girl, Walter. That's what he needs," she said

"Not much chance of finding one of them out here, love. How about a top-up, eh?" he asked, holding out an empty tea cup.

"You'll be lucky if it doesn't land in your lap," she said walking toward him, teapot in hand.

At breakfast the next morning, his mother tried a different tack. "I've been thinking, Pete. Why don't you give that nice young John a ring? See how he's getting on."

"Yeah, maybe, Mum. Later on."

Pete thought about it during the day. Not such a bad idea.

Perhaps his mate was feeling it too. That evening while his mother was having her bath, he dialled John's home number.

Mrs Thompson answered. "Yes Peter, he's here. I'll get him for you straight away." Pete could hear her calling. "John, it's your friend from the army on the phone."

Pete's grip on the receiver tightened as he heard John's footsteps.

"G'day, you bastard. How's it going?" John said picking up at his end.

"Good mate, can't complain. How about you?"

"Yeah, good to be back at work. How about the sheep?"

"Stupid as ever."

"Your old man?"

"Yeah, he's okay. Just getting on a bit, I reckon."

"So, what's happening?" John asked.

Pete thought he might tell Johnno about the kid on the train. But now he wasn't so sure, Johnno sounded like he had it all together. A few weeks ago, he'd gone to Dubbo to pick up his new ute. A kid was sitting opposite him and had his feet up on the seat. *That's not the right way to sit on a seat.* Pete kept repeating to himself. *Not the right way to sit on a seat.* There was a right way and a wrong way to do things. He knew that now, so he told the kid twice to get his feet off the seat but he took no notice. Pete picked him up by his shirt collar, threw the little twerp back into his seat, then took the kid's two feet into one of his huge hands and pinned them to the floor. Pete got out at the next station, because along with everyone in the carriage, he was shit scared of what he might do next.

"You still there?" John asked

"Yeah, I'm here. Had to pick up a new ute last week. The old one carked it."

"Yeah. I bought meself a Triumph. Not much good for hauling sheep though."

"Good for picking up sheilas I bet."

"Yeah, you'd be right about that."

The conversation stalled as they navigated the distance between them. Silence had never been a problem when they were together, never awkward, but this felt different.

"You must be going well at work then mate," Pete said.

"Yeah, guess so."

"Keeping your hands off the secretaries are you?" Pete asked.

"Yeah, not interested in them, mate. Don't get your meat where you get your bread."

They shared a laugh, then nothing. The phone line crackled.

"Better get going then." Pete broke the silence.

"Yeah, thanks for calling."

"Come up and do a bit of shootin' some time."

"You're on buddy. Sooner than later."

"See ya."

John continued to hold the receiver to his ear long after the line had gone dead. No one told them coming home would be this hard.

He should have told Pete about the secretaries. He'd been churning through them like you go through ammo in an ambush. Maude Templeton had been working in the office for fifteen years, and the second week he was back she typed up her formal resignation, handed it to him and was out the door before his father had time to intervene.

The next one was Mary the Mouth. Apart from the nattering, she couldn't get a thing right and he wasn't paying to train her. She was gone in the third week, for general incompetence and extreme annoyance.

Sandra was shaping up better. A better shape too, he decided, as he lay in bed thinking about work. Sleep was a real bastard but the pills were a help. Used to think his mother a bit of a druggy with her Valium. Now he was hooked too. He stared at the ceiling waiting for it to kick in, remembering the taste of the ripe mangoes they used to get in Nam, which were also the shape of Sandra's arse.

The alarm was set for six thirty but he didn't need it, was always awake, listening, waiting for it to go off. Its ringing would replace the whine of the tinnitus. They said the blasts of the gunfire caused that one.

"Morning, Mum."

"John."

She was shitty again. He couldn't even be bothered recalling what it was about last night.

He sat at the table and opened the paper, searching for news of the war. They were pulling out at last. Some good it would do the villagers, or what was left of them. A plate of scrambled eggs landed in front of him.

"Thanks Mum." He dare not ask for extra toast. "Dad gone?"

"Yes. An hour ago. Got to sort some stuff in the factory."

John ate in silence and turned to the comic section. Might be the only laugh he gets all day. Tentatively he approached his Mum from behind as she stood at the sink and kissed her cheek.

"You know we love you John, don't you."

"Betcha, Mum. You too."

She turned to see him retreat through the back door.

He loosened his collar as he approached the office. So hot in there. Stuffy, stifling, like there was no air. But no-one else noticed it.

"Morning, Sandra."

"Morning, Mr. Thompson."

The mail was opened and waiting on his desk along with usual assortment of order confirmations, shipping manifests, sales reports.

He buzzed the intercom.

"Come and take a letter please, Sandra." He admired the shape of her legs as she walked to his desk and watched as she adjusted her skirt, doing a little wiggle as she sat down. His train of thought had gone so he doodled on the clean blotter with his fountain pen.

"Change of plans. Can you ring Ray Cantrell and confirm lunch on Friday. And I'll need a copy of the order from GHK." Would be a good idea to show it to his Dad.

Ten minutes later, he buzzed her again. "Sandra, the order?"

"Sorry Mr. Thompson, I'm still looking."

He had definitely put it in her filing tray the day before. He listened to the slamming of the cabinet drawers then decided to get out of the office before he said something he'd regret. His father was in his office.

"Morning, Dad. Mum said you needed to get in early."

"Yes, son. How's things your end?" His Dad looked up from his paperwork.

"Good. Got a good order from GHK yesterday."

"I knew we were in the running. Get what we expected?"

"Yep. And a bit more. Anything I should know about down here?"

"Not really. Bit of a timekeeping problem."

"Brian?"

"No, actually it's Jock. Been getting in a bit late. It's okay."

"Bloody oath, it's not."

"I'll sort it, John. Not your worry, son."

Hands in his pockets, he sauntered away. It was time his father let him take a bit of responsibility in the factory. He'd be looking after the lot soon enough. He walked past Sandra on the way back to his office. "The letter, sweetheart. I'm ready now."

She sat down, shorthand pad and sharpened pencil resting on the desk.

"Any luck with the GHK order?"

"Not yet, Mr Thompson. But I'll find it. I promise."

Her shorthand was good, he'd give her that. Kept up with him no problem.

"Type it up while I'm out please." An early lunch today he decided. Pie, peas and a schooner.

He was whistling as he walked back to his desk forty minutes later. The letter he had dictated was on his desk with a bloody spelling mistake in the second sentence. His heart began to race, his breathing shortened and he could feel the anger about to burst out, explode all over the office.

"Sandra!" he hollered, "get in here." She stood in the doorway and took off her glasses to look him.

"What's this shit." He waved the paper at her. "Don't you check your work? A bloody typo and that's all you had to do while I was out. He scrunched up the letter and threw it in the bin. He wasn't asking too much. Just wanted her to do her job. Orders were orders. Pete would have understood.

The next day, she handed him her resignation, said her old man told her she didn't have to put up with his abuse. He thought about apologising . Instead he told her to pack her things and go. He marched her down the stairs and out the door then back-tracked to the factory to check the bundy clock. Yep, Jock was still getting in late.

"What the fuck's this, Jock." He waved the bundy card in the air. "You've already been told. Starting time is starting time."

"I think you need to speak to your father, son."

"Stuff my father, Jock. If this keeps up, you're finished!"

His father heard the exchange and called him into the office "Son, I've let you handle the secretaries – didn't interfere, and that's something you still have to sort out." Mr Thompson tried to keep his voice low. "This is different. Jock's got some personal stuff going on. It will sort out. He's a good employee and I don't want to lose him. Let me handle it."

"I don't see why he can't be on time. In the army Dad, being on time wasn't an option." His voice broke as he explained, "It was the difference between life and death sometimes, Dad.".

They were all looking at him, everyone in the factory. Like the eyes of the Vietcong but nowhere to hide. His father took him by the arm and guided him towards the canteen.

"Sit down and have a coffee, son. Pull yourself together." John turned away and backtracked through the factory where the men were working, heads down as if nothing had happened. He had to get out of there. His car keys were in his desk drawer, and sitting underneath was the GHK order.

That night he was sitting on the verandah when he heard the screen door open.

"John, that's your fifth beer, love."

"Leave it off Mum."

"John, what's happened to you? I don't know who you are since you came home."

"Why don't you just get off my back! Mind your own business for God's sake."

"You are my business Son. I try to do everything to keep you happy but I don't know why I bother." She threw the tea towel in the sink and ran up the stairs. He heard the door slam and threw the beer bottle over the fence into the bush.

The next morning his Dad told him about a flat he'd bought a couple of years ago, right on the beachfront.

"Was an investment in your future, Son, a bit of a surprise," his father said, "somewhere for you to live when you marry and settle down. But maybe the time has come for you to move in."

"Sounds cool, Dad." It would be near the sea, away from the tension of the house. "Thanks, Dad, I guess. Thanks a lot." The ocean was one of the few places where John felt at peace. Whenever he was surfing, his mind calmed and his blood cooled. Thoughts became focused and weren't rat-tat-tatting all over the place. There was solace in the sea. Maybe his father knew that, or maybe he just wanted him gone.

They agreed to have a family dinner every Tuesday night so he could see his Mum. Although conversation was strained, at least he wasn't reducing her to tears and he thought it was going well. An extra Valium in the morning was helping to keep the lid on things, so he was surprised to find after the third week that he wasn't the only guest. Sam and Lee were having cocktails with his oldies when he arrived.

"Enjoying your new pad, Johnno?" Sam asked. "Get a good view of the bikini market from your balcony, I bet."

"Yeah, it's good. And being so near the water and all." John replied.

They ate the first course while his Dad and Sam talked about where the housing market was going. Then Sam, for a good ten minutes, bemoaned the extra charges the builder had tried to claim for the recently completed extension to his already enormous house – a pool and a new rumpus room that would be Sam's private den. Sam wasn't having any of it and his hard-line tactics to wear the builder down were shared over a bubbling pot of chicken chasseur. The conversation during dessert was dominated by a discussion as to which motor cruiser Sam should buy for the upcoming season. The women feigned interest for a while then began to natter away to one side. Lee was concerned that Paul, her son, would marry a Pommy now he was living in the UK and she'd never see him again.

John couldn't be bothered joining in so he said nothing and no one seemed to mind or notice. He sipped his decanted wine and thought about the very different world he had left behind. What would the villagers have had to talk about over their bowl of rice? Whether their home would survive the last of the bombings? Would it still be standing the next day? Would their children survive into adulthood? Travel had sure broadened his horizons.

9

Churchies

WHEN BRAD SPED AWAY, LEAVING the table and his marriage in pieces, he instinctively headed for the water. There was no logical reason for his lethargy but he felt absolutely stuffed so sat for a moment on the sea wall. As he watched the seagulls squawk over a few dried-up chips and listened to the breakers slap the sand, he wondered what he and Emma would do now. Perhaps the answer lay out there, across the ocean where the world fell away, beyond the horizon.

"Hello."

Brad twisted around in the direction of the voice and the afternoon sun and raised an arm to block out the harsh backlight. It took a few seconds for his eyes to focus on the silhouette of a woman.

"Emma?" Her bikini was the one she wore when they first started going together. Pink with green hibiscus flowers. But her hair was really long again. "Emm, is that you?"

"No silly, it's me. Sally."

"Sally?"

"Yes, Sally Watson from school, Mr Emery."

"Oh, sorry," he said, moving to position the sun to one side, "I couldn't see you."

"You don't usually hang out here, Mr Emery."

"No, I don't, you're right."

"I'm here with Mazza." Sally pointed to a girl lying face down on a striped beach towel."

Brad hadn't seen Sally since school broke up and probably wouldn't have recognised her out of uniform. It was apparent that she had been spending a lot of time at the beach. Her skin had darkened to the colour of liquid toffee. Her sun-bleached hair was being teased about her face by the cooling breeze. With a puff of breath, she released a strand caught between her lips.

"Your wife here?" she asked.

"Nope."

"Doesn't like the surf?"

"Yes, she does Sally. But she's at home."

"You got kids?" She twirled a strand of hair around a finger.

"No, no kids," Brad said, trying to hide his irritation. She had disturbed his solitude and he wasn't in the mood for small talk.

"I don't know if I'd ever have kids," she said.

"Well, you've got a while to think about it."

"No, I mean, with all the problems in the world."

"What would you know about the problems in the world, Sally?"

"Oh, I don't mean to sound sorry for myself. No, I haven't got any problems. But you've got to admit that the world's a pretty screwed up place?"

"Yeah, I'd admit that."

"Hang on a minute." Sally leapt sure-footedly, from the sea wall onto the sand. Brad watched her skip towards her friend who had dozed off in the haze of midday heat. When Sally knelt down and spoke to her, Mazza raised her head, then looked up at Brad. Sally made her way back up the beach towards him, towel slung over one shoulder, sand prints on her knees.

A particularly feminine figure, Brad decided, as bodies go. A lot of women have a boy's torso, straight up and down with only their breasts to distinguish their gender. Sally, however, was curvaceous. Her body swerved, rose and fell like undulating sand hills. He imagined the whiteness of her skin where the tan mark ended. The demarcation line between the public and the private. The places that were untouched. He averted his eyes in time to see her towel flying through the air. He caught it as she reached the foot of the wall then she looked up at him, her arm extended. He reached down and hoisted her up. Without asking permission, she spread her towel next to him and sat herself down.

She intrigued him. Brad couldn't remember ever feeling relaxed around a teacher. But maybe this was something he could take credit for. He tried to make his students comfortable from the beginning, talking their language, sharing a joke. Had a go at telling Emma about it once while she made dinner and he knocked back a beer.

"…It was really funny," he said, the hinges on one of the desks had come apart so I sent Joel to get a screw and screwdriver from the handyman."

Emma listened as she turned the chops under the griller.

"Anyway, he got it wrong, so I told him when I ask you to get me a screw, make sure it's a good one! You should have heard them, Emm. They cracked up." Brad chuckled to himself as he waited for her to share his mirth, congratulate him on his quick wit.

"You sure you should be getting that friendly with them?"

"It was a joke Emma." He rummaged in the fridge. "You just don't get it," he said and ripped the top off a third can of beer.

Sally shook out her towel and spread it beside his. "It does confuse me, you know," she continued as if they had been in full flow of conversation, "why God would let all the shit stuff happen. I mean, if he's that smart…" She bit her lip and her hand covered her mouth. "Sorry, I can swear out of school, can't I?"

"Go for it. But I don't think God has much to do with the problems that we cause."

"Yeah, you're right." She was leaning back on her hands, kicking with her legs against the sea wall. "He just lets us get right on making our own mess."

When she raised her face to the sun her hair hung down past her waist. How small her ears were, dainty sculptures like the inside of a Nautilus shell. Perhaps he could hear the sea if he got close enough.

"And sometimes it's pretty hard to get out of," he added "if you've caused it – the mess, that is."

Sally sensed that he wasn't talking in the abstract. She turned to face him. "There is always a way out. You've just got to ask him to show you." She tucked a strand of hair behind one of her seashell ears and waited for his reply.

"You mean God?"

"Yeah, God."

"I haven't believed in him for years." Brad threw a loose stone onto the beach.

"That must be hard."

"You reckon?"

"You don't go to church?"

"No point." He threw a second stone but it landed short of the first. "Think I'll hit the surf," he said and stood up.

Sally brushed the sand from her hands and stood next to him. "Well if you ever want to start going again, you can come with me." She shook out her towel and draped it over her shoulder. "I go every Sunday."

"Thanks for the offer, Sally."

She retrieved a two dollar note from between her breasts. "I'm going to buy a thick shake. Want me to bring one back for you?"

He tried to appear uninterested as she readjusted her bikini top, but his voice had gone up an octave. "No thanks," he said.

"See you at school then."

"I'm teaching your year twelve class this year."

"I know."

She waved the money at him and was nearly out of earshot when he called, "Sally, where's the church?" A few people turned to look at him.

"On the corner, across the road from the new McDonalds,"

she shouted back. "Have a good surf, Mr. Emery." As she sprinted away her hair was caught by the wind and lifted up like a pair of wings, giving the impression that she was airborne.

Why had he asked her that? He had no intention of going to church. Now he felt unsettled, irritated by her certainty that God or Jesus or whoever it was, could show him a way out of the mess he was in. Churchies. They get that smug air of superiority. Think they've been chosen and know what's good for everyone else. He sat back down, picked up another stone and threw it along the sand. Would be nice to have their faith, to share their certainty. Although most of them don't get it until they've hit a wall. And here he was sitting on one.

"No fucking way, man!" he called out. Heads turned. He jumped up, grabbed his board and raced towards the surf.

As he paddled out, he nodded to a few of the regulars, the more confident riders who had laid early claim to the best place for a good take-off. When he reached the mob out back, he sat and waited. The first two sets he let go, resting for a moment, then paddled hard as the next swell approached. He thought he had the wave to himself, then from the corner of his eye he spotted a goofy footer coming straight at him. Brad was closest to the break so the wave should have been his.

"Fuck off, mate!" he yelled just before their boards collided, then felt the slow-motion thrashing of their arms and legs as they floundered in the glass green of the receding wave. His lungs cried out for air as he broke through the surface and hauled himself onto his board, gasping as another set rolled in.

"You arsehole!" he called to the bloke treading water next to him. "What the fuck...Johnno?"

"Nice way to welcome home a mate, you prick." John spat water at him.

"Shit, mate, didn't know it was you."

They began to paddle in synchronised strokes.

"When'd you get back?" Brad asked.

"While back."

"Enjoy the overseas holiday?"

"Yeah, five star luxury mate."

"Least you're all good, eh?"

"Fucking fantastic. You hanging around?"

"While it's good."

"How's Emm?"

"Yeah. Good." He tried to sound convincing.

John powered away in strong smooth strokes. Judging by the size of his torso he spent a lot of time in the water and Brad had trouble keeping up. Conversation ceased as they negotiated two breakers then moved beyond the swell to the back of the pack. They turned to face the beach and sat back on their boards to rest a moment, their legs sliced off at the knee by the deep black of the ocean. Rays of sunlight dried the saltwater on their skin to a crusty white.

"Having a turn tonight. You wanna come?"

"Yeah, maybe. At your oldies?"

"Nah, got my own pad." He pointed up the beach. "The flats on the front, number six."

"No shit, man."

"Yeah, me old man's way of saying he was glad I didn't get my fuckin' head shot off." Listen, I'm outta here. Can't sit round like a sheila all day." He paddled into position and lined up for the last wave of the set. "This one's mine, buddy," he shouted over his shoulder as the sea took him. "See you tonight."

It was a flawless take-off and Brad watched as John slid from sight down the face of the wave then took up a crouching position in the barrel and let the water cascade over his shoulders.

"Stoked!" he yelled as he pulled out and thrust a fist into the air.

From time to time during the day, they passed each other, silently. Around two thirty the wind picked up and the conditions began to deteriorate. Brad decided to call it quits. He'd have to go home some time and Emma should have calmed down by now. John was still sitting way out back on his own, when he drove out of the car park and cruised past John's block of flats. You'd be able to see the beach from the balcony. He'd go to the party on his own tonight if she wouldn't come.

A wet towel hung over his shoulder as he began the climb to the second floor. The door was ajar and Emma was standing with her back to him, cleaning the sink.

"Your Dad's been," she said.

"How come?"

"We were supposed to go for lunch. Remember?"

"Shit yeah. I forgot."

Emma turned her back and resumed cleaning the sink. "He cleaned up the garage," she said, her voice breaking.

"I didn't notice. I parked on the street."

The towel dropped onto the floor as he approached his wife and held her by the shoulders."

"Emm, I didn't mean it, you know." He turned her around to face him.

"Oh God. I do know, it's not your fault, it's both of us, We'll be okay, wont we?" she whimpered.

"I meant I didn't mean to break the table."

Her eyes widened. "Is that all you think happened?"

"You're being difficult, Emma. What's got into you."

"Why is it always me?"

"Emm, can we drop it, please. I've got some news."

"What?"

"I ran into Johnno in the surf."

"He's home then. That's good, I guess."

"Actually, he ran into me. Bastard cut in on one of my waves."

"They're not yours you know."

"Point is, he's having a party tonight. Maybe it's what we need. Haven't been to a party in years."

"He asked us?"

"Yeah. Defo."

"At his oldies?"

"No, he's got a new pad on the beach."

"How did he score that?"

"Old man."

"Should have guessed."

"Come on Emm, it will do us good. How about you wear those hot pants you made. You look good in them."

"I'd like to see him, I guess. It's been ages."

"Great," he said, relieved. "We need to leave about seven. Come on Emm, give me a cuddle."

"Oh, Brad. I don't know what is happening with us."

"Emm, I'm trying. I really am," he said as he walked to the bathroom. "We should get ready."

The primal thump of a base rhythm led them to an open door on the second floor of John's units. Emma hung back as Brad checked they were in the right place.

"Yeah, this is it." He led her inside.

Emma's eyes adjusted to the smoky gloom. A guy was twirling around in circles in the middle of the room, arms flailing above his head. He held a beer can in his left hand and every now and again his hips connected to the pelvis of a barefooted girl with straight blonde hair that hung over her bare midriff to below her navel. It was John for sure, and a girl Emma didn't recognise, making out to Mick Jagger's second chorus of *Brown Sugar*.

"Get a go at him." Emma squeezed Brad's arm. "Looks like the army taught John how to party."

Brad recognised the girl. Remembered her from the surf club and vaguely recalled them leaving together and pashing out the back. He watched as she flung her hair away from her eyes. They met his, moved to observe Emma, and then returned to him. She remembered too. John had come along that night and dragged him off to the pub just as he was about to give her a knee bender in the back lane.

"Mate, come in to my parlour." Johnno slapped Brad on the back. "Emmy, gorgeous Emmy, come and give me a big tongue kiss."

"John Thompson, where's the nice young man I used to know?" She offered him her cheek.

THE TEACHER, THE PUPIL AND THE WIFE

"Beers in the bathtub, Mate." He pointed down the hallway then faced Emma, pulled her close and nestled his nose in her hair.

"Missed you heaps, Emm."

"Glad you're safe, John." She reached up and stroked his cheek.

"Yeah, me too. Wanna drink?"

"I'll have one to celebrate your homecoming. Red wine if you've got it."

"Your wish is my command." As he turned towards the kitchen, the long-haired girl grabbed his arm.

"Dance with me," she said.

"Piss off, Janice," he snapped as he pushed her away.

Emma watched with concern as the girl sauntered back to the lounge room.

"Don't worry about her, Emm." His free hand guided her towards the kitchen. "Now what were we doing? Oh yeah, a drink." He opened a cupboard door and rummaged around for a glass, held it up to the light and, satisfied that it was clean, poured the wine.

There was only one other person Emma knew who drank wine that came in a bottle. Her father-in-law. She took a sip and licked her lips. "Tastes better than the stuff out of flagons, John."

"Nothing is too good for yourself, Emmy and life's much too short to drink crap." His beer can was thrust unsteadily towards her as she proposed a toast.

"To our returned soldier."

"Listen. You be all right if I go find her ladyship?"

"Yeah, sure."

"Catch you later." He winked at her and wove his way through the crowd, grabbed the girl's hand and led her towards the bedroom. Emma found a seat in the corner of the lounge and watched the hungry mob devour the only food on the table, her plate of chived mashed potato wrapped in devon.

"Hi Emma." She swung around. It was Martin's wife.

"Kerry, haven't seen you for ages."

"You look great. Love your hot pants."

"Thanks, I made them."

"You're so clever. Wish I had your legs."

"Yeah and I wish I had your hair," Emma laughed, "guess we're never happy with what we've got."

"Probably right." Kerry said and threw back most of her glass of wine.

Emma took another sip of claret. "Anyway, how are you, Kes? How are the happy married couple?"

"Don't ask me." She shrugged and polished off what was left in her glass. "I mean, how would I know?"

Emma suppressed a look of surprise. She and Martin should be on cloud nine. A block of land, a gift from the oldies, and a new house underway. Wasn't it every girl's dream? Kerry had boasted she only worked because she wanted to. Martin said she could quit any time. They'd definitely be able to afford kids.

Kerry began to sway back and forth and Emma took hold of her elbow. "You okay?"

"Yeah," She held her glass up to the light and squinted. "Nice wine."

"Let's sit down Kes. My feet are killing me in these shoes. Tell me about the house then. How's it going?"

"How would I know, Martin does it all. I just go along with it."

Emma lowered her eyes.

"Sorry Emma. That was mean. It's a gorgeous house and I know I'm sooo lucky. Been told a hundred, no, a thousand times."

"Two storeys?" Emma asked.

"Yes, with a rumpus room. And en-suites. Posh, eh?"

'You're kidding."

"Nup. All the bells and whistles. Take me forever to clean." Kerry laughed at her own cynicism, then hiccupped. "How're youse guys, anyway?"

"Good Kerry. Nice to have John home, isn't it?"

They turned to see him coming out of the bedroom with the girl, the pair of them looking dishevelled and red-cheeked.

"Yeah. He's changed though, dirty bugger."

"You reckon?"

"He's wild, not like he used to be." She made for the Ben Ean Moselle on the table and helped herself to a refill. "You're drinking red," she said as she finished off the bottle.

"What were you saying? About John?"

She nestled down next to Emma. "He's the same as them all. Just took him longer to catch up. In the end, they're all just after sex, sex, and more sex." She raised her glass and finished off the contents.

"Suppose so." Emma said. Even Brad had been once.

"I thought Martin would settle down, you know. After we were married. 'Scuse me." Kerry covered her mouth as she belched. "But he's still like a rucking bull if you want to know the truth. And I'm fed up. Not to mention sore," she snorted, "I suppose Brad's the same?"

Kerry kept on, before Emma was obliged to think of an answer. "You know, he even wants to have sex when I've got my periods."

Emma wondered what that would be like.

"To tell the absolute truth, I can't stand him coming near me anymore." Kerry's bottom lip started to shake and she put the empty glass to her mouth to still the trembles.

"It's probably only a phase, Kes," Emma said hoping it might be true, for both of them.

"You don't understand." She grasped Emma's forearm, red nails digging into flesh. "I don't want my husband coming near me. Ever, ever again." Then she burst into tears.

"Kes, I'm so sorry. Don't get upset." Emma gave the hand a pat then prised loose the fingernails digging into her flesh.

"I don't know what *you're* sorry for, Emma." Kerry retrieved her arm and dragged it along her dripping nostrils. "Martin's the rampant animal." Emma was seeing him in a whole new light. "No, Emma. I'm the one who's sorry." She leaned over and hissed into Emma's ear. "I'm sorry I ever got married, if you want to know the truth."

Kerry lurched forward to place her glass on the coffee table. It missed the edge and Emma picked it up from the floor. "Thanks Emma, you're a good friend," Kerry said grasping Emma's hand with two of her own.

They sat for a moment, contemplating life, then Kerry stood up, smoothed down her mini skirt and with intense concentration, and without a word to Emma, made her way towards the bathroom, holding onto the wall for support. Emma thought she'd give her a few moments then follow, but before she had a chance, Kerry reappeared with her handbag slung over her shoulder.

Emma watched as she made a beeline for Martin. He was huddled in the corner whispering into Brad's ear. Brad looked like he couldn't wait to get away. He never liked Martin much – used to call him 'Marlin' because of the wet fish handshake.

Kerry placed her hand on her husband's shoulder and whispered to him. She didn't wait for a reply and he didn't watch as she walked out the door. Only the three of them noticed she had gone.

Emma eased herself back onto the lounge, both hands clutching her wine. Kerry had always been a bit unhinged. Some family tragedy way back. Everyone hoped things had taken a turn for the better when she landed Martin. She'd never picked him as randy. Kerry's problem was the opposite of hers.

Emma tilted her head back against the wall, closed her eyes and let the music and wine take over.

"Ya know, they say you're mad if you smile at nothin' Emma." John plonked himself down beside her and moved in close.

"I wasn't smiling at nothing."

"Then tell me."

"Private joke."

"Garn. You can tell Johnno anything." A half empty bottle of port hung precariously from his left hand.

"Why don't you tell me what you've been up to?"

"Well, I carn tell you, Emm-ma. You prob'ly wooden approve." His words were slung together haphazardly, all vowels and muted consonants, not unlike Kerry's.

"Wanna dance?" He yanked his head towards the centre of the room.

Tommy Roe was singing *Dizzy*. Emma decided that it described what was going on inside John's head.

"I think I'll find Brad. See if I can get him to have a dance."

John turned and surveyed the room. "Here, be a gorgeous girl and ged me a beer and I'll fine your old man."

As Emma walked to the kitchen, John headed onto the balcony.

"You fuckin' stupid or somethin' mate?" He grabbed Brad's shoulder, separated him from the girl he had pinned against the wall, and spun him around. "Your wife's lookin' for you. And you're a slut, Janice. Get outta here."

"Easy on mate. Just mucking around. No harm, okay?" Brad reasoned.

"Just fuck off Janice."

"Sure. I'm outta here."

They watched her stomp out of the flat, deliberately knocking over a bottle of wine as she went. Emma was rummaging in the esky for a beer and looked up as the door slammed shut.

John turned to Brad. "Your wife wants to dance," he said, then walked to the end of the balcony and lit up.

Brad used both hands to push his hair into place and walked back to the party.

"That for me?" he said to Emma as she came towards him, beer in hand.

"For John actually. You have it. I'll get him another one."

"Leave him. He's having a joint, he won't want it now." They turned to see John leaning over the railing, one leg cocked on the second rung, his face turned towards the hushhh of the waves.

"Hear you want to dance?"

"Yeah, love to."

Brad took Emma's hand and pulled her towards the centre of the room. A Roberta Flack LP was on the turntable. Emma snuggled into him as they swayed to her version of *The First Time Ever I Saw Your Face*.

"Do you remember our first time?" she murmured.

"In the back of the station wagon?"

"No, when we first met, when you walked into the dance with the guys when the pub closed. Remember how we couldn't stop looking at each other?"

"Sure I do." He tightened his arms around her.

"Brad, move your beer. It's icy on my back."

"Sorry." Their arms fell away.

As he emptied the can, Emma turned towards the balcony. The tops of the waves were like licks of whipped cream in the dappled moonlight. John was still there, looking out into the night. "He looks lonely, Brad. I think his girlfriend left."

"Leave it, Emm. He's pissed. Get your bag, we're going too. I'll say goodbye for both of us."

"It's a bit early isn't it?"

"They'll all be stoned soon. You don't want to be here, Emm."

"Guess not."

"Get your stuff. I'll say goodbye." Brad tapped John on the shoulder. "See ya, Mate."

"Fuck off. You don't deserve her." He looked past Brad and found Emma standing in the kitchen with her empty plate in hand, staring at them. He held her gaze for just a moment too long. When she started to walk towards him, he turned away and looked back out to sea.

As they lay in bed, Emma asked. "Brad, did you tell John why we were leaving?"

"Yeah."

"Maybe he needs to have a joint, Brad. After what he's been through."

"Maybe."

"He must think we're wowsers."

"I don't think he'll remember much about last night, so I wouldn't worry."

"Kerry told me she's not happy."

"She say why?"

"I don't think she loves him."

"He's a funny guy."

"No more than the rest of us."

"Go to sleep, Emm. It's late." She rolled onto her side and he listened while her breathing became shallow and slow.

Brad lay awake, staring into the darkness. He saw Janice pinned against the wall by the biggest erection he'd had in months. She had turned him on instantaneously, like a light.

Bloody Hell. They were in his head again, the squatters, taking bets this time that he was on his way back to his old habits. He was so screwed up. It was after two am when he finally accepted that he had no idea what to do next and fell into a fitful sleep.

When he woke he knew from the wan daylight that it was early so he lay with eyes closed hoping to go back to the oblivion of sleep where the guilt and confusion let him be. It was then that he recalled the dream. There was a girl, with hair like gossamer wings.

"Ask God for help," she said.

10

Breaching the Forbidden

THE WARDROBE DOOR SQUEAKED AS it opened. Emma didn't stir. Unsure of what the dress code was these days, Brad chose a white short-sleeved shirt and long brown trousers, badly creased, but they'd do. He dressed in the bathroom and grabbed a granny smith on his way out the door. Plenty of time, and Emma would think he was on his way to the beach.

It was 8.30 when he pulled up just short of the church grounds and polished the apple on his trouser leg. The first bite told him it was sour so he chucked it into the garden bed on the nature strip.

Two couples were standing outside the main door chatting. *Keen to get a good seat*, he mused. They all looked pretty normal, nice actually and happy. So maybe there is something in this religion stuff. He always thought he could do it on his own, make his own decisions, didn't need anyone or anything else. But there was no way he could pretend he hadn't stuffed up so far. Big time. Maybe he did need some help. He detected a faint cheer from the squatters.

While the idea of talking to God, someone you couldn't see, seemed silly, it also had its appeal. God wasn't going to give him a hard time if he didn't listen. He couldn't if he wasn't there, could he?

People were moving towards the church door, but he would wait until everyone was inside then creep in and position himself discreetly at the back. That's if he didn't chicken out in the next few minutes and head to the beach. A knock on the windscreen glass startled him and he watched her lips move as she mouthed the words,

"You coming in?"

He wound down the window. "Just making sure I've got the right place."

Couldn't quite get his bearings with Sally. The ease with which she addressed him made him forget she was a pupil, and she had a worldliness about her. Mature for her age, definitely.

He fumbled with the door handle then dropped his keys as he stepped out of the car.

"Butterfingers," she joked. "Come on, follow me."

As they crossed the road, she waved to a group about her age. A family of four greeted her by name, kissed her, hugged her and then two young boys waved from the door of the church. Brad stood back, unsure if he would stay or chuck a runner at the last minute. Sally let him have his space and only as she entered the church, as she tossed her hair back over her shoulders, did she turn and beckon for him to follow.

The pews were pretty full so he got to sit at the back and could still make a quick getaway. As she sat down, Sally bowed her head and he saw her lips move. They were soft full lips and he wanted to reach over and touch them. She looked up as the minister climbed into the pulpit. A hush came over the congregation. Brad jumped in his seat as the sermon began. He didn't need a microphone, this bloke. His voice bellowed out, bouncing off the stone walls. Sally giggled. Evidently, he did this every week because no one else flinched.

"If we confess our sins, he is faithful and just and will forgive us our sins and purify us from all unrighteousness. 1 John 1, Verse 9," he bellowed.

Brad was sure that the minister was speaking to him. Nah, no way was he being singled out. Couldn't be, not even Sally knew he was coming.

"Repent, then, and turn to God, so that your sins may be wiped out, that times of refreshing may come from the Lord. Acts 3, Verse 19."

There's no way this bloke could have known the relevance of the verses that just kept on coming.

"God is in control of everything." This reassured and at the same time terrified Brad. Was God there all the time, watching maybe? The screwing around? The infection – was it a punishment?

"God's love is a gift of hope." That was exactly what he had lost. Hope for his marriage and for himself.

And the minister kept right on firing the salvos. "Redemption and absolution is God's gift to every sinner." God was onto him, that was for sure.

The rest of the sermon was lost to Brad as his mind became consumed with tantalising thoughts of forgiveness and purification. According to the bloke up the front, all he had to do was ask God. Too easy. A cinch. But what about Emma? Would God be able to make him desire his wife again? That'd be a bloody miracle. But that's what God's supposed to do, make impossible things happen. Maybe they could start again with a clean, fresh slate.

Sally passed the hymn book and pointed to the title *Cleanse Me*. The congregation raised their heads and their voices rose. Brad mumbled the words and noticed that Sally occasionally glanced at him and grinned as she sang along.

Search me, O God,
And know my heart today;
Try me, O Saviour,
Know my thoughts, I pray.
See if there be
Some wicked way in me;
Cleanse me from every sin
And set me free.

From the pit of his stomach, he felt an expanding wave of emotion. When it reached his chest, he thought the compression was the beginning of a heart attack and was terrified that he would cry out with the ache of it. He clamped his mouth shut, turned his eyes to the vaulted ceiling and held his breath until the clot of guilt dissipated and he could breathe once more.

When the congregation silenced, then knelt to pray, Brad stayed in his seat and took the opportunity to draw his sleeve across his eyes. He was sure no one noticed.

"Will you come again?" Sally asked as they queued to shake hands with the minister.

"Not sure," he said.

She nodded. "Whatever you want."

The couple in front of them ushered their children away and it was their turn. "Hi, Reverend Turner, this is Brad," Sally chirped.

"Your Mum and Dad not here today?"

"No, they went to help Uncle Sam with his new boat."

"See them next week then. You're staying for Bible Study?"

"Yep. As usual."

Brad shook the minister's hand and then moved away as quickly as possible. The sky was overcast and it looked like it could rain. He'd surf anyway.

"Glad you came?" Sally asked with a side-ways glance as they moved away from the steps.

"Yeah. Thanks for the invite."

"See you Tuesday then." she said casually.

"Sure." It had started to spit raindrops. Brad turned his palm towards the sky. "Don't get wet," he said, "see you," and sprinted towards the car.

Sally moved to shelter under a tree. As he drove away, she waved. He hoped she would.

The next week, he surfed in the morning and on the off-chance, took the turn-off towards the church on the way home. He spotted her coming from one of the outbuildings.

"Want a lift?" he called through the passenger window.

"Yeah, sure."

He cleared the front seat then opened the door.

"Hop in."

"Thanks."

"You'll need to show me the way."

"Straight ahead."

"Surf was great today."

"That's good. Turn left here."

He liked how she didn't pressure him. "How's this year going for you?"

"Hard, but okay."

It was Brad's turn but the words were stuck. They drove on until Sally broke the silence.

"I'm down the end of this street. Just let me out here. Thanks heaps. See you." And she was gone.

He didn't understand why he felt elated.

The next week, he went back to church and sat at the back, on his own. She was sitting with her parents in the front pew and he watched her eyes close as she prayed, her pouted lips open and shut as she sang and her neck lengthen as she threw her head back for the high notes. Her father put his arm around her and whispered in her ear during the sermon and she nodded in agreement. Brad left before the end of the service and waited out of sight until she finished Bible Study. This time, when she saw the car, she walked quickly towards it.

He pulled over well away from her house. She never asked him why, nor did she suggest he drive her to the door. After all, they were only talking. Doing nothing wrong. Chatting about school and the beach. He started the engine and drove home feeling a light-heartedness he hadn't felt in years, so he went back the next week, and the next and the next.

When the May school holidays arrived, he would occasionally glimpse her sunbaking in the sheltered dip of the sand dunes with friends, lying face down. The straps of her bikini top were undone, her arms spread cactus-like over her head, her breasts partly exposed like half scoops of vanilla ice cream.

June was a wet month with big seas and little chance of good surf. Still, he went to the beach and sat with the rain dripping down the windows, watching the waves crash on the seaweed littered shoreline, waiting for church to finish. On the last sodden Sunday of the month, with the windows of the car steamed up and the air muggy with the heat from their bodies, she asked why he looked so down in the dumps.

"Things aren't too good at home, I guess."

She didn't pry or try to convince him otherwise. Simply listened and he began to tell her things he'd never told anyone else.

"Maybe I shouldn't have got hitched in the first place… I had second thoughts…couldn't tell her."

The confessions seeped out and it felt good to tell someone who didn't judge.

He told her how he felt trapped now.

"How can you stand it?" she asked, the sympathy a gift.

"I don't have a choice."

"You always have a choice."

"You reckon?"

"Sometimes we don't like the choices we have, but you should never feel trapped. If you pray, you'll find a way. Even if it means acceptance."

"A way to stay?"

"Is that what you want?"

"I dunno."

"You'll work it out."

"I think it's you that helps me work things out."

"I just listen."

"I like that. Can we keep doing this?"

"What, meeting up?"

"Yeah."

"To talk?"

"Yeah," he replied, "no harm in that."

He repeated the words to himself as he drove home. *No harm in that*, and this time, the squatters went wild, mocking his self-deception.

At the beginning of second term Sally began to hover near the staffroom with lame queries about homework. At day's end she would appear alongside him as he walked towards his last class. At first, he thought their meetings were coincidental and couple of times when he expected to see her and she didn't turn up, he felt an aching disappointment. When he reciprocated, arranged to be in her path, she would respond with a knowing smile.

The coincidences increased in regularity and became more daring. He was convinced they were deliberate. Sally would drop a text book when he walked past her locker and simultaneously they would reach for it, hands brushing against one another, lingering. They held each other's gaze and only when their instincts told them that they were being observed did they avert their eyes. As they walked to class, he would hold the door for her and she would reach out her fingers and maintain contact for longer than necessary. Every day, each smile said a lot more than 'hello'. Their interaction at school had none of the intimacy of their tightly cocooned talks in the car, but it was electric and he was elated. He hadn't strayed, he'd kept his promise and maybe God was rewarding him with a newfound contentment. They'd done nothing wrong. He had never touched her. He made sure of that. Yet, he sensed that the time spent with Sally was a greater act of betrayal, than anything he'd done in the past.

On a Monday afternoon early in July Sally lingered at her desk, stalling for time, rummaging in her backpack. "You go on Marilyn," she said. "I've got to sort out some stuff." Marilyn threw her books in her bag and left in a huff. As usual the room emptied of pupils at twice the pace it had filled.

Brad continued to clean the blackboard. He shook out the duster, topped up the sticks of chalk, repositioned his chair, examined papers on his desk. When the door closed, he raised his head and looked at Sally with an understanding that evaded words. He walked towards her, pulled out the seat from the desk in front of her then sat legs astride, leaning his elbows on the chair back and head on his arms. He watched as she arched her back, gathered up her hair and tied it in a knot on the top of her head, meeting his eyes as she did so. He waited for her to speak.

"I really love your classes. You know that don't you?" she said leaning forward and resting her crossed arms on the desk. "You make the lessons so interesting, I'm really stoked that I took the subject."

"What do you want to do next year?" Brad knew the answer, they had talked it over many times but he couldn't think of anything else to say to make her stay just a little longer. "You should be able to take your pick, Sally."

"True. But we don't always get to choose what we want. We both know that."

"Sally, I can't do this much longer."

With trepidation he slid his hand along the desk, across the divide, the gap that existed between pupil and teacher, breaching the forbidden. His fingertips brushed her closed fist. Her eyes look directly into his. In the moment of stillness that followed, he panicked. Had he misread the signs? Then her childlike fingers unfurled, and one by one they coupled with his own.

"Meet me tonight," he said.

11

Gossip

It had gone eight o'clock and Emma could hear Greg's car pulling up as she ran down the stairs. "Morning," she said a little breathless.

"What you got there?" he asked as she laid a plastic bag onto the back seat of the Mini.

"A dress I'm making for a party on Saturday. I'm going to finish off the hand sewing at lunchtime."

"Party at your place?"

"No, at Sandy's."

"She a friend from school?"

"Yep."

"You'll look nice in red."

"Oh, thanks. Nice to get a bit dolled up for a change."

They drove in silence for a few miles then Emma cleared her throat. "Greg, can I say something, about looking nice, can I give you some advice?"

"Sure."

"You should comb your hair and maybe iron your clothes. You look like you've just got out of bed."

"Yeah, I know. Just got a lot on." He used the fingers of his left hand to push his lanky, black hair back from his forehead then smoothed down the sides."

"Doesn't take long, Greg. It would be good for you, at work and all."

"Yeah, you're probably right.

They made the rest of the journey to the factory in silence. Emma also worked on the dress that night and again on Friday, while Brad was at Uni. She ironed out the seams, gave the frill around the neckline a final pressing and, pleased with her handiwork, hung it in the wardrobe ready for the party.

On Saturday while he was at the beach, Emma whipped cream and hulled the strawberries to decorate the pavlova that was cooling in the oven. Sandy didn't have to ask, Emma knew what to take. Her pav's were always a hit at parties. At two o'clock while she was in the bathroom colouring her hair, the front door opened. A few moments later, a commentator's voice drifted from the TV. While the match played she dried her hair, painted her nails, applied make-up then retrieved the dress from the wardrobe. When she heard the final whistle, she emerged from the bedroom,

"Brad, what do you think?"

"What?"

"My dress. What do you think?

"Oh, you look lovely. When did you make that?"

"Last week. After you said we could go to the party."

"Hair looks good, too. Like the red toenail polish." Occasionally, he could see her for the good sort that she was. He knew other blokes eyed her off and tonight he understood why. She'd got a bit of a tan over the last two weeks, sunbaking against the factory wall at lunchtime. Her skin glowed and highlighted her pale green eyes. The red dress was sexy, low neckline and really short. Not much to it actually. Emma always said she could make a dress from a metre of fabric, which cost less than two dollars.

"Can you get dressed please, Brad? We need to leave in fifteen minutes."

As they backed out of the garage, Emma turned around to position the pavlova on the back seat and noticed a pair of brown trousers and a white shirt on the floor.

"You been wearing these?"

"Yeah."

"What on earth for?"

"Been going to church," he confessed.

"You what?"

"Going to church…if the surf's no good."

"You're kidding! You hate church."

"Some kids from school talked me into it."

"You really think you should get that friendly?"

"We've had this out already. Go on, tell me why not?"

"I don't know. My teachers never had anything to do with us."

"Thought you were okay about it. You know I've been surfing with the some of the kids from school."

"What about John? Why aren't you surfing with someone your own age?"

"He's a weirdo, Emma. You saw him at the party. Listen, it's good for me to get on with the kids."

"No one ever had anything to do with teachers at school."

"Times change, Emma."

"You aren't going to get all religious are you?"

"No chance. I just go now and again to look good." They pulled up in front of Sandy and Rob's house.

Brad was out of the car like a shot and walked around to open the door for Emma.

"Wow, a real gentleman tonight."

They made their way down the steep driveway. Garden lights floodlit the bushland that surrounded the clinker brick home. Emma wondered what it would be like to live here, to have a home with space and trees and an outdoor area.

Sandy met them at the front door. "Hey, you two. Love your dress kiddo. Hey Brad, you're looking fit. Come on in."

Rob padded into the kitchen in his socks.

"Evening all. Emm, hi." They embraced. "Caught any good waves lately, Mate." Rob shook Brad's hand.

"Been a bit too busy to do much surfing."

"Sandy, where do you want this?" Emma held out the Tupperware container.

"On the bench please. Looks yummy," she said opening the lid.

Rob padded over in his socks. "Pavlova. Wow Emm, thanks."

"Keep your fingers out, it's not all for you," Sandy called.

"As long as I get a big bit later."

"And put some shoes on, please. Then get the barbie going, love."

"Sandy, give me a break."

"People will be here soon."

"They've seen me in my socks before," he drawled. "Help yourself to a beer Brad, while I follow orders. Outside in the esky. Shoes coming up, Darling."

Emma admired the way they could banter without a hint of irritation. She watched Brad wander into the yard, hands in pockets, and busied herself by sticking toothpicks of cheese and gherkins into the carcass of a pineapple while Sandy counted out forks and knives.

"Glad you could come, Emm." She laid the cutlery aside and kissed Emma's cheek. "Work good?"

"My job's okay but there's talk of putting people off in the factory. Gee, the house looks great, Sandy."

"Yeah, you know Rob – Mr Perfection, but I don't complain."

"Listen, before anyone gets here," she pulled Emma aside, "Kerry and Martin have split."

"You're kidding."

"Nope. Last week. She's gone back to her Mum's."

"Is she okay?"

"Don't know. Michelle told me. She found some matches in his pockets from a brothel up the Cross. He confessed the lot when she confronted him."

"Poor thing. We saw her at John's party a while back. She wasn't too good then, but I never thought…"

"She wasn't happy, Emma."

"I suppose so. Who's coming tonight, Sandy?"

"The usual gang – Michelle and Tony, Barney and Bernadette and I think Darren and Ros have just arrived.

The doorbell rang. Rob ushered his brother and sister-in-law into the kitchen.

"Hi darls." Roslyn kissed Sandy then turned to Emma.

"I haven't seen you for yonks. You look great. Brad, hi there."

"Oh, sorry. Hi Ros. Just admiring the work Rob's done in the yard."

"Darren, Brad's here."

"G'day, mate." Darren strode towards him. They shook hands.

"You still studying?" Roslyn asked.

"Yeah, still at it."

"My Dazza hasn't got the brains," Ros said as she put her arm around her husband, "but he makes a great plumber." Darren shrugged his shoulders as he pulled the ring on a beer can.

Emma turned to see Michelle making her way down the driveway. Tony trailed behind, carrying a teak salad bowl. Michelle's long halter neck dress highlighted her bony shoulders. She had legs like stovepipes, poor thing.

By the time Barney and Bernadette arrived, the barbecue coals were glowing and ready. Rob bought his steaks in Mascot from a butcher that cut them two inches thick. Too bad if you wanted well done.

The men had already formed a huddle near the barbie, standing legs astride, one hand holding a coldy and the other tucked into the top of their jeans. John was the topic of conversation.

"Yeah, I hear he's off the air a bit."

"Went troppo up north, now he's living it up in the pad his old man bought for him."

"Lucky bugger."

"Poor bugger you mean, getting called up. Glad I missed the roll-call."

Opinions were tossed back and forth about the rights and wrongs of the Vietnam war.

In the kitchen, there was general agreement from the girls that the breakup of Kerry and Martin was on the cards.

"He was a sleaze," Roslyn said.

"Yeah, and she was an iceberg," Darren chipped in over his shoulder as he made a beeline for the bathroom.

"Get lost, you," his wife shouted as the door closed.

"Steaks nearly ready, Sandy," Rob called.

"Salads are on the table Darling. Can everyone grab a plate please," Sandy called as the girls filed outside.

Brad was seated at the opposite end of the table to Emma. She watched as Darren and Tony talked across him as if he wasn't there. No-one except herself seemed to notice and he didn't seem to mind. He kept his head down, tucking into his steak while polishing off several glasses of claret.

After dinner, the girls cleared up and the blokes huddled around the warming embers of the fire, beer cans exchanged for glasses of claret. Emma glanced over from time to time and found Brad staring into the darkness. When he left the group and sat on the stone bench, she went to join him.

"You okay? Not enjoying yourself?"

"No, it's all good."

"We'll go soon if you want."

"Whenever," he said.

"You hear about Martin and Kerry?" Emma asked. "They broke up."

"Yeah, I heard."

"Was that what you were talking about at John's?"

"Nah, just car stuff."

"Oh." They sat in silence.

Emma smiled at Michelle who was watching them from the kitchen window. When Rob turned up the music, she gave it a few minutes then pulled Brad up to dance.

"Two tracks, okay? And then we'll go."

"Sure."

"You've been somewhere else all night," she said and leaned onto his shoulder.

"Just tired I guess."

When the track finished Emma said, "I'll get my things."

"You're not leaving?" Sandy said as she scraped the leftover pavlova onto a plate and began to wash the Tupperware. "I've hardly seen you."

"Brad's been at Uni late this week. Sorry."

He came up behind them. "Yeah, sorry Sandy. Great party."

"Let's catch up at the beach, eh. The four of us."

"Sure," Brad replied. "Better take a leak before I hit the road."

"Well if you've got to go, you've got to go, I guess." Sandy kissed Emma's cheek, held her by both shoulders and asked, "All good with you guys?"

"Yeah, sure. He's just tired."

Their car hadn't left the curb before Michelle tapped Sandy on the shoulder.

"Everything okay with Brad and Emma?"

"Yeah, why shouldn't it be?"

"Just some stuff I heard"

"Like what?"

"Not saying, but seems he and Martin were pretty buddy-buddy."

"So?"

"He told Tony they used to go out together, up the Cross." Michelle rolled her eyes.

"So? There's no law against that."

"What about picking up prostitutes?"

"That's bullshit." Sandy blew smoke in Michelle's face.

"Not according to Martin. Seems Brad never had any money so he had to pay for them both."

"Michelle, I don't think I'd believe a thing that guy says. Kerry didn't leave him for nothing. He's a jerk."

"Maybe, but he's got nothing to gain by making it up. If it's true, Brad's a real bastard. I feel really sorry for Emma. Do you think we should tell her?"

"Don't you bloody dare. It's just bullshit."

"Yeah, maybe but I wouldn't want to be sleeping with someone who's doing it with pro's. Might catch something you don't go fishing for. Know what I mean?"

"Come on, help me finish the wine, and swear you won't say anything."

Sandy wondered for how long Michelle could keep her mouth shut. It was 1.15 am when the last couple left.

While they were clearing up, Sandy confided in Rob, "Should I tell Emma?"

"No way. It could all be bullshit."

"What if it's not?"

"You can't be the one to tell her, Sandy."

"What if she finds out I knew?"

"Say you didn't believe it… Do you?"

"Don't know. He was miles away tonight."

"Even if she does find out, she'll probably make up an excuse and forgive him."

"God knows what she sees in him."

"Something we don't."

"Guess so."

"Sand, remember when Jane and Eric separated and we told her what we thought of her old man?"

"Said he'd always been as tight as a fish's arse, always managed to be missing when it was his turn to shout." Sandy took a pile of plates and scraped the leftovers into a garbage bag.

"And then they got back together. Bloody hell, you put us in it."

"Hang on, you told her how when we all went out he took our cash to pay the bill and then booked it up on his company credit card."

"Oh God, yes. I remember."

"Can't think why they don't want to have a bar of us now, can you?"

"Can't say I miss them actually." Sandy began to rinse the wine glasses in a sink of clear water.

Rob came from behind and wrapped his arms around his wife.

"What do you think you're doing?" she said, bending over and responding with a wiggle of her bottom.

"Just playing with my favourite toys," he said, as he caressed her breasts and kissed her neck. "Leave that. Come to bed."

"Don't think I've got much choice, have I?" Sandy tossed the rubber gloves into the sink with a grin and followed her husband up the stairs, massaging his bum cheeks as they went.

12

Predator or Perfect Love?

SALLY WOULD HAVE MISSED HER stop if she hadn't caught sight of Marilyn standing at the curb, arms crossed.

"Next stop, please driver," she called as she dragged her schoolbag from under the seat and raced out the door. "Mazza, sorry. I had to stay back. You been waiting long?"

"What do you think?" She kicked the grass with the toe of her school shoe, head down, then glared at Sally.

"Said I'm sorry."

"S'pose you were with him, again."

"With who?"

"Give it up Sally. You know who. Mr Emery."

"Don't know what you're talking about."

"Yeah, sure you do. He might be your teacher, but what's he teaching you?"

"Get lost."

"Come on Sal. I've seen youse at school, pretending you just run into each other. And where are you on Saturdays? Not studying with me like your Mum thinks."

"So do you still want to come home for a while? We can play

some records. I've got a new Black Sabbath single."

"Stop changing the subject. Fess up."

"Nothing to tell. Come on, let's go." Sally set off up the road with Marilyn following behind.

As soon as they were alone in the bedroom, Marilyn started up again. "No more crap Sally. What's going on?"

Sally slouched across the bed, rolled onto her back and stared at the ceiling.

"Sal, I'm your best friend." Marilyn lay on her tummy and raised her head. "I know you. Don't lie to me", she said looking straight at Sally. "What's it like, being with an older man?"

For months, Sally had felt like shouting it from the rooftops, telling the world how amazing he was. So far, she hadn't said a word, had kept her promise. Now Marilyn had sussed them out.

"You swear you won't tell anyone, Mazza" Sally glared at her. Absolutely promise on your life, no-one."

"Course. Promise, promise, promise." She sat up. "So, tell me."

"Well," Sally began, now sitting against the wall, hugging her knees to her chest, "he's not like other boys, I mean the kids that I used to date. He's mature and intelligent."

Sally didn't notice that Marilyn's eyes rolled towards the ceiling.

"We just get on so well, you know." She sighed. "He just kind of knows what I'm thinking and feeling."

"You're so not serious. You mean it's true? You're off your bloody head. Are you kidding me or what?" Marilyn pushed herself into a sitting position and moved closer. "When did youse get together?"

"I felt it as soon as we came back this term and so did he," Sally explained, with more patience than she felt Marilyn deserved. "Then one day, we were in the classroom when everyone left and he was sitting opposite me and his hand slid along the desk, and we touched and well, that was it."

"Far out. You're sneaky, Sal." She elbowed Sally so hard she lost her balance.

"Didn't really have any choice, did we?" Sally hopped off the bed, sauntered to her desk and began to rearrange ornaments.

Marilyn was sitting on her haunches and leaned towards Sally and whispered, "Have you?"

"Have we what?"

"You know." She threw a cushion at Sally.

"What, kissed? Of course we have." Sally said, catching it on the full.

"No, gone all the way."

"You make it sound sordid." The cushion was returned to Marilyn.

"But have you?"

"Don't be stupid."

"You're lying."

"I am not."

"You are. You always do that thing with your tongue when you lie. You did it then."

"Mazza, you don't understand. He's not like that."

"You mean he's not a guy."

"You don't understand." Sally smoothed out the pleats in her uniform. "We've got the rest of our lives together."

"Whoa, you mean you've talked about getting hooked up." Marilyn's neck was protruding from her school blouse like a tortoise from its shell.

"Well not exactly, but he loves me and well, he's got to get out of his horrible marriage first."

"Divorce, God. But his wife's really nice. Everyone says so."

"She might look like nice but she's not. Picks on him like you wouldn't believe. Anyway, I'm in no hurry. I'd wait forever."

"Far out." They both stopped to listen to a sound at the door but it went away.

"What about school?"

"No one will know until after the HSC."

"And your oldies?"

"Definitely not the oldies. They'd freak out. But they'll come around when they get to know him."

"You reckon?"

"Yeah, why not?"

"Mine wouldn't. My Dad'd murder him." Marilyn ran her index finger across her throat.

"Look, when I've left school, I can pretty well do what I want."

They had forgotten to play the record which was a shame, because the music would have drowned out their conversation. The bedroom door flew open. Sally's mother was grasping the handle for support, her free hand covering her open mouth, as if she was about to vomit.

For what seemed like a long time, no one moved. Mrs Watson let go of the door handle but grasped it again when her knees went from under her. Sally and Marilyn saw her lips move but no words came out.

Mrs Watson swallowed hard then cleared her throat. "You'd better leave, Marilyn."

"Sure Mrs Watson."

Marilyn was up and off like a shot. "See ya Sal." She glanced back expecting to find her friend cringing on the bed, but Sally was standing tall, her feet firmly planted on the ground. Mrs Watson waited until she heard the front door close then locked eyes with her daughter.

"Did...I...hear...what...I...thought...I...heard? Sally?" After each word there was a pause, a gap that shouldn't be there. "Are, you, having an, um, affair with a teacher?" Sally hadn't known until then that people could scream softly.

"No Mum. I'm not..." Her fingers drew quotation marks in the air, "...having an affair..."

"Then what on earth were you talking to Marilyn about? And don't get smart with me, young lady." Mrs Watson had another voice now, with a shrill and hysterical ring to it. "Who is this person that you intend to spend the rest of your life with given that you've only just started it!"

"His name is Brad."

"And how do you know him? Where did you meet him?" The

pitch was an octave lower now, more controlled and less hysterical but with a hint of menace.

"I met him at school and yes, he is my teacher. But it's not like you think. He respects me."

Her mother looked around the bedroom as if it was the first time that she had been there. The room where she laid her newborn in a bassinet that seemed to engulf her. The room where her sweet baby had grown into a beautiful adolescent. Sally's Bible was on her bedside table and the rag doll that she took everywhere for the first four years of her life was slumped on the windowsill. There was the picture on the bookshelf of Sal with her friends at the snow, her first trip away when she started high school, the school where she was now, where this hideous thing was happening.

Mrs Watson gripped the back of the chair beside the desk where Sally studied late into the night to achieve the marks that had made them so proud. She turned the chair around, intending to sit down, but stopped short as she saw her daughter anew, and for the first time in her life found it hard to talk to her. As she lowered herself onto the seat, Mrs Watson clasped her hands on her lap, looked up to the ceiling, took a deep breath and then exhaled slowly.

"When did it start, Sal?"

"What start?"

"This thing with this man.'

"This year I guess."

"When this year?"

"I don't know. After the holidays I suppose."

"So, it's been going on for months behind our backs. What on earth do you think you're doing?"

"I'm still studying hard, if that's what you're worried about. I'll still do well and I'm going to go to uni."

"Sally Watson, that's the least of my worries. How old is this man?"

"He's twenty-four, not much older than me." Sally welcomed the chance to explain, to get her mother to understand. "He's a good man Mum, and he is serious about us but he's in this really bad marriage."

"Married?" Mrs Watson whimpered, "I can't do this without your father Sally." She used the desk to lever herself into a standing position and left the room, knocking over the chair as she went.

The tray with the two glasses of lemonade and two pieces of homemade chocolate cake was still on the floor outside the door. Mrs Watson wasn't sure that she could safely carry it back down the stairs so she left it where it was. Derek would be home in half an hour. She would wait until then and they'd decide what to do. Overcome by a wave of nausea, she wrapped her arms around herself and fell into a forward bend. When the urge to vomit passed, she straightened up and with the aid of the banister, made her way downstairs.

The hands of the kitchen clock showed seven minutes before her husband would be home. In a dreamlike state, she walked towards the kettle. Five minutes now and he would turn into their driveway, stop the car as he did every day by the kitchen window and wave to her as he opened the garage door. Any minute he would come into the kitchen and delicately kiss her on the cheek as she poured the clear bubbling water into the celadon teapot they had inherited from his mother. He liked his Earl Grey weak and black so Mrs Watson would begin straining it into his cup, before it brewed for too long. As he sat down she would drop in a thin slice of lemon. No-one else knew how to make the perfect brew. "You've got the touch, Jewel," he told her so often.

She must have looked normal when he first walked in, because he didn't seem to notice anything different. He couldn't see what was tumbling around her head and tearing at her heart. She would let him settle, before telling him and give herself time to find a way to explain the things she'd overheard, the words that grew to be phrases that turned into hideous sentences.

"Good day?" he enquired as he pecked her cheek, "get my dry cleaning?

"Of course I got your dry cleaning. Do I ever forget? Here's your tea, Dear."

He detected the shrill note in her voice that someone who didn't know his wife so well may have overlooked. He chose a kitchen stool, picked up his tea cup and blew on the steaming brew, as was his habit.

"I only asked," he said taking a sip and raising his eyes from the bone china rim. "Just making conversation. Not a good day then?"

Jewel arched her neck and looked towards the ceiling for inspiration. She found it impossible to know where to begin.

"Okay, let's have it. What's got you so uptight?"

His gaze moved to her fingers, watching as she twisted the ends of her handkerchief. He reached across the kitchen bench and with a gentle touch, stilled her hands.

"Come on Honey, nothing's that bad. Is it your Mum?"

"No, it's Sally."

He jolted upright. "Where is she? Is she all right?"

Jewel nodded her head. "Yes, she's upstairs."

"So, what's happened?"

Jewel explained how she baked a chocolate cake because she knew Sally was bringing Marilyn home and Marilyn loved chocolate cake. They all knew that. Step by step, she described how she had carried the tray with two plates and two glasses of lemonade up the stairs, careful not to spill the drinks, and laid them on the ground while she opened the door.

She could sense the drawn-out explanation was frustrating Derek but she needed to tell it from the beginning. Jewel made it clear she hadn't intended to eavesdrop but as she bent down with the tray there were a few words that had filtered through the keyhole, snippets of the conversation, that made her catch her breath, straighten up and stand with her ear to the door. She said she felt guilty doing so because they had always assured Sally she had their trust. But she couldn't ignore what she heard. Jewel paused, trying to find the words that wouldn't come, even though she sensed her husband was just about at the end of his tether and his tea was going cold.

"Well, go on, what did you hear?" He was expecting to be told Marilyn was in some kind of trouble or that Sally had failed an exam. What he heard came out so fast he couldn't quite catch it, but the dam had burst and the pace quickened and Jewel couldn't control the words that overflowed.

"Oh Derek, she's in a secret relationship. Our Sally and a teacher at the school. She's gone crazy Derek. I can't get her to talk sense. She's not normal, not like Sally. I couldn't stay there, she's still in her room, I didn't know what to do but I knew you would so now I…"

"Whoa. Hang on. Tell me that again. Slowly. About Sally, not the cake or anything else. You must be confused. What exactly did Sally say?" Derek's hands were clenched around his teacup.

"Oh Derek, I hope I'm wrong but she was defiant. She…"

"Jewel, calm down, just tell me what you overheard."

Jewel related the conversation word for word as best she could remember. When she got to the bit where Sally told Marilyn that she and Brad had talked about marriage, Derek hung on to the benchtop and lurched back in his seat.

"Jewel, you're sure about this? You talked to her. What did she say?"

"That's it Derek. She didn't deny any of it. She wasn't my Sally. She was someone else."

"Bloody hell! Where is she now?"

"Still in her room."

"I'll have his guts for garters if he's touched her."

"We don't know that yet. We have to find out." Jewel was whimpering now, her handkerchief completely knotted around her fingers. "Derek, how could he? He's her teacher."

"Not any more he isn't!" His hand sliced across the benchtop, knocking over his tea cup, spilling tea into the saucer. "He's finished."

"It's been going on for months, Derek. We didn't know. How could we not see it? What are we going to do?"

"I know what I'm going to do. I'm going to stop this here and now. Nip it in the bloody bud." Derek unbalanced the kitchen stool as he stood up then bounded up the stairs, two at a time.

He didn't knock, something he never did. There she was, lying on her side, holding her Timmy in her arms, the toy tiger that he had bought the day she was born. His baby tigress he nicknamed her because she fought so hard to come into the world. Nearly thirty-six hours in all and she still had the strength to cry out loudly when she finally made it. His heart softened and he spoke gently to her.

"Sal, it's Dad. Sal, can we talk?"

She rolled over and looked at him, her eyes swollen and her hair tousled. Derek sat on the edge of the bed next to her.

"What's going on Sal, what's this I hear about a teacher?" He couldn't comprehend that Jewel had heard right. He would hear it from Sally and then he could explain it to Jewel, calm her down.

"What did Mum tell you?"

"That you had some sort of relationship with someone at school."

"Yeah, that's right."

"With who Sal?"

"With whom Dad."

"Sally!" he cried out.

"He's a teacher Dad."

"He teaches...you, Sally?"

"Yes."

"Right." Mr Watson's shoulders went back and his chest rose.

"I thought you'd understand Dad."

"Well, I do, Sally. I understand it's normal for girls to fall in love with their teachers, or boys for that matter. I remember having a crush on my English teacher when I was just about your age."

"Dad, this isn't a crush."

"You can't be sure Sal, crushes can seem pretty serious you know."

Sally laid Timmy to one side and wriggled upright, leant against the bedhead, cleared her throat then looked directly at her father.

"Dad, I do know. I've thought about this for a long time. It might have started out like you say early on, but not now. This isn't just a silly schoolgirl thing."

"How on earth could you know?" He wanted to say, *you're just a silly schoolgirl.* "You're too young to be in a position to make a sound judgement."

"What's too young Dad? Anyway, he feels the same."

"You mean you've spoken about it?" Derek got to his feet.

"Yes, Dad."

"How old is he Sally?"

"He's twenty-three, nearly twenty-four actually. So, you see, he isn't that much older than I am."

"Sally, he's your teacher."

"I can't help that," she reasoned.

"Tell me how you know this, I mean, what he feels."

"Because he says it, he says he loves me. He wants me to be part of his future. Once he's divorced, that is."

Derek's hands involuntarily flew to his head and pulled at the hair near his temples. When he became aware of what he was doing, he crossed his arms and stuffed his hands under his armpits, holding onto his body for support.

"Sally, has this man ever touched you?"

"Dad that's none of your business."

Derek held out his hands in supplication. "Then whose business do you think it is?" he whimpered.

"Mine and his."

"No Sal, you're wrong! At your age it is definitely not." Despite his determination to control his emotions, Derek's eyes filled with tears. "I'm your father Sally, and it's my job to protect you."

"There's nothing to protect me from, Dad. He hasn't done anything, so don't get all narky." Sally was playing with what was left of the tiger's tail, twirling the shafts of cotton in her fingers. "Dad, can't you remember how you and Mum felt when you fell in love? You were this young too. Well this is just the same."

He wanted to shout but it came in a whisper. "This is nowhere *near* the same. This person is in a position of trust and he's breached it."

"You're wrong, Dad." Sally stood her ground. "It was me as much as him."

"Sally what on earth's come over you? What's this person's name?"

"His name is Brad Emery."

"Right, thinks he can get away with this, does he?" Derek turned to leave.

"Dad, what are you going to do?"

"I'm going to sort him out, that's what I'm going to do. Tell him to keep his hands off my daughter." He shook a pointed finger at Sally. "Go to your headmaster if I have to." From the corner of his eye he glimpsed Jewel standing in the hallway.

"Dad you can't, I might get expelled and I won't be able to finish my HSC. No-one knows at school."

"You've really thought this through, haven't you? But it doesn't stop me giving him a bloody nose when I see him."

"If you hurt him, I'll never speak to you again!" Sally threw her tiger onto the floor.

"And what about what he's done to us, to you, Sally. Don't you understand this man has betrayed us. Don't you realise that what he has done is reprehensible – to seduce you like this? You, Sally. A seventeen-year-old girl who hasn't started her life yet."

"Stop treating me like a child!"

"Well stop acting like one, Sally. He's nothing but a filthy predator!"

He's not. He's not! Get out! Get out of my room! He's not a predator, he's my perfect love." Sally threw herself onto the bed and buried her head in a pillow. "I hate you!"

Derek thought he was about to fall over then felt Jewel's hand grip his elbow. He looked to her and she nodded reassuringly. "Come on dear, let's go and finish our tea." Together they retreated to the kitchen.

Derek sat at the kitchen bench, head in hands as Jewel caressed his back. The ticking of the clock could be heard in the silence of the room.

"I'll kill him, Jewel" he whispered.

"Just calm down, Dear. We have to work this out."

'How can the school let this happen?"

"They don't know about it, Darling."

"Well they'll bloody well know soon!"

"Derek, let's think this through."

"This isn't Sally's doing, Jewel. He's got to her."

"Derek, I think he has. It's not our Sal upstairs. She's shut down. But we have to keep her talking to us, stay close to her."

"How come you're so calm all of a sudden?"

"You know we always take turns having our breakdowns." She attempted a smile. "Look, I'll go up and say we want her to come down for dinner."

Derek was shaking his head back and forth as he toyed with what was left of his cold cup of tea. "There must be some mistake. How could he do this to her?" His hand stilled and he looked at his wife. "Is he the one we met at Parent Teacher Night? The one we liked?"

"I've been thinking that, too. I guess so."

"Well he put on a bloody good show. This was happening then, you know. He was doing it then, when he met us. My God, he didn't even flinch and we trusted him with her."

Jewel ran her hand along her husband's as she left the kitchen and hauled herself up the stairs with the aid of the banister.

"Sally, it's Mum." She knocked at the door. "Dad and I want you to come down to dinner. In about half an hour. Okay? Sal, did you hear me?"

There was no answer. "We'll see you in half an hour, Sally," she said as she descended the stairs and heard Sally call out that she wasn't leaving her room.

"Well?" her husband asked.

"She said she feels sick. She's not up to eating now. I'll take a tray up to her later."

Derek flew out of his seat and Jewel's hand lightly touched his chest.

"Leave her, Derek. Not now."

He was a breath away from telling Jewel that he'd do what he wanted where his daughter was concerned. He stopped himself because he realised that she was, after all, on his side.

"Okay, I'll give her until the morning to come to her senses. Talk to her then."

Jewel patted his arm, then stirred the beef goulash and put water on to boil for the noodles. They ate in the kitchen accompanied by the sound of the wall clock and the dying cries of magpies on the evening air. In silence, Jewel cleared their plates and scraped the half-eaten meals into the kitchen tidy.

Next morning, Derek rose early after a disturbed sleep. His morning shower did little to revive him. All night he had been rehearsing what he would say to Sally.

Preoccupied with his thoughts, he took a white shirt from his side of the wardrobe. A straightforward choice as there were no coloured shirts to be had. As he buttoned up, he reassured himself – *I'm a good negotiator* – and he was, but this was very unlike the commercial negotiations he had been party to. On this occasion he had so much more to lose. He tried to work through the issues in his mind with a detached and dispassionate approach, but the strength of his emotions and the high stakes were clouding his judgement.

Every Sunday night Derek would sit in front of *Sixty Minutes*, his favourite TV show, polishing and buffing his business shoes. They stood dutifully in line on the floor of his wardrobe, under his suits, waiting for their day of the week to come around. Jewel had banned him from the edge of the bed, so he sat in the tub chair and bent over to do up his laces. As he righted himself it was crystal clear that he had to convince Sally there was no future for her in this relationship. Once she had that clear in her mind, it would follow that she would choose to end it of her own volition. And she would thank her father for helping her to see the nonsense of it all. Because that's what it was, a lot of nonsense, this teacher crush that she was having.

He took a moment to choose a tie, the one item in his attire that expressed individuality and today he chose a subdued blue and black stripe to go with his dark suit. He tightened the Windsor knot and thought through what approach he should use to get Sally to see sense. Jewel's wise words to keep her close were firmly in his mind. He had to bring her around to his way of thinking, but last night Derek had detected an unfamiliar stubbornness and independence in his daughter that alarmed him. This other man was changing her. He would have to tread carefully.

He knocked on Sally's door at 7 am, calm and focused.

"Sal, are you awake?"

"Yes, Dad. What do you want?"

"I want to talk to you Sal." Silence

"Sally I'm coming in Sweetie. Okay?"

Derek turned the door handle tentatively and hesitated before he entered. Sally was on top of the bedspread, her legs drawn up to her chin and she was picking at the skin around her nails. Last night's dinner tray was untouched on the desk chair.

"Gone off your mother's cooking?"

"Not hungry."

He moved with small steps towards his daughter who continued to be distracted by her nails, and noticed that his hands trembled as he shifted the tray onto the desk and wheeled the chair to Sally's bedside.

He tried to remain calm as he lowered himself onto the seat but the consequences of failure weighed heavily upon him.

"Sally." He cleared his throat. "Tell me what's going on, this thing with Brad."

"You seem to think this 'thing', as you call it, is trivial – that I've got some schoolgirl crush going on."

"Well, don't you think that's possible?"

"No I don't."

"Just think for a minute, Sal. Remember last year, Marilyn had a crush on Mr Robertson didn't she? Thought he was the most amazing thing since sliced bread."

"I don't remember bread before it was sliced, Dad."
"Sally, don't. The point is, these things pass."
"But this is different and I'm not Marilyn."
"How do you mean, Sally?
"You know she's dippy, Dad."
"And?"
"The more I know him the better it gets."
"Look Sally, it isn't long before you go to schoolies week with your friends. The pressure of the exams will be off. You've got a brand-new life ahead of you. Can you see that you could feel quite different then? You might even meet someone your own age."

"I know that's so not going to happen, Dad."
"Well. Have you thought about after you leave school? How's he going to feel when you're not around?"
"It's not up to me to speak for him, but I can tell you I'll feel the same."
"Your mother tells me he's, um, he's married." Derek's eyes closed as he asked
"What about Mrs Emery?"
"What about her?"
"Sally, we've always brought you up to do the right thing by other people. What do you think this is doing to her?"
"Dad, are you saying I'm a marriage wrecker?"

If her father had responded immediately, Sally may have left it at that. Instead he turned to look out of the bay window to the gum trees, their leaves still in the silent morning air, and beyond to the horizon to buy time that he needed to gather his thoughts.

So Sally kept on…"You're wrong," she said, "their stupid marriage was wrecked before," and the words continued to tumble out like a slippery eel from a net, "anyway, they're separated now," she added in a whisper.

Momentarily, Sally believed her father was appeased by this revelation but as he turned to face her, she knew otherwise. As calmly as his voice would allow he said, "Sally, what I am going to do is forbid you to see this man."

She shot back at him, "You think you can do that Dad? Well, you can't."

He stood up, slid the chair under the desk and left the room. He used to be able to guide her, but she was being influenced by something stronger than the bond they had forged as father and daughter. It used to matter what he thought, but not anymore.

His soft-boiled egg was still on the table when he reached the kitchen. It would be hard by now, and cold. He ate it in silence, Jewel allowing him his thoughts.

"No good, Love?" she said. Derek confirmed with a nod of his head, what she already knew. "I'm going to see if she wants breakfast."

"Hang on a minute. Give her this."

"What is it?"

"It's a note, telling him to ring me."

13

Don't Go Buying a Shotgun

"Brad, we need to talk."
"Hi Sal. Haven't you got a class?"
"They know."
"What?"
"Mum and Dad. They know."
"Your parents?"
"They know about us."
"What?" he said, staring at Sally as if he she was speaking in a foreign tongue.

The class began to file through the door. "Meet me after school," she whispered and was lost amongst a bustle of noisy fourteen year olds.

"G'day Mr E."
"How ya going Mr. Emery?"

He watched them pass by, their lips moving, but he registered nothing. One by one they took their seats. An unfamiliar hush came over the room.

"Anyone home, Sir?" The silence was broken by whispers and sniggers from around the room.

Brad tried to pull it together, thoughts tumbling around his head, interfering with the words that he was trying to articulate. At first, they thought his faltering speech was a joke but when they tried to imitate his stumble, he shut them down with a glare. This wasn't the teacher that they were used to. Cool Mr Emery who was willing to share a joke, treat them as equals.

"Not feeling too good Sir?"

"Big night, eh?" A burst of laughter from the back of the room brought him into the moment.

"Um, yeah, not too good, so if you guys could just get on with it that'd be really great. Just read through the next chapter."

"What one's that"?

A round of laughter that died away to whisper quiet.

"Six," he said, looking down at the book open on the desk, "just get on with it."

With his head lowered, he attempted to focus his thoughts but his mind refused to co-operate. It kept regurgitating one phrase. *They know. They know.* He sank into the chair. *How could it happen? I've been really careful? What if the school finds out? Fuuuck.* The next hour was a stretch of time that seemed interminable.

When the bell rang, he was out the door before anyone else. "Got a hot date Mr. Emery?" someone called from the side of the room. *Far out. What if they all know?*

He saw Sally exit the school gate as he backed out of the staff carpark and passed her walking in the direction of their meeting place. He drove around the block to give her time to arrive and himself time to think.

It was not a particularly warm afternoon but he wound down the window hoping that a rush of air would flush his mind free of the racing, pacing questions and ambiguous answers that were clogging his head, making it impossible to think clearly. The cicadas were bleating out a rhythm that paced his own heartbeat – only louder and stronger as if they were conspiring to make it burst.

As he pulled up, she was sitting on a rock, hands in lap, head lowered. In response to the rumble of the motor she leapt up and ran towards the car. Brad reached across, opened the door, took her school bag, laid it on the back seat and waited. She squatted on her haunches, her back to the passenger window, and began to fiddle with the end of her school tie.

"Sal," he tilted her chin upwards and looked into her eyes, "why did you tell them?"

"I didn't tell them. I wouldn't do that. Mum overheard when Mazza and I were talking. We ..."

"Marilyn? Jesus Christ, if you told her, the whole world knows."

"That's not true. Mazza isn't like that. She's known for ages , didn't need me to tell her. And she hasn't said anything to anyone." Her rocking back and forth disturbed him and he asked her to sit still.

"And your Mum heard?"

"And she told Dad."

"Far out."

"It's foul, I know."

"This wasn't supposed to happen."

"Dad was furious."

"That figures. What did you expect, Sally?"

"I've never seen him like that. I wanted to climb out my window in the middle of the night and come to you and run away."

A stray blowfly was persistently buzzing around the windscreen. Brad swiped at it menacingly until it flew outside. He wiped the sweat from his forehead.

"Brad, they can't stop me seeing you, can they?"

"Probably, I don't know."

She unravelled her legs and turned towards the windscreen. In the silence that filled the car, she examined her nails that were short but not bitten. There was a callous on the middle finger of her right hand, a legacy from writing copious class notes and essays. The fly was back and Brad killed it this time, using the end of his towel as a swatter. Sally reached into the pocket of her school blouse and took out a crumpled piece of paper.

"Mum gave me this."

In block letters was the name, *DEREK WATSON*. Underneath, *375 1111 – PHONE ME.*

"Mum said you'd better ring him or he'll go crazy."

"Far out."

"Brad, look at me." She held his gaze. "I told him you were separated."

He continued to stare at her, open mouthed. "You what?"

"I had to. Dad was freaking out about your being married."

"Oh Sally, this is such a friggin' mess."

She whimpered.

"Come here." He opened his arms and she fell into them. "This wasn't supposed to happen, was it?"

"No. Not like this."

He tightened his arms around her. "You'd better get home."

"You'll ring him?"

"No choice Sally. You'd better go. They'll be waiting for you."

She stood her ground as he reversed into the road, called to him that she loved him but his thoughts were elsewhere. He felt the knot in his stomach tighten at the thought of facing up to her old man. He'd managed to keep it together at Parent and Teacher Night. He'd liked her oldies, they were funny. Mr Watson cracking jokes about having a daughter finishing school and how old it made him feel. They looked young and seemed 'with it'. Mrs Watson had on a mini skirt and was really friendly. Maybe they'd be okay about it? *Not a fucking chance.*

A hundred yards down the street, he spotted a public phone and stopped the car. A blast of heat hit him head-on when he stepped inside so he leaned his back against the shelf and propped the door open with his leg while he rummaged in his pocket for a fifty-cent piece. For years, whenever he was in a phone box, he felt the urge to urinate and put it down to a subconscious response to small spaces, triggered by recollections of the outdoor toilet he'd used as a boy. Today, it was the thought of phoning Sally's father that nearly made him piss himself.

The phone rang only once before he slammed the receiver back into the cradle. He just couldn't do it, not now. He'd head for the pub on the corner and use their toilet. A few drinks to steady his hand wouldn't go astray either.

He left the pub at 9.30 knowing that Emma would still be awake and convinced himself that he would tell her when he got home. An hour later, Emma in bed and none the wiser, he turned off the shower and walked into the darkness of the kitchen. The full moon was a spotlight in the cloudless sky and he wished he could fly off into space.

First thing in the morning he'd have to ring Mr Watson. Would set the alarm for early, to get his headspace right. Give himself time to work up a bit of Dutch courage.

By 7.45 am he was sitting in the car outside a phone booth two blocks from the school. He committed to make the call at 8 o'clock. The phone rang out. His relief was soon replaced by the daunting prospect of a day spent dreading the afternoon to come. At 4.15 pm he rang again in the hope that it would be too early for Mr Watson to be home from work.

A male voice answered. "Three seven five, double one double one."

"Hello, this is Brad Emery."

"This is Derek Watson, Brad. I've been expecting your call. Are you in the area?"

"Yes sir."

"How soon can you get here? Do you know where we live?"

Shit, thought this was just going to be a phone call.

"Um yes, Sir, I do. Twenty minutes," he said, swallowing hard.

"See you in half an hour then. You'd better be here, son."

Mr Watson replaced the receiver on the wall then turned to Jewel who, at the mention of Brad's name, had stopped peeling the potatoes. She lowered herself onto a stool, a half-peeled Pontiac in one hand and a paring knife in the other.

"He knows where we live," Derek said as he faced his wife. "He could have been here, in our house. Could have been alone with her when we were out. I thought she was old enough to leave on her own. I trusted her."

"Take it easy, please, Darling." His face was rhubarb red and a throbbing vein had appeared near his left temple. Jewel worried it was going to burst. "Darling, you don't know if he's been here." She laid her hand against his twitching cheek. "He might have driven her home once. Or he could have gotten the address from school records. Don't jump to conclusions, calm down, Sweetheart. Let's just wait and see what happens."

Derek ran his hands through his hair.

"Mum, Dad." They turned to see Sally standing in the doorway. Faces turned to the kitchen window as a cream Volkswagen rumbled to a halt in front of the house.

"Go to your room Sally," Derek said.

Jewel saw her daughter's defiant stare before her husband did. She stepped into his line of sight and put her arm around Sally's shoulder to guide her to the foot of the stairs.

"Come on Sal, it's for the best. Wait in your room, honey," she whispered as she swept a loose strand of hair behind her daughter's left ear. Sally broke free and Jewel watched her sulk away, holding the banister with both hands while continuing to look over her shoulder. She stopped at halfway when the doorbell chimed. Jewel indicated for her to keep going, then turned to Derek for guidance.

"I'll take him into the lounge room Jewel."

"Don't you think I should be there?" She didn't trust her husband alone with Brad Emery.

"Okay, but let me do the talking."

Derek Watson opened the door. He was a polite man and would normally have shaken Brad's hand but he saw no reason to comply with convention. What's more he was surprised at how often he thought about hurting this person, given that he, in principle, abhorred physical violence.

"Follow me, son."

Mr Watson sat on the three-seater wing back lounge and Mrs

Watson chose to sit next to him. Brad had to choose between two chairs and decided on the one nearest the door. It was a low-slung seat and his knees came up around his armpits. He tried leaning back but it looked too casual so he spread his legs and slid forward, trying at the same time to adjust his shorts that had ridden up around his crotch. Mrs Watson averted her eyes and Mr Watson cleared his throat.

"Brad, I've called you here because we have learnt some things that have distressed us, upset us immensely in fact, concerning you and our daughter. I'd like to hear what you've got to say."

Brad squirmed, looked to the ceiling, to the floor, and began the speech he'd rehearsed the night before when he couldn't sleep.

"Mr Watson, and Mrs Watson, I just want to say, I respect your daughter and I would never do anything to harm her. I understand Sally is young and I am her teacher and I've thought about that a lot but it doesn't change the fact that my feelings for Sally are genuine."

"And it doesn't change the fact that you've deceived us. You've carried on a relationship behind our backs for what I believe, is quite some time."

Jewel nodded in agreement, relieved that Derek appeared calm and rational.

"I know how it looks Mr Watson, but I didn't want to jeopardise her schooling," Brad continued on the off chance that it was the deception which most concerned the parents. "I didn't think we could be open about our relationship until after Sal finished year twelve."

Jewel Watson spoke up. "So your wife knows all about….about this?

Brad hesitated and Derek Watson intervened. His voice was raised and the index finger of his right hand pointed at Brad. He leaned forward in his chair and spat out the words, "you are, as far as the law is concerned, still a married man, Brad Emery and Sally is … she's still a child! She's barely seventeen." The accusatory finger began to move rapidly up and down for emphasis. "You, however, are an adult!!" His free hand gripped the arm of the lounge and he learned further forward. "But obviously not a responsible one!" At which point, the finger stood erect and began to move from side to side. "If you had Sally's interests at heart you would never, NEVER have let yourself get involved with her." Brad and Jewel Watson sat stock still and speechless.

Then Derek Watson rose up and began to pace the carpet in the middle of the small lounge room, three long steps in one direction then a turn. "What happened between you and your wife is of no consequence to us because I forbid you to see Sally again." He turned, faced Brad then paused. "She needs protecting from people like you." And he was off again, pacing up and down. "I take some responsibility for this, we should have been more watchful, but we won't be derelict in our duty from now on." Derek Watson faced his opponent, legs astride and arms behind his back. "I don't have anything more to say to you, Brad. I'd like you to leave our house and I repeat, you are not to contact Sally or talk to her outside of the classroom."

"No, no, no Dad!" The shrieking came from the bottom of the stairs. "That's not fair. You can't stop me seeing him. Mum, tell him he can't do that."

"Sally, your father is only trying to protect you." She wrapped her arms around her daughter.

"Brad," Sally pleaded, "make them understand!" Jewel Watson held Sally as she tried to break away.

"Please leave this house." Mr Watson stood between Brad and his family.

"Sal, I have to leave," Brad said, unsure whether or not he should offer his hand.

"Bloody oath you do. Just go." Mr Watson had dispelled any doubt he may have had.

Sally broke away from her mother and her father caught her by the shoulders. Brad felt sure Mr Watson would have hit him if his hands hadn't been full. In one swift movement he was out of the house and up the path. Black smoke spewed from the V-dub as it accelerated out of the cul-de-sac.

"I hate you. I hate you!" Sally screamed as she broke away from her father and ran to her room.

Jewel and Derek faced each other and for once, neither of them were able to find words of consolation.

Jewel sought solace in her kitchen. "I need to turn off the stove."

Derek retreated to the garage. Twenty minutes later, he reappeared. "Where is she?"

"In her room."

Derek began to pace the kitchen floor, then paused, hands in his pockets, his eyes downcast. "Jewel, I've been thinking, about what Sally said. What would the consequences be if the school finds out? Would they suspend her? Even if they let her sit the exams, it would have a terrible impact." Derek paused for an intake of breath. "Jewel, what if the wife goes to the school?"

"I hadn't thought about any of that. Why would the wife go to the school?"

"Revenge? I mean, we don't know if the break-up was amicable. If she's angry and she's found out, she might want to hurt them."

"Oh Derek, this is horrible."

"Jewell, I think we have to talk to her."

An empty saucepan clattered onto the bench top. "I'm not sure I'd be up to that."

"It's the only way, Darling. We have get the facts for ourselves. I need you to come with me. It'd be too confronting for her if I went on my own."

"And what do we say to her?"

"See what she's thinking. Maybe she's already on the war path. If she's going to expose them, we should get in first. If the headmaster knows we're on top of things, maybe he'll agree to keep it quiet at least until the exams are finished. My guess – he'd want to keep a scandal like this under wraps. Then again, maybe she's not vindictive, but we've got to know. Maybe she's as distressed by all this as we are."

"What if she doesn't know it's Sally?"

"You're right, that is a risk. But she'll find out eventually. You're right, that could be the case, but I think we are better off being one step ahead."

"Can't we just wait and see what happens? Get through the HSC."

"No, I really believe it's too big a risk Jewel."

"It's so complicated." Jewel threw the tea towel onto the bench.

"And how do we contact her?"

"Sally probably knows."

"You think she'll tell us?"

"Actually, I do. She knows she needs to keep this under wraps for the time being. We agree with her and are trying to help her."

"I guess you want me to talk to her."

"I think you'd be better at it than me. I still find it hard to be calm with her. Jumping Jesus, what a mess."

Jewel watched the swollen, throbbing vein in Derek's neck. She resolved to get him to the doctor for a blood pressure check as soon as possible.

"I'll give it a go," she agreed as she dried her hands on a tea towel, took off her apron and made her way upstairs.

Derek flicked through the sports section of the *Sun Herald*, eager to find something that would hold his attention. The absence of raised voices gave him hope.

"Well?"

"She works at Jacksons, in the office."

"Jewel, what has our daughter been doing with her life right behind our backs?"

"Darling, don't think the worst of her. Remember she's the victim here."

They sat listening for any sound from upstairs.

Jewel broke the silence, "Darling, I think you might have been right. I explained it to her and she didn't argue. She seemed to know we were on her side on this one."

"She'll thank us one day."

When Jewel heard Derek's shower running, she double-stepped up the stairs.

"Sal," she whispered, the door held slightly ajar, "you've got to get up and get dressed and eat something."

"Mum, come in."

"What is it Sally?"

"How old were you when you fell in love with Dad?"

"I was the same age as you Sally, you know that."

"And Dad was older."

Sally, your father wasn't my teacher and neither of us were married to someone else."

"Mum, I haven't done anything I'm ashamed of."

Jewel paused, the question she wanted the answer to hanging in the silence, waiting to be asked. A dread of what the answer might be, stopped her.

"Did you hear me, Mum?"

"Sally, we've always trusted you and we still do."

"Then trust me with this, please Mum."

She brushed Sally's hair from her eyes. "Sal, I've got to go back down."

"Mum, I'll die if I can't see him."

"Look, it would be my advice to get up, have a shower, get dressed and come downstairs. You have no hope of getting your father's co-operation if you behave like this."

"And yours?"

"We'll see. Now up you get."

She closed the door and made it back in time to pour a strong scotch and soda for Derek. She passed it to him as he came into the kitchen.

"Is that the shower I hear?" he asked, taking a first sip.

"Sounds like it."

Sally trotted down the stairs, her hair still damp.

"Come here Sal." Derek opened his arms. She hesitated then walked towards her father. "You know we love you, Sal," he said as he held his daughter.

"I know, and I love you and Mum." She allowed herself to be held, then asked, "Want me to set the table?"

"Yes, please."

The parents turned towards each other, eyebrows raised as Sally began counting out knives and forks.

When Sally was in the dining room and out of earshot, Derek spoke, "Maybe she's got some sense in her head at last?"

"I wouldn't presume she's changed her mind about him, Dear."

He looked at Jewel, his anger and defiance dissolving and as he spoke, his voice broke. "I really don't know what to do Jewel. For the first time in my life, I don't know what to do with Sal. I don't want to lose my girl and I don't want him to have her. Can I have both of those things? Can I? I can't lock her in her bedroom forever." Derek's head fell into his upturned palms and Jewel came up behind him and placed her hands on his shoulders.

"Darling, don't you remember how grown up we felt when we were her age? We were so sure of everything and you know, it turned out okay."

He opened his mouth to interrupt.

"No, let me finish. I agree with you. This isn't the same and it's not what either of us want but, if we're going to have influence, we've got to keep her talking. She's just made the first step, shown us that she's willing to work with us. So, let's see what happens. Try to keep your cool and don't go buying a shotgun yet. Promise?"

He nodded. She was right – but he knew where to get one if he needed it.

During dinner, Jewel watched her daughter and husband, the two most precious people in her life, and feared for the future of their relationship. An intruder had shifted the dynamics of their tight knit family in the space of a few short hours.

"I don't know if I can go to Church tomorrow, Jewel."

"We can't hide away, Darling. We have to carry on as normal," she said with a lump in her throat, "as much as we can, anyway."

He rose from his seat and looked out the window. "I think I'll go for a walk around the block."

"You want company?"

"No thanks. Not tonight."

When she heard the door close, Jewel walked briskly upstairs, closed the bedroom door, locked herself in the bathroom and silently bawled her eyes out.

14

It's All Over Rover

BRAD STOOD AGAINST THE GARAGE wall, feeling the chill of the concrete through his summer shirt. If the squatters would just shut up he would be able to think more clearly. The stairs to the apartment felt steeper and his legs heavier. He stopped at the landing and slid his hand into his pocket where the note lay. The last time he'd received a message on the cream, watermarked paper it was from Derek Watson. But not this time. In Sally's neat hand were the words *They're going to call your wife*. Maybe they'd done it already. Either way, he was dead meat.

The door was slightly ajar and as he pushed it open, Emma greeted him with a turn of her head.

"Hi, how was your day?" She was washing a lettuce then drying it with a tea towel. "We need to decide about tomorrow night," she called, glancing over her shoulder. "If we're going to your oldies party. It was nice of them to ask us, bit of last minute I know, but I think we should say yes."

Unaware that he was frozen on the spot in the doorway, she continued, "Brad, are you listening? Can I tell them we'll come?"

"There's another party." he replied. He hadn't known he was

going to say it. The words tumbled out as his briefcase slipped from his hand.

"What party?"

"I'm going to a party." He cleared his throat for emphasis. "You shouldn't be there."

She stilled. "You can't go to one party and me the other."

"You shouldn't come, because you might not like what you see."

Emma turned around, a jar of homemade salad dressing in one hand and salad bowl in the other. "What?"

"Sally will be there."

"What are you talking about?" Her voice was strained and she was becoming distressed by second guessing the inferences.

"I don't want to go with you Emma. I'm going with her."

She laid the salad bowl on the sink.

"Sally from school?"

"I've got to tell you this, now." His tongue rasped against his dry lips. "We've been seeing each other."

Emma's lips parted and turned up a little at the corner, nearly a smile but more of a question mark. She recognised the man standing opposite her but these words could only have come from someone other than her husband.

"What do you mean, you've been 'seeing each other'?" A faint bewildered voice. "You mean studying?"

"No. Don't you get it Emma? Sally and I are together."

The salad dressing was running from the upturned jar. It fell to the floor. "She's your pupil. She… she's still at *school*. You told me if we had kids you'd like them to be like her. You did, didn't you?"

"She might be a student, but she's not a kid." He began to rub his thumbs and index fingers together at a rapid pace. "Sally and I want to…"

"Want to what?" she shouted.

"Listen to me for once. Just for once will you hear what I'm saying."

She reached for a chair and held onto the table as she sat down.

"Look, I didn't plan it like this," he went on, "it just happened, at the beginning of the year." His shoulders moved as if to shrug off the responsibility.

Emma stared down at her clasped hands then looked once again towards this man whom she loved, then back at her hands, as if she might find some explanation in the knot of fingers.

"But, we're married," she whispered.

"Maybe you should go to your mother's in the morning," he said. "Take the car. We're finished, Emm. I want to be with her." Brad took the keys from his pocket and laid them on the table. She heard the bathroom door close and the lock snap shut. He never did that.

She should go to him, but her limbs were not responding and she looked around for a clue as to what to do next. After some time, she had no idea how long, she pushed herself into a standing position and lurched forward until she reached the fridge. Like a sightless person, she felt her way along the loungeroom wall to the bathroom then leaned against the door.

"Brad. Please come out. I don't understand what you're saying." There was a quivering in her voice as if she had been taken by a bone-deep chill. "Brad. Please. Answer me."

"Go away, Emma. It had to end. You know that. Just think about it."

She lacked the initiative to move and slowly slid to the floor. With her ear pressed against the door she thought she could hear the sound of his breathing but was unsure that it wasn't her own. After a while she remembered she hadn't finished making the salad. She stood up and made her way back to the kitchen.

It's all too silly, she decided and began to slice the cucumber. *He will come out of the bathroom any minute and say, "Joke"*. She waited, motionless, staring at nothing. But he didn't come out. Slowly, she laid the knife on its side on the cutting board and listened. Still no sound from the bathroom. The soles of her slippers were sticky with salad dressing so she picked up the dishcloth and began to clean the floor, then she cleaned the sink, rubbing back and forth, ringing out the Wettex, a little more Ajax, more polishing, more scouring, wiping away the dirt, the doubt.

She took off her slippers and pulled out a chair. "No good," she said aloud, "I'll think better standing up," But her legs were no longer there and she caught the windowsill as she was about to go down. Her chest tightened and it became difficult to breathe, as if the air had been sucked out of the room.

Slowly in, slowly out. Think rationally. Today is Friday. Only last week he brought me chocolates. Caramels, my favourite kind. Someone who was leaving you wouldn't do that, would they?

A part of her believed it would all be over in a minute, that things would sort out quickly enough, but there was a terrifying glimpse of another reality – that this could be the end of her marriage here and now. A panic rose up and she began to shake her head no, and stopped only when she heard the bathroom door open. Her breath came even more quickly now and she felt dizzy as she waited for him to come to her and say he was sorry, but instead he went into the bedroom. She thought she heard him call, "Emma, come here." But there was only the hum of traffic two streets away, and the occasional car engine starting up.

Sometime later she stood in the entrance to their bedroom and could see him lying on the bed, facing the wall, with the sheet pulled up to his chin. He had placed the matching scatter cushions neatly on the floor on his side of the bed, an orderly scene of comfortable domesticity.

Emma unzipped her skirt and folded it on the dressing table stool. She unbuttoned her blouse and laid it over her skirt, then slipped out of her petticoat. On tiptoes she moved to the bed and slid her nightie from under the pillow. Then with her back turned, took off her pants and bra and pulled her nightie over her head. With care, she loosened the top sheet, lowered herself onto the edge of the mattress and drew her legs up then slid them under the blanket. Her head settled onto the pillow and her eyes focused on the outline of the plaster rose in the ceiling.

He wasn't asleep, she could tell from his breathing, so she waited, lying corpse-like, for him to acknowledge her presence. After a few moments, she stretched her hand towards him. When her fingertips brushed his back, he flinched and moved from her and she began to weep. He ignored her and eventually the distance between one sob and the next lengthened and she turned away and lay in the dampness of her pillow, listening. When his body rose and fell with the long breath of deep sleep, she dared once more to move herself nearer. With the hesitancy of an intruder, she positioned her face as close as she dared, to capture his scent and feel his warmth. It was late when she found solace in sleep.

A few hours later she stirred and the shock of it hit her like the time she had been dumped by a six-foot-high wave. Her lungs fought for air as she struggled to comprehend the meaning of it all.

He was awake, lying stretched out with his hands behind his head. She lay motionless and when the street lights went out she whispered his name. "Brad."

"Yeah?"

"Do you mean what you said last night? You want me to go to my mother's?"

She felt him nodding, telling her to go, then he moved to the very edge of the bed and turned on his side.

The bile rose so quickly it was in her throat before she realised that she was going to vomit. Her hand flew to her mouth and held it shut as she raced for the toilet. It felt good to be spewing it out – the sickness that had infected their marriage. The cold water hit her face like a slap and the tiles were cool on her legs as she slid down the side of the bath, onto the floor.

He wouldn't come to her now, she knew that. She would have to do for herself. She couldn't face her parents. Not yet.

Emma crept into the bedroom and took the small change from the cut glass dish on the dressing table. He lay motionless as she picked up her clothes from the night before and retreated to the loungeroom to dress.

The sun was rising and the street empty as she made her way

to the phone booth. Her whole body shook as she dialled Sandy's number and waited, holding the receiver in both hands.

"Hello". The paucity of words and the deep voice were Rob's trademark.

"Rob, it's Emma."

"Oh, hi gorgeous, you're up early. What's happening?"

"Rob, I'm sorry, I need Sandy."

"Sure hon. You okay?"

Emma bit her lip and nodded her head.

"I'll get her for you. Just hang on Emm."

"Emm, what's happening?" Sandy could hear the sniffling. "Tell me, what's wrong? What is it?"

"It's Brad, Sandy." Emma blew her nose. "He says he doesn't want to be married anymore."

When Rob passed the phone to Sandy he had stayed by her side, snatching snippets of the conversation.

"He said what? You're not just being an hysterical git, are you?"

"He told me last night."

"We shouldn't talk about this over the phone. I'll get Rob to come and get you." She put her hand over the receiver as she turned to her husband. "Okay?" He jangled his car keys at her. "He'll be there in twenty minutes, Emm, hold tight."

"It's okay Sandy. He said I could have the car."

"Tell the bastard to shove it up his arse. You don't sound like you're in any condition to drive. Just stay where you are."

"I'm sorry, Sand."

"Look, Rob's leaving now. Throw some clothes in a bag. Go wash your face, you must look like the wreck of the Hesperus and you're not getting into my place looking like a dag. You still there?"

"Yes."

"Now go do what I said and get out of there. Wait downstairs. Clock's ticking Emm. You need to get a move on. Okay?"

"Okay." Emma let the door of the phone booth slam behind her and made her way back to the flat.

Sandy turned to Rob.

"Dickhead says he wants to split up. I knew something was going on."

"Arsehole." Rob threw his thongs into the corner near the lounge and grabbed a pair of sneakers.

"He's a bloody weirdo, isn't he," Sandy said. "I knew things weren't right with them." She reached for a packet of Alpine and Rob threw her a lighter. "You could sense it," she said as she paced back and forth. "It was like his stupid head was somewhere else the other night." The smoke trailed from her nostrils as she searched for an ashtray.

Rob finished tying his laces then hitched up his shorts. "Didn't tell you this, but I ran into Martin. I think Michelle might be on the money."

"Oh God, I don't want to know," Sandy shook her head then proffered her cheek for a kiss. "You'd better get going."

Forty-five minutes later, she watched Rob open the van door for Emma then help her navigate the driveway. She began to fill the kettle but changed her mind and found the cooking brandy in the top cupboard. Rob made a discreet exit to his workshop as she laid the bottle aside and opened her arms. Emma responded by crying for a good nine minutes. The sound of an electric drill reverberated through the house.

"Here." Sandy passed Emma a box of tissues. "And you look like you need one of these."

"What is it?"

"Just drink it."

"Sand, I can't, I'll be sick."

"Ciggy then?"

"You know I don't smoke."

"Never too late to start." Sandy patted the couch next to her. "What happened Emm. Tell me, word for word, you know... a 'he said – I said' version. Go on, tell me all of it."

It's all over Rover, Sandy concluded as she listened to Emma's story and it concerned her not in the least. Brad had never been good for her friend. Always felt sorry for himself, moaning last year because he had to work through the school holidays to earn a bit of extra money. Self-pity when he had to study after school, which finished half way through the afternoon anyway. A real whinger. Rob had longer working hours than Brad. Started earlier and finished later, then kept at it in his workshop most nights. It was the only way you could get ahead, but Brad and Emma never seemed to.

"So that's it. Finished, is it Emm?"

"Oh, I hope not Sandy. I still love him you see." Emma shook her head as if puzzled by her own stupidity.

Sandy's first reaction was to tell her what she had always thought of Brad. Try to convince her she'd be better off without him. She hesitated, remembering the consequences of the last time she had spoken her mind.

Emma noticed Sandy's hesitation. "I know he's not the ideal husband, and I know you think I'm an idiot, but I can't help it."

"Honeybunch, no man is so bad that either a dog or a woman won't love him. Mum used to say that about Dad."

"Your Mum wasn't silly."

Sandy took Emma's hand in her own. "Maybe this pupil thing is just an infatuation?"

"You think so?"

"Did he say he loved her? The bit of fluff?"

"No not exactly. He said he wanted to be with her. Sounded like he meant forever. He just shut me out. It was horrible Sandy."

"Do you want Rob to talk to him?"

"He says he's going to a party tonight," Emma whimpered, "with her." Sandy caressed her back.

"Probably bullshit. He'll be at the beach tomorrow morning. Rob'll get hold of him and get some sense into his thick head. You're staying the night by the way."

"Do you think he could? Talk to him? You think he'll listen? You know how he is."

"He'll tie him down if he has to."

"I would like to stay tonight if that's all right?"

"Course dumbo. You don't have to ask." Another back rub.

"I'll have to go home tomorrow, to get ready for work and Greg is picking me up. Though I don't know how much longer I'll have a job." Emma blew into the crisp cotton handkerchief Sandy had ready on the coffee table.

"What do you mean?"

"Remember, I told you the company hadn't been going too well? They've already put off a dozen guys from the factory and they're talking about more lay-offs."

"Look, don't worry about that now. You'll get another job, if it comes to that – the next day. Why don't you go and have nice hot bath and then come and help me make some lunch?"

There were new cakes of soap in the hand basin and fluffy white towels on the bed. Emma sat on the rim of the bathtub as it filled with water, running her hand back and forth to get the bubbles going.

Soft sounds of pan flutes drifted up the stairs as she rested, eyes closed, until the water began to cool. The bathrobe felt luxurious and although it was her intention to rest on the bed for only a moment, then go downstairs to help, the sleep she had forfeited the night before staked its claim.

15

A Rock and a Hard Place

ON SUNDAY MORNING DURING THE church service, Derek asked God for forgiveness for the white lie he was about to tell.

"No morning tea for us today, folks," he called as he ushered Sally and Jewel to the car, "got to visit the in-laws."

The family drove home in silence. "Going to study, Mum," Sally muttered as they came through the front door and ran up the stairs to her room.

Derek turned to Jewel. "Funny how a world turned upside down can look quite normal from the outside. We've been to Church, Sal's going to study, we'll have lunch – just like any other Sunday," he shook his head, "but it's not." Jewel's comforting hand rested on his shoulder.

As the day wore on, Mrs Emery weighed heavily on his mind. By early afternoon he'd decided he needed to clarify a few things before the meeting with her. What he needed to know, was where he stood legally and Sam Thurgood was just the man to speak to, discreet and no beating around the bush with Sam. There was no need to tell Jewel, he decided, in case there was nothing to tell.

"Think I'll duck out for a quick one at the club, Darling," he announced when the evening news finished and mentally added this white lie to his earlier request for forgiveness.

"On a Sunday night?"

"I feel like getting out for a while, Love."

"What about dinner?"

"Couldn't eat a thing after that lunch. I'll have a quick beer and be back."

"Might do you good I suppose," Jewel conceded. "Darling, before you go, I was thinking."

"Here's trouble."

She laid a hand on her husband's arm. "If all goes well with the wife, what if we let Brad come here, under our supervision? If he's really serious about Sally, he can't object to that and it will put those good intentions of his to the test, having to be chaperoned."

"You know how I feel about him," he said, covering her hand with his own. "I don't want that man anywhere near her, under any circumstances."

"I understand, I do, but what if he refuses, if he's not willing to do something that simple to be with Sally? You've got to agree that would solve a lot of problems. And if he does come, we know she's safe here."

"I'll think about it, Jewel. But right now, I don't believe I could be in the same room with him."

As Derek kissed her cheek, she asked "One more thing, Darling, you think Marilyn will do the right thing?"

"I hope so, Jewel. I don't think she would hurt Sally and my guess is she knows the trouble she'd be in if she talks."

"And you won't mention it at the club."

"You don't even have to ask, Jewel. See you in an hour or so." He kissed her other cheek. "Now stop that mind of yours working overtime, you hear? Go and watch one of your TV shows."

Derek parked outside Sam's two storey, six bedroom, red brick home where he lived with his wife Lee. Their son Paul was still living in the UK. Their daughter Carol's wedding a year back had been a big event. Of course, the Thurgood's didn't have a bell or a chime. The heavy brass knocker announced Derek's arrival and the door was opened by the man himself, his thick fingers circling a stubby holder with *Thurgood Properties* in red letters on the black Styrofoam.

"G'day Mate. Haven't seen you in ages. Come on in." Sam moved aside.

Derek wiped his feet on the doormat and stepped into the marbled foyer. "Looking fit, buddy," he said to Sam, all six feet two of him.

"You're kidding aren't you?" Sam patted his belly. "Put on a few more pounds than I'd like to admit to. Can't play squash any more, legs given up." He raised his beer can. "But the liver's in surprisingly good nick." A glance over Derek's shoulder confirmed that Jewel wasn't in the car. Together they walked through the lounge and into the dining room where Lee was clearing the table.

"Derek, good to see you." She kissed him on the cheek. "Jewel here?"

"No, just me, Lee. She wanted an early night." He pointed to the half empty dishes. "Still cooking up a storm I see?"

The table held the remnants of a lamb roast, the empty bottle of red wine testimony to a leisurely meal.

"You know, I'm still not used to just two of us. Cook for a family. Lee nodded in Sam's direction, "but he'll eat the leftovers later, one way or another. What about you, Derek? You eaten?"

"Yes thanks, Lee, we had a big lunch."

"How are Jewel and Sally?"

"Both really well. Sal's about to do her HSC."

"God, I remember it with my two. Such a trying time."

"Right about that. Feels like we're all sitting these damn exams. Actually, I'm here for a bit of advice on the property market from my old mate here. Thought I might catch him in."

"Come on down to my new den, Derek. Glad you came by." An arm rested on Derek's shoulder.

Derek turned as he was ushered towards the stairwell. "You'll excuse us, Lee. I'll catch you on the way out."

"Good oh, give me a hoy if you want a coffee."

At the foot of the stairs, Sam stood back to let Derek pass. He had spent the last few weeks fitting out the interior of the new extension.

Autographed football memorabilia covered one of the clinker brick walls. On the other, was a photo of Marilyn Monroe standing over an air vent, her dress billowing skyward. Alongside, was a framed print of a red Ferrari, next to a family crest that looked disconcertingly similar the one Derek bought recently for $150. The recliner-rockers were facing the biggest TV screen he'd ever seen. Through the sliding glass doors at the other end of the room, blue floodlights highlighted a rock feature with iridescent water cascading into the kidney shaped swimming pool. The palm trees were there and all that was missing, he decided, were the hula girls.

Sam fetched two beers from the fully stocked fridge behind the studded black leather bar. "What do you think, mate?" Sam passed over a Tooheys as Derek perched on one of the matching bar stools. "Very impressive. Nice hideaway."

"Sure is, do some of my best thinking down here. Every man needs a private space."

"Know what you mean."

Sam lit up a Marlboro and fetched an ashtray from behind the bar. "And I can smoke to my heart's content without Lee opening windows and spraying that stuff that smells like a public toilet all over the house."

"Here's cheers," Derek took a mouthful of the beer that he didn't want.

"You thinking about an investment property?" asked Sam.

"Actually, mate, I said that to let Lee off the hook. I hope you'll excuse the subterfuge. I really want to talk to you about something that's a bit sensitive, if that's okay."

"Got the feeling you just didn't happen to drive by. What's up?"

"It's Sally, Sam. I've got a problem and I'd like your opinion on a few things. Always appreciated your advice mate, you've always been straight up with me. But before I go into it – and I feel bad about asking this – you won't mention it to anyone, not even Lee?"

"Well, of course, you can be assured of my discretion. What's troubling you, buddy?"

Derek went through the events of the last few days in detail, exercising self control to make his account as factual and devoid of emotion as possible.

Sam cleared his throat. "Let me recap, make sure I understand you clearly."

Still the lawyer, thought Derek, even though he hadn't practised for five years. Sam blamed tedium on his departure from the legal profession but talk was he'd sailed a little too close to the wind. In fact, it was money that called to him louder than any fear of reprisal for a few dodgy transactions. Sam could see firsthand the wealth his developer clients had accumulated. He wanted to be able to write cheques the size of his own fee with the same ease that his clients did, so he sold his practice and joined them. Sam Thurgood possessed the street smarts, as well as intelligence, and Derek wasn't surprised he was making a motza.

"Your daughter is seventeen years old?"

Derek nodded affirmatively.

"The teacher is what – nearly twenty-four did you say?"

"Yes, but that's from Sally."

"This has been going on since the beginning of the year?"

"Once again, that's what Sally told us."

"How long before she leaves school, Derek?"

"Well, the HSC starts end of next month. I presume she's officially at school until the exams are over."

"And you're sure this is consensual?"

"That's what's so bloody hard to take," he said, shaking his head, "she thinks she's madly in love with this bastard."

"I see. So, she wants it to continue?"

"She's talked about marriage Sam. At seventeen!"

"Don't judge her too harshly, Derek." Sam took a last drag on his cigarette. It fizzled as it disappeared into his beer can. "What I mean, mate, is that she didn't have a chance. Him being her teacher and in a position of authority."

"Yes! That's what's been getting at me. His abuse of his position, of her naivety."

"What about the school, they know?"

"Don't think so." Derek began to pace the floor, striding back and forth.

"Messy. What about the wife? She going to make trouble? Go to the school?"

"Don't know. I thought I should go and see her."

"Good idea. If you can get her to keep her mouth shut, you can focus on getting Sally through to the end of the year. And you want to know what she's going to do about a divorce. I presume that's on the cards. Makes Sally's situation precarious."

"What about him, Sam? I can't just sit back and let him have his way with her. Can I get the police involved?"

"I don't think you can. I haven't asked if the relationship has been consummated because legally it doesn't matter, she's over sixteen. Unless you know for sure that sexual intercourse took place while she was a minor, the way I see it, he hasn't broken any law."

Derek let go a deep sigh. "What about the school, the Department of Education. They must have some rules to stop this happening."

"I'm not sure they have mate. I can find that out for sure. I'll have a look through the Act but it was written a long time ago and unless there's been a recent amendment it's unlikely – they just didn't acknowledge this kind of stuff back then. Still don't, really. Sweep it all under the carpet." Sam straightened up. "Certainly the teacher's behaviour has been unprofessional, but you can't prosecute him for that."

"Sam, this isn't right. There must be something I can do."

"There's one thing you might have going for you. Even if the relationship is consensual, maybe it could constitute a form of abuse. You see there's a big power differential here. She's young. He's someone she would look up to, respect, you know, and that, I believe, would create a dynamic in which 'mutual consent' as such, is impossible. But it's a long shot."

"So, he's seduced her but probably not broken the law."

"There's a discretionary role that the School Principal could play. I don't think he'd want this bastard on staff if he knew what he was up to. But then you'd have to bring him in on it."

"Feels like this bloke has got us over a barrel. There's nothing I can do at the moment to stop it and keep Sally on track? She's worked so bloody hard for these finals."

"Well you are still Sally's father, mate. You can lay down some rules. Do you think she'd see him if you forbade her?"

"I'm sorry to say this Sam, but I don't think I'd believe her if she said she wouldn't. I think he's got her mesmerised. She is so far from understanding what she's done. She thought because I met Jewel when she was seventeen, we'd be okay about it."

"And so we're back to square one."

"Between a rock and a hard place. Anyway, if you could check out the Act, mate. I'd better be on my way."

Sure you don't want one for the road?"

"No mate, driving."

"You know, I think I'd be having a quiet word with him. Mate's advice now." Sam put his arm around Derek's shoulder as they walked upstairs. "Run into him in a back lane, but make bloody sure you've got a witness. I mean you don't want to be accused of hitting him, you not being a violent man and all that."

Would it come to that?, Derek wondered. He had never menaced anyone in his life, but never before had something so precious been under threat.

16

Passion Pit

B RAD SQUINTED INTO THE SUN'S rays breaking through the salt smeared glass of the windscreen. What did he feel? Relief? *A little.* Sad? *Yes.* Frightened? *You bet.* He arched his back and stretched out the ache that came from a night spent curled up in the back seat of the V-dub in the beach carpark. Despite the discomfort, the car was better than the cold, hard sand and better than confronting Emma back at the flat.

A clear morning ahead and so far no wind, the sky a dappled flamingo. Pink sky in the morning. He didn't need a warning. The shit wasn't finished yet. His thoughts turned to Sally. She would be waking up for church. He imagined her sitting in the pew, wearing one of her summer dresses, her shoulders smooth and tanned, then shook his head to get his mind back to the present. His head was spinning. When he wound down the window to get some fresh air he smelt the sea. It was always there for him.

By seven o'clock he had half a dozen good rides under his belt and although the waves were holding up, hunger drove him back in. The smell of Joe's bacon and egg rolls drifted up from the beachside milk bar. It was as he headed towards the ramp that he spotted

Rob walking purposefully towards him, surf ski balanced on his head. Brad could never work out why he preferred it to a board.

"G'day mate. You're at it early," Rob said.

"Yeah, too good to miss."

"Got a minute mate?"

"Yeah. Guess so."

Rob laid his ski on the sand, and after an awkward moment, Brad did the same with his board.

They stood facing out to sea. Rob flicked the sand with his toe.

"Mate, Emma's at our place. She's pretty cut up."

"Yeah, I suppose she would be."

"Says you told her you want out?"

Brad ignored the question. His head dipped forward and he ground his heel into the sand.

"Sure you know what you're doing mate?" Rob was unsure if Brad shrugged because he didn't know the answer, or if he couldn't care less. "Big call, I reckon."

"I didn't kick her out. She can come back."

"Don't you think you should tell her that?"

"Just thought since you got yourself involved, you might want to tell her."

"Not trying to interfere mate. Just trying to help."

"If you say so." Brad picked up his board, tucked it under his right arm and ran his free fingers through wet hair. "But if she's there, I won't be, mate." He walked towards the shoreline, wondering where he would be.

Strong strokes drove him quickly through the breakers towards the riders out the back. He headed for the rear of the pack, seeking solitude and the soothing rise and fall of the swell. Rob should mind his own bloody business. Sandy had put him up to it, for sure. Two sets went by and half a dozen dudes fought for each ride. He was the first to sense a new set coming in, a stirring beneath his feet. The wave would build from nothing, rise up briefly then disappear in a mass of white water. A bit like his relationship with Emma, he thought. Good start, then all downhill, finally to be thrown around like flotsam, drowning, gasping for breath, suffocating. He really was hungry now so he let the next wave take him in. When he reached the shoreline, he checked out the beach in case Rob was still around. Coast clear. He looked further on past the roadway and smiled as his eyes rested on the block of flats where John's new pad was.

Three times around the block and into a spot right out the front. The intercom buzzed.

"Yeah."

"It's Brad mate."

"Come on up." The door was ajar. Johnno appeared and offered his hand. "Good to see you mate."

"Yeah. Been a while. Surf's good."

"Big night mate. Only just got up. How you going, anyway?"

"Listen, sorry about the last time, Janice and all that. Beer in, brains out I reckon mate."

"Forget it mate. Anyway, want a coldie?" He was halfway to the fridge, and Brad noticed his blonde locks were nearly to his shoulders. A better look than regulation short back and sides and his skin had darkened, or did it just look that way because of those ice blue eyes? Rumour had it he had continued to put his good looks to good use, pulling the honeys back to what was widely known as 'Johnno's Passion Pit.' Throw in a new Triumph sports car and it was a safe bet Johnno was going to score with any chick he fancied.

"Bit early ain't it?" Brad said with a raised eyebrow.

"Hair of the dog for me," John said ignoring Brad's question and tossing him a beer. "Verandah, buddy," he beckoned as Brad caught the can in mid-air, "get the passing parade this time of day. Sometimes I think they're doing it just for me."

They settled into deck chairs and rested their beer on the railing. It took Brad another twenty minutes before he got to the point of his visit.

"Not going too well with Emma and me at the moment, mate. Wondered if I could crash here tonight." Brad was unsure if John took a swig of beer to buy time.

"Yeh, no problem," he said, wiping the excess moisture from his lips, "there's one bedroom that doesn't get much use. It's yours."

"Other one gets a bit of action I hear?" Brad couldn't help himself.

"Then you've heard right mate."

"What's your success rate, you keeping score?"

"You mean do I keep score of the chicks I score with, eh? About ninety eight percent hit rate I reckon. Once I get them into the passion pit, the game's over."

"So what happened to the two percent?"

"Had the rags on mate, red sails in the sunset, know what I mean?'

"Yeah," said Brad, sorry he'd asked. He was tempted to brag about his own conquests but decided the fewer people who knew, the better.

"How many do you reckon?"

"Dunno. Lost count."

"Bloody hell. Sounds like you're onto a good thing."

"Drink to that."

John's women were turned over, literally and metaphorically, quicker than you could get out of your wet board shorts on a cold day. His longest relationship was three and a half weeks. Seems her mother knew his mother and Johnno didn't want to look too much of a heel, giving the daughter the flick a week after he'd got into her pants. And she had taken longer than most to come around, probably for the same reason that he had hung onto her for so long.

"Want to be careful mate, you could end up with a lot of little Johnnos running around."

"Not a bloody chance buddy. Rubbers every time."

"Must be costing you a fortune."

"Mate gets them," he explained, sucking on his cigarette. "Don't cost me a cent."

"Cool," replied Brad, and remembered his agonising visits to the chemist before Emma was on the pill, wandering around looking at razors or zinc cream, waiting for the pharmacist to finish serving a customer, but the phone would always ring, or the bloke would go to the back of the shop to make up prescriptions and some old biddy would come up and ask, "Can I help you, dear?" Then she'd make a big scene, pretending she didn't hear. "What was that you wanted?" and everyone in the shop would stare like he was a criminal or something. Then he'd buy some razors and get out of the place.

"Disaster struck about three months ago though. Supply ran out." John was back from the kitchen with fresh beers. "I had this chick on the lounge and I'd just pants'd her, I reached for my wallet, and remembered. Didn't have a bloody rubber."

"What'd you do?"

"Told her I had one of those pills that stops you getting up the duff."

"She swallow it?" replied Brad, thinking he was being clever.

"Nah, mate you don't put it in your mouth. Up the love tunnel – whoosh."

"She let you?"

"Not a chance, she didn't trust me, did it herself. Nerve racking though, but I got lucky. In the dark, she couldn't tell it was a button I'd just pulled off me shirt. Bit of quick thinking, saved the day."

"And happy endings all round."

"Not really. It was my best bloody shirt, mate! Ripped a hole in it when I pulled the button off."

Brad nearly toppled off the desk chair as he bent over, laughing. "Fuck off mate!"

"Gave it to the old lady to fix. Told her a guy grabbed me in the pub. She was real sympathetic." They were both rolling about now hollering with laughter, the first time in ages for Brad.

The day disappeared in a haze of alcohol. After a dinner of Kentucky Fried, Brad lay in the dark, listening to the waves crash onto the shoreline.

By 5.30 am, he was wide awake, with a bit of a hangover. It was a gas to be able just to wander to the end of the room and check out the conditions. He could see by the light of the rising sun that the beach was a mass of white water, so he went back to bed until he heard Johnno moving about the kitchen.

"Might be here a couple of nights if that's okay with you."

"No worries, mate." John was shaking out a packet of rice bubbles. "Just make yourself scarce if I'm making out."

"Yeah, no problem."

"You're welcome to breakfast if you like this stuff," he said, holding up the carton. "Milk's a bit off though."

As he was leaving, John threw Brad a key.

"Listen, all jokes aside. You and Emm, what's going on?"

"Dunno Johnno. Things just gone off the rails a bit."

"Maybe you can get it back on the rails eh?"

"Anything's possible I guess."

"Shit man. She must be really cut up. She know you're here?"

"Nah. Didn't want to involve you. Don't have to stay if it's a problem."

"Nah, see ya tonight – if you're not married again before then."

A look around the flat convinced Brad he'd struck it lucky. A beach, free beer and a mate. A bloody trifecta. The perfect place to start life as a single bloke.

17

Deal's a Deal

"I'm sorry. Rob couldn't talk sense into him." Sandy said as she backed the ute out of the driveway."

"I know he tried. Say thank you for me. I can't remember if I did."

"I'm not happy with you being on your own tonight, Emm. You know you can grab your stuff and come back to us."

"And how do I get to work tomorrow morning? I have to earn money."

"You're not counting on him to come back, are you Emma?"

"I heard what Rob said."

They pulled up out front then checked the garage.

"Bastard took the car," Sandy said.

"Well he needs it and I don't."

"Not the point, Emma. Come on let's go upstairs. At least he kept his word on this one," Sandy said as they opened the door to the flat, "it's all yours, Kiddo."

"I wonder where he is?"

"Emma, listen to me. Try not to think about it too much. I know it's nearly impossible but let your head get a bit of a rest."

"Sure," she replied unconvincingly, "I'll try."

"I'm going to go now. You've got the leftovers for dinner, so don't forget to eat them. Call me tomorrow after work. Promise? I'll be waiting."

"Promise."

"Think you'll manage to sleep?"

"I'm exhausted Sand. I think I will."

Emma woke after a few hours and lay listening to the rumble of every passing car, willing the motor to quieten, to idle and for the garage door to open. Instead the sounds died away and the night once again fell silent.

When the sky began to change from black to pale gold she pushed herself into a sitting position then made her way to the bathroom to prepare for the day. The mind-numbing repetition of her job, the shorthand, the typing and the filing would be a respite from the mental gymnastics of the last two days, the regurgitation of thousands of questions that had no answers. When at last her watch read seven fifty, she left the flat and waited by the kerbside for Greg to arrive.

"Morning," she mumbled, avoiding his gaze, her cheek pressed against the cool glass of the car window.

"You look tired, Emm." A note of concern in his voice.

"Didn't sleep much last night. That's all."

"You sure you're all right for work?"

Shit shit shit. The tears were there now and wouldn't be held back. They overflowed onto her cheeks.

A hand rested on her shoulder. "What's wrong Emma?"

An emphatic shake of her head and the drops flew around like rain spatters.

"Geez Emm, I can't stand to see you cry. Here."

He pulled out a crumpled handkerchief.

A loud honk as she blew her nose made them laugh. "Oh God. What am I going to do? I'm a mess. He's gone Greg. I haven't seen him since Friday."

"Brad?"

"Who do you think?"

"I'm really sorry Emm."

"I can't believe it's happened."

"You're sure?"

She nodded. "Afraid so. I don't think he's loved me for a long time."

"Then he's a stupid git."

"You can't make someone love you, you know."

"Yeah, I do know."

"That happened to you?"

"You could say that."

They pulled into the carpark. He turned off the motor and rested his arms on the steering wheel. "You know Emm, I don't think you've been happy for a long time."

"Really?"

"You sit there all tensed up and pick at the skin on your fingers."

She felt the remnant of a whitlow on the thumb of her left hand and tucked it under her armpit.

"You let me know if you need anything today," he said as he locked the car.

"Yeah. Thanks. Greg, please don't say anything to anyone."

"Course not. See you this arvo Emma." He walked away slowly, head bowed, shirt untucked, hands in pockets and turned in time to see Emma disappear into her office.

The phone rang at ten fifteen. "Technical Department, Emma Emery speaking."

"Mrs Emery, this is Derek Watson. Do you know who I am?"

"No sorry, I don't."

"Your husband teaches my daughter Sally... Mrs Emery, are you there?"

She clutched the phone in both hands. "Yes."

"I'm sorry to phone you at work but I didn't have any other way to contact you. Can I speak with you briefly?"

Emma swallowed hard. "Yes."

"Mrs Emery, my wife and I would like to meet with you." A pause to allow her take it in.

"What for?"

"We realise this is very difficult dear but we would really appreciate it if you could see us, my wife and I, for a short while. Could we meet tonight, about 6 o'clock? We could come to you if that's easier?"

"He won't be there."

"It's you we want to see, not your husband." Derek was grateful for Jewel's steadying hand on his shoulder. "Emma, we are desperate. Please."

Silence.

"6 o'clock then," Derek said convincingly. "Could I have your address please."

When she put the phone down, Emma grabbed her handbag and headed to the ladies' room. It wasn't long before she heard the swinging door slam shut followed by footsteps.

"Everything all right sweetie?"

"Yes Mrs White, I just got my periods."

"Oh, poor little thing. I was so glad when the curse left me. I'll leave you to it, sweetheart."

Emma got back to her desk in time to hear the rattle of the tea trolley.

"Morning Emma. Here luvvie, your morning tea." She glanced up to see Mrs O'Toole's tea ladies' arms place her rock cake and teacup on the desk. "You're looking a bit peaky today, no colour in those cheeks."

"Just a bit tired."

When Mrs O'Toole moved on, Emma picked up the phone and dialled the number she knew by heart.

"Hello. Five eight nine two three two three"

"Mum, it's me."

"Hello Darling. Wondered where you've been. Haven't heard from you for a while."

"It's been really busy. At work."

"Not working too hard I hope. Did you have a nice weekend?"

"Yes Mum. Just thought I'd give you a ring." Silent sobs.

"Good Darling. You and Brad like to come over for dinner on Thursday?"

"I think he's got to study. I'll talk to him and ring you back?"

"Yeah, sure honey. Everything all right?"

"Yes Mum," was all she could manage.

"Okay honey. You're sure though? Anything you want to talk about?"

"No Mum. Got to go. At work, remember."

"Love you lots. Ring me when you know about Thursday, or before if you want."

"Love you too. Bye."

Maybe this will all have blown over by then. Maybe Sally's parents can talk some sense into their daughter, maybe Brad will change his mind, maybe Mrs White will mind her own business one day.

At 4.30 Emma was out the door. Greg was waiting. She sat clutching her handbag, head down, wondering what she would wear to show the Watsons that she was still young and beautiful.

"You feeling better?" he asked tenderly.

"Just want to get home to lie down."

"Sure. You need anything, you let me know."

"Thanks."

"Emma, I mean it. Just ask. You hear?"

"I mean it too Greg." She was halfway out of the car and turned to him. "Thank you. You're kind."

As Greg leaned over to pull the door closed, he called to her. "If you see him, tell him for me, he's a dickhead of the first order."

She barely registered his advice as she ran up the stairs. There was just enough time to wash her hair and change her clothes.

The uncarpeted stairs were a good warning system for anyone making their way to the second floor. At exactly two minutes to six, she heard the hollow clunk of shoes on concrete.

Her hands trembled as she stood poised on the other side of

the door, waiting to release the lock after the first knock. When it came she counted backwards from ten then opened the door.

"Hello, Mrs Emery." Mr Watson held out his hand.

"My name's Emma."

"Emma, I'm Derek and this is my wife, Jewel."

Mrs Watson seemed much younger than her own mother, who wouldn't be seen dead in high heels or a mini skirt and who said that you couldn't wear your hair long after you turned thirty, but Mrs Watson looked good. He eye liner was perfectly applied and the pale pink lipstick matched the colour of her blouse.

"May we come in?"

"Sorry, yes. Please." Emma stood back to allow them to pass. Should they sit at the table or on one of the divans? She hesitated long enough for Mr Watson to decide.

"All right if we sit here, Emma?" He chose the divan near the door and propped two cushions behind his back for support.

"Yes, of course. Would you like a drink, or tea or something?"

"No thank you dear. We don't want to put you to any trouble."

As they settled themselves, Emma looked around the flat and saw it as if for the first time, through their eyes. The back of the fridge stuck out from the kitchen alcove. She had made a hessian curtain to disguise the overhang, but it looked tatty. In the middle of the dining table was a relic from her six-week pottery class. She had been proud of what she now recognised was an ill-proportioned vase, fashioned from misshapen, concentric coils of clay with an arrangement of dried wild grasses from the sandhills.

Her eyes moved to the lounge room. When she and Brad had first put the bookshelves together, they were proud of the result but now she saw nothing but bits of rough cut cedar and old bricks stacked on top of one another. The Watsons were seated on what had been Brad and his sister's divan beds. Emma had made corduroy covers for the mattresses and cushions to match but they still looked like beds. Rob's coffee table was the only decent piece of furniture in the flat.

Mr Watson spoke first. "Emma, we wondered if you would tell us what you know? About what has happened."

Mrs Watson sensed Emma's unease and her eyes darted to her husband and back. "My dear, we mean you no harm. On the contrary. I think we all wish things were different."

"I met your daughter once, at a school dance," Emma said. "Brad and I spoke about her last year. I mean, he said how she was a good pupil and everything. I thought that was all there was to it."

"Emma, it is our understanding that Sally wasn't the cause of your marriage break-up?"

"My marriage break-up?" Emma couldn't hide her shock at hearing the finality of those words but Mr. Watson kept on.

"Yes dear. We believe the decision to separate was mutual?"

"I don't know how to answer that." Emma fought to maintain her composure. She needed time and shook her head as she scrunched the tissue in her hand. Her reply came out much louder than she had intended, like the shot from a gun, an explosion of emotion.

"No! I mean, it wasn't. I didn't know anything. I still love him, I love my husband." Her voice was breaking and the tears began to well up.

At the sight of Emma's distress, Mrs Watson reached over and grabbed her husband's arm. "Oh, Emma, we're so sorry. We were hoping it wouldn't be like this for you."

These people have no idea. A sharp pain in her stomach made her bend over. "I've been blind," she said righting herself. "I should have known he was so unhappy." The tears were running freely now and she paused to blow her nose.

"Emma, we're incredibly sorry. We don't condone any of this." Mr Watson looked to his wife who nodded in agreement.

"I thought he was at the library marking papers and everything. Said it was because of school, you know, extra work with year twelve. He's doing a degree. Did you know that?"

"No dear, we didn't," said Mrs Watson. "You don't have to talk about this if you don't want to."

Hiccups, one after another. "He started to exercise with, *hic*, weights and things and, *hic*, I think now, he must have wanted to look good for her. Should have known, seen the signs. Had no idea. Believed what he, *hic*, said." She took a deep breath, "I've been so stupid," and exhaled. "Now it's too late."

Mr Watson spoke. "Do you want to take a break, dear. Can I get you some water?"

"Excuse me." She headed for the bathroom. It would have been a relief to rinse her face but her mascara was already out of control. *What do they want of me? I wish they would just go.* The flushing of the toilet camouflaged the hooting sound from the clearing of her blocked nose. She drank from the tap, pushed her hair behind her ears and went back to the lounge room.

When she sat down, Mrs Watson spoke. "Emma, we really feel for you and we're as keen as you are to get things back to normal. We feel sure they will come to their senses, but if this gets out now, if the school finds out before the term finishes... well..."

Emma looked from one to the other, it made sense now. "You're wondering if I'm going to say anything. To the school?"

"It would be best for everybody if we keep this between ourselves. Don't you agree?" Emma noticed the furrow in Mr Watson's brow.

"That's right, dear," Mrs Watson agreed. "I think it would be best for everyone."

Emma looked from one to the other. She hadn't even considered involving the school. It would really stuff things up for their daughter, even if it didn't work out between her and Brad. The Watsons were now perched on the edge of the divan, waiting for her answer.

"I won't go to the school."

"Oh, that's incredibly kind of you Emma. We can't imagine how hard this must be for you." Mrs Watson lightly touched her husband's shoulder as they adjusted their positions.

"If there's ever anything we can do for you, be sure to let us know," said Mr Watson. The meeting was over, they stood up.

"Yes, dear, anything at all."

He turned at the doorway. "We can count on you then? To keep this between us?"

"Yes. I won't say anything." Mrs Watson kissed Emma on the cheek and she watched them walk to the landing, then as she was about to close the door, Mr Watson turned around.

"Thank you…and I mean it. Anything that you need, Emma, just ask."

They have no idea, she thought. *What does he think I need, except my husband back? Do they really think I have done this because I'm a good person? Do they think I've done it for them or for Sally? I couldn't give a stuff about their daughter. There's only one reason and it's not what they think. It's because Brad would never forgive me if I did anything to hurt her.*

18

A Thoughtful Boy

"Hi Darling," Jewel said as Derek walked into the kitchen, "I just hung up from Sam. He said he missed you at work."

"Oh, does he want me to call back?" he asked, kissing his wife on the cheek.

"Well actually, and I hope this is all right with you," she continued while pouring the tea, "I mean, I know Lee isn't our favourite person but they're old friends and I've invited them to dinner tomorrow night. Shouldn't be a late one, being a weeknight and we haven't seen them for ages. It might be good to have some company."

"Good idea, Darling," Derek replied, sipping his Earl Grey.

"Well that was easy. I'd better think about what we're going to eat."

The next morning, Jewel left early with her shopping list in hand. For most of the afternoon, she worked in the kitchen and had just finished laying the table when the Thurgoods arrived, spot on at 7pm. She felt confident that the menu would please everybody. Pumpkin soup was always a safe bet, then steak and kidney pie. Derek loved that and it would satisfy Sam's appetite. Lee, usually picked at her food and was more interested in sharing the local gossip than eating. Her pre-occupation with her own conversation was so complete that over dinner, Jewel was able to tune out for most of it.

That was a really beautiful meal, Jewel," Lee said as she stood up from the table.

"Let me help you clear up." She stacked the dessert plates and carried them into the kitchen along with the leftover cheesecake.

"Grab the port bottle Sam," Derek said. "Meet you in the lounge room." When Sam was out of sight, Derek whispered, "he wants to talk about his new property deal love. Can you entertain Lee?"

"She does that for herself." Jewel replied with a grin as she walked past, into the kitchen.

"Sally swatting away upstairs I suppose?" Lee asked as she helped to stack the dishes.

"Yes, exams start soon." Jewel ran the hot water into the sink, picked up a dinner plate, rubbed it vigorously with the sponge and placed it in the dish rack.

"I'm sure she'll do well."

"Hope so, Lee."

"Always was a good girl your Sally, never any trouble."

"That's true."

"I thought our worries were over once Paul left school but how wrong was I!" Lee paused as if she had said too much, and perched on a kitchen stool, resting the tea towel and dinner plate in her lap.

"He's not enjoying the UK?" Jewel asked.

"On the contrary but he is coming home at Christmas."

"Bet you can't wait."

"I suppose I'm looking forward to it. Of course I am. He's still my boy, even though..."

The silence between them lengthened as Jewel debated whether to probe further.

Lee began to sniffle and dab at her nose with the end of the tea towel. "I'm sorry Jewel, I don't want to spoil our lovely night." She rummaged in her handbag and took out a small plastic bottle.

"I've been wanting to tell someone, but there's no-one." She unscrewed the bottle top and took out a pink pill. "I don't mean for you to take that personally. It's just, well, I feel ashamed." She popped it in her mouth and swallowed hard.

"Ashamed of what Lee?" Jewel turned to face her friend, rubber gloves dripping dishwater onto the lino.

"I think Paul's a homosexual," Lee said. Her eyes rolled to the ceiling as she clasped the plate to her chest.

Jewel turned back to the sink in an attempt to act as normal as possible, as if Lee's news was inconsequential, an everyday event. "Paul? Are you sure? He told you?" She placed a handful of cutlery into the drying rack.

"Well, not in so many words, but you know how he's never had a girlfriend…"

"Of course Lee, but he might be a late starter. It doesn't make him, you know, what you said."

"Jewel, I wish you were right," Lee took a deep breath and continued, "he rang me yesterday, all the way from England, to tell me he's coming home for a visit.

"That's exciting, Lee," Jewel interjected.

"I thought so too at first then I asked him if he had some news. I thought he might have met a nice girl." Lee paused to position herself on a kitchen stool, still clutching the plate, "he sort of told me then, in his round about way."

"Oh dear." Jewel's rubber fingers touched her lips as if to censor her thoughts.

"I think he rang me because he doesn't want it to be too much of a shock when he comes home. Always been a thoughtful boy."

Jewel peeled off the kitchen gloves and threw them onto the draining board then pulled up a stool and sat next to Lee. She reached across and patted her on the knee. "More than that actually. He's one of the nicest young men I know. Never failed to do something to impress me every time he was here. Let's just wait and see shall we. You might be wrong." Then she added "I can't believe it, not Paul."

"What if it is true, Jewel?" Lee laid the plate aside and smoothed the tea towel onto the bench top with the flat of her hand. "Was it something I did bringing him up? I remember buying him those paper parasols when we went shopping. I should have been more careful."

"Lee, you mustn't think that. I mean, I don't believe anything *causes* it. Certainly not a few paper umbrellas. It's just the way they're born. There's been a lot of talk about it, what with the new laws coming in. I think they said it's in their genes."

"Must be from mine. I'm sure it's not in Sam's."

"What about Sam? Do you think he knows?"

"Oh God no! He'll be a disaster. You know what he's like. Blokiest bloke around. We've been listening to the talkback about these new laws. Everyone's calling them 'poofters', 'shirt lifters'. And he sits there nodding his head and saying 'hear, hear'."

"I think you should change radio stations Lee."

"But that's what people think, isn't it? That's what they'll call him. He'll never have a normal life Jewel," she sobbed.

"I can tell you now it won't matter to me, or to Derek. If Paul's still the same boy, and I'm sure he is, there's a lot to love about him." In truth, she wasn't all that sure about Derek. He had liberal views and she knew he supported the new laws, but he'd said, when he thought about what they did, he knew why they were called 'queer'.

"Maybe it's the crowd he's been mixing with over there," A loud honk as Lee blew her nose. "I'm sorry to burden you with my worries."

"That's what friends are for Lee. Come on, let's make a cup of tea. Got England through the war didn't it?"

Lee checked out the lounge room as the kettle was filled. "They're still outside smoking," she said as Jewel came in with the tea tray.

"Let's put on some music, eh?" Was Johnny Ray a good choice Jewel wondered? There had been rumours about him and other men.

"Thank you. You really are a good friend." Lee added three teaspoons of sugar to her tea and spoke as she stirred. "To tell you the truth, I've been suspicious for a while, but I didn't want to think about it."

"I can understand that."

"Oh Jewel, what sort of life will he have? Never be married. Have children." She looked at her friend and sobbed, "How can he ever be happy?"

"Lee, we don't know for sure yet. Try not to think about it."

Jewel's advice fell on deaf ears. "Nothing anyone can do. It's hopeless," Lee wailed. "Poor thing. Oh God, how will we ever tell his father?"

"I always find a good dinner and a bottle of wine works when you've got to break bad news."

"I think it will take more than that with Sam."

Jewel was still trying to come up with something that would calm her friend, when the men came into the room.

"We should make tracks, Lee. Great dinner, Jewel."

"You're such a good cook, my dear Jewel." Lee kissed her cheek and held her close. Sam raised his eyebrows.

"Derek mate, see you soon?"

"You're on Sam. Let's catch up for the game next week, eh?"

As he lay in bed, waiting for his wife to take the stuff off her face and then put more on, Derek thought over Sam's news.

"Sorry to say, mate," Sam said in a rare show of sympathy, "but I don't think there is anything you can do legally. The Crimes Act, Section 73, does refer to a teacher-pupil relationship. Specifically, if the pupil is under seventeen, the teacher is liable to eight years imprisonment, but here's the rub mate – you've got to have proof of sexual intercourse. You going to put Sally through that?"

And there it was. Nothing more to say really. He was beaten, afforded no justice by the law. If Brad had stolen his car, he'd have a case against him. But he had taken his daughter. Maybe Sam's other idea wasn't such a bad one. A dark alley on a dark night. But could he do it? It went against everything he had ever taught Sally – the abhorrence of violence, for any reason. And, if he hurt Brad, would she ever forgive him? So was he really a good man, or would he stay clear of Brad out of self-interest? Too tired to ponder the philosophical, Derek closed his eyes and listened for the reassuring patter of Jewel making her way from the bathroom. He sensed the weight of her dressing gown being laid across the bed and waited for her cold feet to search out his warmth and for the soft peck on his cheek as she bade him good night.

19

The Letter

Mrs White slammed down her phone, jumped up from her desk then raced to the end of the office where she stood on tiptoes to peer over the glass petition.

Emma's fingers rested on the keys of her typewriter. "What's going on?" she asked.

"Oh Emma. They're going through the place like a dose of salts, handing out retrenchment notices."

"You mean firing people?"

"On the spot, dearie," she said straightening her back and added. "That was Doreen on the phone. She's gone already."

"Are we going to lose our jobs too?" Emma stood up and strained to see what Mrs White was gawking at.

"Looks like it. There's a delegation walking this way."

Emma's boss, glasses in hand, joined them in the corridor.

"What's happening Jock?" Mrs White was in no mood to be put off. "Don't spin me stories, I can see well enough what they're doing."

"Muriel, I'm sorry but it looks like we're in for it too." They're closing down this section completely. I've just heard. Bad news for us all."

Graeme the Sales Engineer was still at his desk, staring open-mouthed.

"Looks like you're going as well," Mrs White piped up, "so, don't just sit there as if nothing's happened."

"I'm sorry Emma, Graeme," Mr Mott said, "nothing I can do."

"Oh sweet Jesus", Mrs White wailed, "we've just bought a new car."

"I've booked a holiday in Fiji," Graeme added, standing up slowly. He was followed by Mr Mott who declared that he had just enrolled his daughter in a very expensive private school.

Emma raised the stakes, in a whisper to herself... *and my husband has just left me.*

One at a time, the staff were called into Mr Mott's office and handed a letter and an envelope.

Emma counted the money, four weeks' pay in all; a week in lieu and three weeks holiday pay. "What do we do now?" she asked.

"Well I'm damned if I'm staying here a minute longer." Mrs White already had the cover on her typewriter.

"Do you want me to finish this letter Mr. Mott?" Emma asked, more than a little bewildered.

"Thank you, dear, but no. Muriel, why don't you hang around for a few minutes while I pack up then we'll all go and have a drink. There's a few people from the other sections going to meet up." She slumped in her chair, coat and handbag over her arm and waited.

"Right, that's it then," Mr Mott said as he looked around the office for one last time. They followed him single file out the door, piled into his Fairlane and drove down the road to the bowling club.

Drinks were a real fizzer. The mood was sombre and most people left as soon as was polite. A few of the young guys with no responsibilities and a taste for free beer stayed on.

Greg tapped Emma on the shoulder. "Emma, I'm really sorry. This on top of everything else for you. Are you all right?"

"None of it feels real."

"Emm, I've got to get home."

"That's fine by me. I can't stay here much longer."

"Be back in a minute then."

He meandered towards the gents as Mrs O'Toole came up to Emma. "He's a nice bloke, isn't he," she said.

"I guess so," Emma agreed although she'd never really thought about it.

"I know he doesn't look the best but he doesn't have much time to look after himself given that he has to do everything for his dad."

"What do you mean?"

"His father has some disease that makes him shake all the time and he can't walk. Greg does everything for him and he's trying to do his study at the same time."

"Really?" Emma bit her lip. "I thought he was just lazy."

"He's a good boy Emma. Not many like him."

"You 'bout ready Emm?" he called, standing a few feet away. She wondered if he had overheard.

"Yeah, sure. I'll say a quick goodbye to the others," and added "if that's all right?"

"Yeah, off you go."

"My Dad used to tell me the bosses don't give a damn about us," he said as they walked to the car. "Looks like he was right."

"Greg, I didn't know about your dad."

"Doesn't matter Emm. Knew you didn't."

"I'm so sorry. I guess I didn't understand a lot of things."

The trip home was speedy in the absence of peak hour traffic.

As the mini turned into her street, Greg asked. "You hear anything today? From him?"

"No."

"You still hoping?"

"Yep."

"You're really forgiving, Emm."

"Or stupid."

"This happening at work, on top of everything else. Like I said, it's hard for you."

"It's like someone took my life, put it in a jar, gave it a good shake then scattered the contents all over the place."

"It will be okay Emma, in time."

"At least I've got some money to keep me going." She wrapped her fingers around the brown envelope.

He pulled into the curb and let the motor idle. "Same time tomorrow, eh?"

"I'll miss our morning rides, honest Greg."

His bottom jaw quivered and Emma thought he might cry. "You'll get another job," she said reassuringly.

"Yeah, sure I will." He let go of the steering wheel and turned to face her. "Promise you'll let me know if you need anything."

"I'll just wander down to the spare parts department. That easy." She patted his hand.

"Seriously, Emma," he flicked his hair from his eyes and looked directly into hers, "if there's anything I can do…"

"Thanks Greg. I really mean it, thank you." She unfastened her seatbelt, stepped from the car, then turned around and leaned in. "And I'm sorry I was so mean."

"No you weren't Emma. Like you said, you didn't understand, that's all."

He pulled the door closed and backed out of the driveway. Emma stood at the curb clutching her handbag and watched someone she wished she had known better drive away.

A letter in a blue envelope was sticking out from their mailbox. As she retrieved it, the sound of a V-Dub motor caused her to look up. Brad got out slamming the door and came running towards her.

"I didn't think you'd be here, I…" He stopped in mid-sentence. "Give me that!"

"What?"

"The letter."

Emma looked down at the envelope held in her hand. *S.W.A.L.K.*

was scrawled in purple marker pen across the seal. Underneath were the words *Tomorrow is the First Day of the Rest of Your Life.*

"Give it to me." He tried to snatch it from her.

"No," she said, clutching it to her chest.

"Give it here! It's addressed to me."

"I know who it's from. It's from her," Emma hissed. "Why is she writing to you at our house? She's got no right." She backed away and he paced her retreat. "Nooo," she screamed at the top of her voice as he made another grab for the envelope. "Get away from me. Don't touch it."

When he made another move towards her she began to thrash about, flailing her arms in the air, striking him whenever he came near. She was screaming, wailing, and crying out like a mad woman, she thought afterwards.

He tried once more to snatch the envelope, and this time her closed fist connected with his earlobe. "It's not fair. It's not fair," she yelled.

Brad felt a stab of pain and grabbed the side of his head, but she didn't stop.

"Why are you both doing this to me?" Emma kept pummelling his head, then his face. Her nails tore into him. The envelope was scrunched in the palm of her left hand and she wouldn't let go. When he tried to grab her arms, she was amazed at her own strength.

"Go on, hurt me if you want," he shouted. "Get it out Emm."

It was as if a spell was broken. Her movements ceased and she fell, like a puppet whose strings had been cut, onto the footpath, on her knees, her head hanging loose.

A car stopped across the road and the couple inside watched, transfixed. Blinds parted in the ground floor unit. Emma was slumped face down, sobbing into the pavement, then she began rocking back and forth, on her haunches. Brad bent down and hoisted her up by the armpits. "Come inside Emma." The venetians snapped shut as he guided her towards the entrance foyer and supported her up the stairs, through the door and onto a divan.

When he came back from the kitchen, she hadn't moved. "Here, swallow this." He placed the glass in her hand and held it to her lips but she didn't drink.

"Emma it's scotch. Drink it. Will do you good." He touched his ear and his lip and felt the dampness. When he looked down, he had blood on his hand.

"She had no right. How dare she write to you here." The scotch was doing its job.

"It's not her fault. She thought you'd gone."

Her hands shook and he could tell from the rising pitch of her voice that the hysteria was returning. "This is my home!"

"It was a mistake. I'm sorry."

"So that makes it all right?" she howled.

"No Emm. I stuffed up."

"Stuffed up my life. And now I don't have a job."

"What do you mean?"

"I got retrenched today." She laid the glass on the floor and tried to reposition a strand of hair that had come loose.

"What, from work?"

"Well you don't get retrenched from your marriage," she hissed as she undid her hairclip and let her hair fall free.

"No."

"Are we finished Brad? Is this how marriages end?" She began to play with the clip, snapping it open and shut.

"Guess so."

"Guess so? You're not sure?"

"Emm, don't."

"What did I do wrong?"

"Nothing."

"Then why do you want her and not me?"

He looked directly at her. "She makes me feel like a man."

Then she must be a bloody magician. That's what Emma wished she had said – the great comeback which, like most of the really good ones, she thought of weeks later.

"What do I make you feel then?" she asked, wanting to know

but at the same time terrified of what she might hear. She had begun to snap off the teeth of the hair clip one by one, and drop them onto the carpet,.

"You make me feel I'm never good enough."

"I don't think that."

"And I can never do anything right."

She wanted to tell him that he was wrong about that too, but stopped herself just in time.

"I've smothered you haven't I?" she said, not because she believed it in her heart but because she knew it would appease him.

He nodded 'yes' and picked up the empty glass.

"Emm, I've got to go. You shouldn't be here on your own now. Do you want to go to your Mum's?"

"She doesn't know. Not now. No. I can't."

"Well what then?"

"Sandy put a key in the flower pot." She tried make fun of herself. "Knew I'd be back I suppose."

Brad watched his wife more with curiosity than concern, as she stared at the far wall and began the rocking again, and humming. He wondered if she wasn't losing it. As her motion slowed and her eyes became focused, she looked at him as if she was surprised to see him standing there.

"Come on Emm, you should get some clothes. Emm, hear me? Then I'll drive you." He helped her up and steered her towards the bedroom.

"Yes. I'll need clothes." Having a task at hand seemed to revive her. Brad returned to the loungeroom to retrieve the envelope lying on the divan.

They drove to Sandy's in silence. There was nothing to say. He left her standing on the curb, clasping her bag in both hands.

A breeze hummed its way through the tops of the trees and she looked up to see a washed blue sky visible between swaying branches. It was peaceful at Sandy's. If you listened hard enough you could hear the house nestling. At the bottom of the drive, she found a sandstone block in the corner of the garden and settled down to wait for Sandy.

Late in the afternoon, a gust of wind deposited a fluttering of wattle blossom across the courtyard pavers. Emma bent down and scooped up a handful of the spun gold and blew it into the air. Humans resist the new, cling to the present. But in nature there was evidence of the process of growth and renewal. She saw it in the aged gums and young saplings, the disappearing blossoms and new green shoots.

"Well, look what the cat dragged in." Sandy said. "I told you where the key was, you didn't have to sit here like an orphan. How long you been on that rock?" She took note of Emma's appearance. Not like her to have her hair straggling about her face. And her blouse was hanging out of her skirt.

"It's nice here. The wattle is so lovely and you've got ladybirds on this bush. I haven't seen a lady for years. Do you remember the song? *Ladybird, ladybird fly away home, your house is on fire and your children all gone.* Horrible really when you think of the words."

"Sure it is, but you're not supposed to take it literally Emm. Come on, I'll make you a cuppa – or you ready for a wine?" They both watched as a ladybird crawled along Emma's arm. "Come on you slacko, get off your bum and get inside. Staying a while, are you?" Sandy said, and hoisted Emma's bag onto her shoulder. She snapped her fingers twice. "Hello. Anyone home? Emm, come on inside and tell me about it."

Sandy held open the door and sat Emma on the lounge. It took two glasses of wine and long periods of silence to get her to talk.

"Okay, so you're out of a job. No problem. I told you before. You'll get another one tomorrow. What about shithead. You see him?"

Emma began slowly, then the words fell over one another. When she paused, Sandy rose to her feet and applauded.

"You beat the bastard up! Brilliant."

"I drew blood."

"Better still. Amazing. I'm proud of you. Where's the letter?"

"I don't know. He must have it."

"It was probably a load of crap anyway. How about you and I have a girls' night. Rob's delivering some tables so let's get in our jamas and socks and watch TV. You hungry yet?"

"Nup."

"How about a bath."

"Yes, a bath."

When Emma came down the stairs in Sandy's dressing gown, the catatonic stare had gone. "I think I'll live in your bathroom."

"You happy with an easy dinner? I'll make some macaroni cheese. Got some Sara Lee for dessert if you want."

"Not very hungry."

"We'll see."

Afterwards, they tucked their legs up and curled into the lounge.

"Lots happening kiddo," Sandy said as she drained the last of the moselle.

Emma held her glass up to the light. "You know, I really like how wine makes everything seem, well, less important."

"No job and no husband eh? Big week. And I agree about the alcohol. A blessing."

"No job, yes but I still do have a husband, it's just that he loves someone else. It would have been better if he had died."

"Well, maybe we can arrange that. I'll get Rob to drown him."

"No seriously, think about it. If he had died, I wouldn't have him, the same as now, but at least no one else would either."

"There's a point," Sandy raised her glass.

"Let's say he drowned catching this enormous wave – I'd be feeling just as bad as I do now but there would be some dignity in being a widow."

"You look shitty in black."

"Much rather be a widow than someone who's been left for another woman."

"You mean a girl."

"Left for a younger woman. At twenty-one."

"Not a bad line." Sandy raised her glass for a second time.

"And if he was dead, at least there'd never be a possibility of us being together again."

"You think there's still a chance?" Sandy cut herself another slice of banana cake.

"That's the problem with him still being around."

"You poor thing."

"Seriously Sand, don't you think it would have been better, for me at least, if he'd carked it?"

"Yeah, I guess it would be. It must feel like shit knowing that he's so close by. Yet he may as well be on the other side of the world.

"You get what I mean then?"

"Dead would definitely be an improvement. You'd get to have a big funeral and as much as I hate them, they are a way for people to have a big cry, say all the nice things and then get back to living. It's like drawing a line in the sand so you can move on. I get that you can't do that." She licked icing from her fingertips.

"I don't really wish him dead, you know that, don't you? It's a terrible thing to say. But if it had happened, I really believe it would be easier."

"Either way, you're heaps better off without him."

"Wish I could believe that."

"I know you can't, not yet, but you will in time. Emm, he really wasn't good for you, you know?"

"I wasn't unhappy."

"Happy snappy. You weren't exactly jumping with joy. He was hard work."

"Then why do I love him so much."

"God knows kiddo, but I wish you didn't. I guess it's going to be tough going for a long time." Sandy stood up. "Going to the loo. You want tea?"

"No thanks. I'd be up peeing all night, on top of the wine." When Sandy padded back into the room, Emma asked, "You remember that woman, Kubler Ross, the one that talks about death and dying?"

"Sort of."

"Well she said there are stages people go through, when they find out they're dying. This feels like that. There are five, I think. The first is where you deny it's happening. I've fast tracked past number one."

"You're making progress then. What's the second stage?"

"You get angry."

"Good one."

"I did that pretty well this afternoon."

"Remind me not to piss you off."

"After that, you make a pact with God, you know, a trade-off, to get him to fix it. Guess you've got to believe in God to do that, so I don't qualify. Though I have sort of prayed, but not to anyone really, and I haven't promised to be a better person or anything like that because I really don't know if I could keep that promise. Do you think people will blame it on me Sandy?"

"I don't know how they could honey. You've been a good wife to him."

"I haven't let myself go, have I? I mean we don't have much money but I do try to keep myself nice. Do you think I nagged him?"

"Only when he needed it. Look Emm, he'd be nothing if you hadn't taken him on. I think he'd be a beach bum or an alcoholic."

"An alcoholic?"

"You remember when we came for dinner and you'd always run out of milk. Rob reckons he used to pour it down the sink so he'd have an excuse to get out of the house, go and pick some up. He used to drop into the club on the way home, down a couple of schooners. Rob reckons he's got a drinking problem."

"I never knew that."

"Anyway, it doesn't matter now. What's the next stage?"

I think I'm there actually."

"You don't muck around do you?" Sandy swung her legs onto the floor and sat up.,

"It's when you get depressed."

"Well it's only natural to feel down after what's happened." Sandy gave Emma's hand a motherly pat. "But I think I'd disagree with whatever her name is. My professional opinion is that depression is what you get when you haven't actually got a good reason to feel miserable. You, however, have absolutely got heaps to feel shitty about. So you're not depressed, just miserable."

"I can't see the point of anything anymore. I would be happy if I was dead too."

"Never say that Emma!" Sandy reached her hand out to Emma and shook her head violently.

"I really don't want to go on Sandy." She wrapped her arms around her bent knees and the rocking started up again.

"Now don't be stupid. You've got such a fantastic life ahead of you. My God, it's not like you're an old woman. Look at you, you're gorgeous." Sandy set her glass aside and moved to sit next to Emma. She began to rearrange her hair, pulling it away from Emma's face, looking into her eyes as she spoke. "My mother always said so. Or was it your mother? Can't remember. Anyway, whoever it was, they said there's always more fish in the sea and there'll be schools of them swimming around you once you get back in the water."

Emma began to whimper.

"Emm, look at me. Promise you won't do anything silly. You know that I can't live without my best friend. Emm?"

"I won't."

"Emm, I'd never forgive you if you put *me* through what *you're* going through. Selfish bitch. Hey, just kidding okay?"

"Whatever you say."

"Anyway, that's only four stages. What's the fifth?"

"Acceptance."

"Right on! Then here's to acceptance." Together they scoffed the dregs of their lukewarm wine, then Sandy once again put her arms around her friend and held her. "Oh God, I must be pissed. Fancy crying over you," she said as she dried her eyes on the collar of Emma's pyjama jacket.

20

What's Normal?

Despite the prediction of early afternoon showers, Jewel decided to take her chances and hang the washing out. She admired the tidy arrangement of socks in a row and underpants side by side, next to singlets that were pegged under the armpits to avoid billowing at the hemline. She saw the sheets flapping, alongside Derek's white shirts and the pillow cases and felt content.

In the front yard she picked a bouquet of camellias and magnolias to arrange like the still life paintings she saw in the art gallery. A row of primulas grew around the thick trunk of a ghost gum. Unable to articulate her intention to contrast the delicacy of the primulas with the bulk of the tree, Jewel nevertheless achieved the desired result. Later that afternoon she intended to visit her parents as she did twice a week. They would spend their time sitting together, sometimes in silence or sometimes listening to the radio, while her mother continued to crochet and her father dozed on his favourite chair.

As she waited for the kettle to boil for her mid-morning cup of Earl Grey she looked past the kitchen into the lounge room. The

Sanderson should have been replaced a few years back and the curtains along with it. Both these things could have been afforded if she had gone back to work after Sally was born but she and Derek had both agreed it was more important to stay at home and spend time with their daughter. She smiled as she remembered Sally and her friends arriving home to a fresh batch of scones or cupcakes and Sally insisting they only came for the afternoon teas. Those years had gone by so quickly.

She rinsed her cup and plate and climbed the stairs to her bedroom. Secreted away at the back of the top shelf of her wardrobe was a shoe box. She lifted it down and removed the lid. Inside was a crocheted pair of lace christening booties, a first edition copy of *Alice in Wonderland* (which she'd found at a fete) and an assortment of vibrantly coloured butterflies framed in antique silver. The shoe box collection that had been gathered over the years, was whimsical and premature. A grandchild was years away, but she excused herself on the basis that she would never consciously seek out an item. It would be acquired only when she came across something that she might never find again and regret, at a later stage, that she hadn't bought on the spot.

She replaced the lid on the box, and a lifetime of imaginings, then turned to face the picture window. The rainclouds she'd feared, were gathering not outside the window, but within.

Up until now she had never contemplated that Sally would leave home until her wedding day, in a white gown, on her father's arm. Would Brad want that, having been married before or would he want to live with Sally? There were more and more people doing that nowadays. The son-in-law that she had dreamt about would have been great mates with Derek. She would often imagine them chatting amiably about the footy, while she and Sally bathed and fed the grandchildren. Jewel's daydreams were so vivid she was sure they were a premonition.

In the last couple of weeks however, these images began to cloud over and she felt a panic rise when she found them slipping away. What chance did she have of making her dreams a reality if

Sally's husband and father didn't get on? How could they ever be a tight knit family if Brad didn't feel welcome and accepted in her house? "Absolutely no chance." She spoke the words out loud as she stood up, smoothed down her apron and replaced the shoe box on the shelf behind her handbags.

One thing became perfectly clear to her. Derek must welcome Brad into to their family and mean it. That was exactly what he must do. If he didn't, it would drive Sally away and she would never forgive him if that happened.

She heard the phone ringing downstairs and raced to answer it.

"Jewel speaking."

"Good, you're home. Any chance of a natter. I'm passing so I could pop around."

"Sure. I'll put on the kettle."

"Yoo-hoo." Lee never knocked and was in the kitchen before the kettle had switched itself off.

"The flowers are lovely Jewel," Lee remarked, admiring the float bowl of camellias at the end of the kitchen bench, "and Anzac biscuits. You put me to shame."

"I'm ready for a sandwich now. Join me Lee?"

"Just a cuppa please, and maybe an Anzac."

"How's Sam?" Jewel asked, as she placed a milk jug, sugar bowl, tea strainer and two cups onto a tray.

"His lordship is his usual self."

"And Paul?" Lee enquired. "He's home isn't he?"

"Got home on Tuesday."

"How exciting. Is he well?" Jewel waited and when there was no answer forthcoming she turned to see Lee rummaging in her enormous handbag, her lips trembling, a sure sign that she was losing control.

"Here," she passed a box of tissues, "you'll never find one in that bottomless pit. Now what's the matter?"

"It's what I thought, Jewel. He has a boyfriend."

"Oh, gosh." Jewel propped on the kitchen stool. "He told you he's definitely a, um, homosexual?"

"He didn't say the word but, yes, he told me."

Jewel arranged six Anzac Biscuits, one at a time on a plate. The simple task gave her time to decide what to say next.

"So you were right, Lee. And how is he, in himself?" She passed over the biscuits and poured water into the teapot.

"He seems happy and sad at the same time. Says he wants me to be happy for him, and I'm trying, but it's really hard, Jewel. He has a partner"

"Have you met him? His friend?" she asked, replacing the lid.

"Oh no, he's still in UK. And I couldn't, now that I know about them."

"Oh dear. What does Sam say?"

"He doesn't know. I can't begin to imagine what he'll do." Lee blew her nose and dabbed under her eyes.

Jewel cut her sandwich into four triangles and put them onto a Royal Doulton bread and butter plate decorated with red roses, matching the tea cups. *Here it is happening again,* she thought. *Every time I think I have a problem in my life, something happens to make me see it isn't as big as I first imagined. At least Sally is in love with a man.*

"Lee, I don't know what to say. Are you sure about Sam?"

"You know the Premier, the one who wore pink shorts who made it legal in his State a while back? Well, the other day Sam said it was a slippery slope. Said he didn't know what the world was coming to letting parliamentary poofters – that's what he called them – decide what's normal."

"Not everyone feels like that. The churches are against it of course and I thought Derek would be too, but he isn't. He thinks it's about time. He told me a story, about when he was at school." She broke a small piece from her sandwich and popped it into her mouth.

"Go on."

"Seems he got bullied rather badly, you see. You can imagine him, can't you? A bit of a dag. Those funny glasses. And he studied too much to be cool. When I met him, he didn't even know what the latest hit tune was."

"Didn't stop you falling for him though."

"Of course not. I think I saw the good in him from the beginning. Anyway, you know how bullies have an instinct for the thing that hurts you most? Well, they started calling Derek names, teasing him about his ears. Seems the only person who stood up for him was a quiet boy who confessed to Derek, later on, that he was a homosexual."

"Oh gosh. Did they find out? About the boy?"

"No, they didn't but it terrified him the whole time."

"How awful for him."

"Anyway, Derek saw that he was actually a nice bloke. The fact that he was queer didn't matter to him back then. And remembering that time, it has made him rethink the whole thing."

"Poor Derek, being teased like that."

"Not really, I've always told him that I love his flappers."

Lee laughed, grateful for the light relief. "I knew you'd make me feel better. And you're right. It doesn't stop me loving Paul."

"Of course not. He's still your son and times are changing, Lee. Paul has every right to be who he is. A top up?" Jewel slid the teapot across the bench.

"But I don't know if a father's love is the same. I'm so frightened of what might happen if Paul tells his father."

"Maybe it would be better if you tell him?"

'Oh, no, I couldn't. I wouldn't know what to say."

"Then does he have to know? If he's staying in England?" Jewel asked.

"I thought that too, but Paul insists he isn't ashamed any more. Went through years of wondering what was wrong with himself but now he thinks that it's just the way God made him." Lee straightened her back. "He has no idea what he's in for if he tells Sam."

"Maybe you'll be surprised Lee."

"He intends to tell him on Sunday. When his sister's there."

Jewel patted her friend's hand. "Lee, I'm sure it will be fine. Don't worry too much."

"I'm not the only one whose son has problems, you know."

"Oh, really?" Jewel stirred her tea. A few moments before she had been tempted to confide in Lee about Sally. Now she was glad that she hadn't, because her problems could easily become the topic of another gossip session across a kitchen bench.

"It's the Thompsons, you know, from the club." Lee didn't wait long enough for Jewel to reply. "Well, Laura rang me last week, so upset. John got conscripted, you remember? He's the same age as Paul. We were all so nervous for them both and poor John got conscripted. Well, he's been back from the war a while and they had to move him out of the house because he was absolutely unbearable to be around. Anyway, he was back at work with his father and they had an enormous blue last week in the factory, in front of everyone. Got himself sacked on the spot, by his own father. What a scene! Can you imagine?"

"Kids eh? They were much easier when they were feeding every three hours and wearing nappies."

"Not only that, John was supposed to take over the business in a couple of years. Maybe they'll patch it up but Laura said her son won't even talk to her, just hangs up the phone. He's clammed up was what she said and she's really worried about him and Steve is, as she described it, absolutely devastated. Terrible isn't it?"

"That's certainly sad for them."

"Got to go Jewel, my dear friend. Got to pick up some T-bones for Sam's dinner. I can ring if I need you, can't I?"

"Of course Lee, anytime."

Jewel settled down to wait for Derek. He too was devastated. Brad had agreed to the strict conditions under which he could visit Sally. To Jewel, it demonstrated Brad's commitment to the relationship. Derek, however, had gambled that Brad would run a mile, and he lost. Now Brad had open access to his daughter.

Precisely on-time, the Falcon pull into the driveway. The kettle was boiling as her Derek walked in the door.

"Honey, I've been thinking," he said as he brushed her cheek with his lips, "it will be good for Sally to go to schoolies when her exams finish. I know they get a bit wild up at the Gold Coast but we should encourage her to go.

"I'm afraid she doesn't want to go to schoolies, Darling." Jewel was focused on thinly slicing a lemon.

"Why not?"

"She wants to stay here."

"God, he's really got her under his spell."

"And I don't think she's going to keep their relationship under wraps when school finishes." She popped a slice into Derek's tea cup.

"You've talked to her about it?"

"Yes."

"How come I don't know any of this?"

"Need to know basis, Darling. Didn't want to worry you."

"Then there'll be no going back for her." His briefcase dropped to the floor and he stood with his arms crossed.

"What do you mean?"

"She'll feel obliged to keep seeing him."

"But she wants to. That's what I'm trying to tell you."

"What I'm trying to tell you is that when it's out in the open, even if she starts to have doubts, she'll keep them to herself rather than prove the gossips right."

"I don't get it."

"Think about it Jewel." He leaned onto the benchtop with both hands. "The way they'll see it is that he's using her. And she'll want to prove them wrong."

"When did you start being the psychologist?"

"I just know my daughter."

"And I want to keep on knowing her Derek." Jewel squared her shoulders. "I don't want to alienate her."

"Can't you see? If she stays with him, we've already lost her." Derek raised his index finger. "He'll call the shots. We won't get a look in. Believe me."

"Then we need to stay close to her. We both agree on that, even if it is for different reasons. Can we talk about it later, please?"

"Why, what's wrong?"

"I've had enough for one day, that's all. Had a visit from Lee this morning. Why don't you go and get changed. I'll keep the tea warm."

Derek left the kitchen and returned in his shorts and open neck shirt.

"More relaxed?" Jewel asked.

"Me or you? Go on, tell me what she said."

Jewel reached for the tea pot and related her conversation with Lee.

"Poor kid, I feel for him. Did you know Sam tried to get Paul to follow him into the law years back?" Derek asked.

"Yes, I did."

"Well, now he's going to ask Paul to come home for good and work in the new business."

Jewel turned to her husband. "That's definitely not going to happen."

Derek stirred his tea, "You know, Sam's not unlike us Jewel. All he wants is the best for his son and the shock of what he's about to find out will devastate him. He's not a bad man, but he doesn't have any understanding of homosexuality. Sees it as a disease, something that can be cured and I've got to tell you, he's not in the minority. Most blokes I know feel the same way."

That night in bed, Jewel propped herself up on an elbow.

"So Darling, you really think Lee's right about Sam? Think he'll go crazy?"

"She's spot on. Probably underestimates his reaction if anything. It's going to be an interesting family lunch."

"Darling..." Jewel paused.

"Yes. What else?"

"Promise me you'll try to accept what we can't change."

"This sounds like an AA meeting. You mean Sally?"

"Yes."

"I don't want to lose her, Derek."

"We haven't lost her yet Jewel. Give me time."

Jewel pecked her husband on the cheek and rolled onto her side. It hadn't been a strenuous day, so she couldn't fathom why she felt so exhausted.

21

Just a Fling

As THE TAXI PULLED INTO the driveway Emma's mother turned around, allowed the basket of washing to fall to the ground, crossed her arms and watched silently as her daughter stepped from the car. It wasn't the overnight bag or the surprise visit, although both of those would be proof enough, it was the slumped shoulders, the eyes that didn't smile and the palpable sorrow that seeped from a broken heart that told her Emma was in trouble.

"Come here, honey," she opened her arms and Emma allowed herself to be held.

"I'm sorry Mum."

"What's happened, Darling?"

"Brad and I have broken up."

Together they sat on the back step and her mother listened in silence to Emma's story, then with a shake of her head dismissed the notion that this was the end. Marriage for Mrs Saunders was a lifelong institution. These problems were just hiccups, a passing thing, she assured Emma.

"Mum," Emma laid her hand over her mother's, "you know how you hear of people getting divorced and you think it happens to those other people, but not you? Well, why shouldn't it be me?" In the silence, in the dusk, while sounds softened and the earth settled, it became easier to confront the reality.

"It's getting dark Darling, let's go inside. Mrs Saunders took Emma's hand in her own and kissed it. "Your Dad will be home soon."

"Mum, there's something else."

"What Emm?" her mother asked, holding tighter.

"I've been retrenched."

"What, you mean lost your job?"

Emma wondered if the loss of a secure income may have been of more concern than the marriage break-up. Her mother had, after all, coped with a husband whose drinking and gambling invariably left them short.

"Don't worry Mum. I'll start looking tomorrow."

"I'll get the Herald from Mr Dillon," she nodded her head reassuringly, "he gets it every Saturday. It has the Positions Vacant in it."

"I'll have to pick up the rest of my clothes from the flat," Emma confided.

"Give yourself a couple of days, Darling. Do you want your Dad to come with you, in case he's there?"

"He won't be, Mum. He's moved out but I will need to borrow the car."

"Where's yours?"

"I'm not going to need it Mum. I've decided to get a job in town. I can catch the train. He can't."

"Emma, Emma, you have to stop looking after him!"

"Sure Mum. Like you did with Dad."

"Talking about your father, I suppose we'd better get him fed."

"I'll be staying for a little while," Emma said as she held the flyscreen door for her mother. The netting had been fixed. So had a lot of things since her Dad got sober.

"Of course, Darling. We wouldn't want you to be anywhere else."

On Thursday afternoon, Emma drove the Holden station wagon to the flat and waited. She stood on the footpath, listening once again for the sound of the V-Dub. Her heart began to race as it turned the corner.

"Hi," he said, sauntering across the road, hands in pockets.

"Hi," was all she could manage in return. He was there, close to her and she ached for him to take hold of her, to rest her head on his chest, to feel his arms close round her, to feel his warmth, to smell him, to be part of him once more.

"How did you lose your key?" he asked.

"I don't know. Somewhere between here, Sandy's and Mum's. Maybe I left it at work." She could tell he didn't believe her.

"Not like you," he replied.

"You can just let me in," Emma said, "you don't have to stay."

"I'm here to help, Emm."

They walked single file to the building entrance then proceeded up the stairs, Emma leading the way.

"You're looking good Emm."

"Thanks." She straightened her back aware that he was watching her.

"I mean you've lost weight. It suits you."

They were at the top of the stairs and she stood aside as he opened the door.

"Where are my cushions?" she cried, "our bookcase? It's gone!"

"The oldies want to sell the flat, get back their deposit and it appears I'm too messy to stay here. Mum wanted to change a few things so she took the rest away."

Emma's efforts to hold back tears were fruitless.

"Don't cry Emm," Brad said as he gently took hold of her shoulders.

"I don't believe she did this. This was my home!" She wiped her eyes on the back of her arm, angry with herself for letting him know how much it hurt. "It just seems so final."

"It was my home too Emm."

"You've moved in with John, haven't you?"

"That didn't last. I'm back with the oldies now."

"I can't believe you're living with them." She wiped her eyes on her sleeve.

"Emm, I'm sorry. You know. About everything." He tried to wrap his arms around her.

"Bit late," she said, stepping back from his embrace. Tears continued to run down her cheeks. He smoothed them away with the tip of his thumb.

"Emm, please don't be upset."

"How can I not be. What you did behind my back. All that time."

"I am sorry Emm."

"For what, for which part?" At this moment she was looking into the face of a stranger.

"I really didn't mean to hurt you."

"Did you ever love me?"

"Course I did. Please, stop crying, come here." He moved towards her and this time she allowed him to take her in his arms, her body softened into his and she inhaled his familiarity. With a gentle hand he lifted her face and kissed her in the way he had when they were first in love.

"Brad, don't." She tried to pull away.

"But I want to."

"Please stop. Don't do this, please."

"You sure Emm? You don't sound like you mean it."

He had a hard on. She could feel it against her thigh. "Why now? After all this time?"

"I don't know. You seem different."

"Help me get my things," she said turning away from him. "I have to get home."

"I still like you Emm. A lot."

"You like me?" she shot back at him, "you've got to be kidding!" She managed to laugh. "You're bloody mad. Here." She tossed him a plastic bag. "Help me fill this up."

When they finished loading the boot, Brad turned to her. "Don't I get a kiss goodbye?"

"I just don't get it Brad."

"I'm sorry, Emm. But I don't get it either. It's just the way it is."

"You're not being fair. Just go."

He wound down the car window. "Sorry, I really am."

"So am I Brad." As he started the motor she asked, "are we finished?"

"Who knows what the future holds," he shouted out the window as he drove away. When he got to the top of the street he sounded the horn and waved.

Could her mother be right? For the first time in years he really wanted her. His kiss was warm and he said it himself, *who knows what the future holds.*

As she closed the boot she glanced towards their letterbox. Amongst the bits of junk mail, nibbled around the edges by the snails, were the car registration papers. In the past, she dreaded the arrival of big bills that they would struggle to pay. This one however, could provide the perfect excuse to see him again. She hugged the envelope to her chest and made her way back to the car.

The next afternoon she rang the school. When he heard her name, he sounded pleased and agreed to pay for the registration.

"I'll drop the papers around on Saturday afternoon," she said. He agreed, but they couldn't talk any longer as his class was starting.

Perhaps the move back to his oldies was a good idea. Maybe they talked some sense into him. They had always liked her. She clapped her hands together when she remembered they played tennis on Saturday afternoon. He knew it too, that they'd be alone.

On Thursday she scoured the boutiques in King Street. On Friday she had her hair tinted and cut into a bob that seductively framed her face. She was humming to herself as she finished clearing the table that night.

"What are you so happy about?" Her mother was folding the washing. "Well go on, tell me. And what's the new hairdo in aid of."

"It's for interviews Mum."

"That all? Aren't you seeing him tomorrow?"

"Yes, and I want him to know what he's missing out on."

"So, you think I might be right? It could have just been a bit of a hiccup?"

"Could be."

Her mother rested the sewing in her lap and inclined her head. "You're not going to pay for it are you? The registration."

"No Mum, I'm not."

"You have up until now."

"Actually, we shared the costs. Just drop it okay?"

A sustained silence, while they allowed the tension to dissipate.

"I rang him at school and when I offered to bring the papers around, he seemed really keen to see me. Not just because of the papers."

"I suppose he could have got you to post them. It could be a good sign then."

"It could, couldn't it?"

"I hope so, Darling. Come here, give your mother a hug."

"It's just so hard." Emma wrapped her arms around her mother. As she stood up, she wiped away her tears with the back of her hand.

"They do come to their senses you know," her mother reassured.

"Rob and Sandy thought that it could just be a fling. Maybe he's flung, if you know what I mean."

This made her mother smile. "Yes, and we do forgive them in the long run."

I know you have Mum, Emma thought as she recalled a scene from long ago that had been cast to the back of her mind. It was school holidays and Emma woke earlier than usual, the humidity of mid-summer making it difficult to sleep. She sat up in bed, alert to the sound of sobbing and sniffling coming from the back of the house. Silently, she had made her way to the laundry, stood in the doorway and watched as her mother scoured and dumped and scrubbed and rinsed the collar of her father's shirt to remove the lipstick stain. As she turned to wipe her dripping nose on the shoulder of her cotton dress her mother saw her daughter backing away. Neither of them spoke about what Emma had seen that morning.

The Saturday morning traffic was light and Emma arrived early, parked under the willow tree at the top of the street, tilted the seat, closed her eyes and tried to calm herself. She imagined him opening the door, reaching for her and this time there would be no holding back.

With five minutes to go, she cruised towards the fibro house at the end of the cul-de-sac. The loose gravel crunched under the wheels as the car approached and she could hear the chorus of frogs in the creek, celebrating the overnight rain. She pulled up on the front lawn and walked along the driveway. A glance at the windows. He was waiting for her inside, out of sight.

The house was silent as she climbed the steps to the front porch, took a deep breath, struck the stiff door knocker hard and waited. Her heart was beating like a new bird's. The timber door opened and he fumbled with the lock on the flyscreen. As it opened, he looked knowingly at her and smiled his familiar smile. She knew it was going to be all right.

"Come on in."

She walked past him and paused in the hallway while he closed the door. It will happen now, he'll do it now. She felt sure. But he didn't, instead he mumbled an "excuse me", as he moved past her into the lounge room and left her standing where she was. Should she follow?

"Come on through Emma."

She heard a sound to his left, where his mother would sit in the evenings in her armchair. She must have waited to welcome her back, but the chair was empty and there was someone else, crouched on the floor, with legs tucked to one side, head down, sorting through the record collection. Emma's immediate thought was that she knew what was in that collection and could help this person find whatever they were looking for.

"Emm, this is Sally. Sally, Emma."

Sally cocked her head and looked at Emma through a veil of silken blonde hair. She was so relaxed, this girl on the carpet, like she belonged. Neither Emma nor the girl spoke for what seemed a long time. The girl laid the LP on the carpet. *She shouldn't do that. It will scratch. Mrs. Emery would never allow it.*

"Hi," the girl said and shook her hair away from her face. Then she turned to Brad and her lips that were pale against the tan of her smooth skin stretched into a smile as she raised her eyebrows and her green eyes locked onto his.

The noise began then, a ringing in Emma's ears.

"Um, er, guess we'd better do the rego papers," Brad said. His voice was muffled as if he were speaking underwater. He held out his hand.

Emma looked down at the papers. They shook up and down in her hand and were making a scrunching sound. The noises became louder, the scrunching and the ringing. She looked up and they were both staring at her, Brad and the girl. If the noises would stop, she might be able to think.

"Here, give them to me Emma," he reached for the papers and she dropped them. The girl picked them up and handed them to him. Then she got up and stood beside him. Her legs were like the colour of molasses. She was wearing shorts. She adjusted them, smoothing out the creases as if it was important.

"You all right Emm?" Brad repeated.

"It has to be paid by the fifteenth," she mumbled.

"Sure, I'll sort it. Thanks for dropping them over." His booming fuzzy voice was louder with each word he spoke. "You right to drive home?"

She knew this meant they expected her to leave, but her legs weren't taking any notice.

Then Moppet ran in on her four short legs and jumped up, wagging her stumpy tail. Moppet who thought everything was the same. Moppet who still loved her.

"Moppet, darling Moppet," Emma said and she fell onto her knees and wrapped her arms around the warm soft fur.

"Come here you stupid dog," Brad called. "Here girl." He held her by the collar. "You need to get up Emma."

She could see herself now, crouched on all fours, cowering like an animal, the two of them standing over her. When bile began to rise in her throat she had to stand and run out of the room, along the hallway, through the flyscreen door and down the steps to the car because she would never vomit on Mrs Emery's carpet.

With both hands she got the key into the ignition then found the strength to depress the clutch, turn the key and slam her foot onto the accelerator. They were on the verandah watching as the car kangarooed along the driveway then down the road.

She drove until she could go no further, until the road ran out at the edge of the walkway to the beach. When she looked around she saw that she was parked opposite Jo's where Brad used to buy his breakfast and his cigarettes. Her head fell onto the steering wheel and she sobbed. The keys were still in the ignition and the door wide open as she leapt from the car and ran to the milk bar.

"Cigarettes please. Matches too," she spluttered and held open her purse for Jo to take the money. Back outside, her hands shook as she tried to light up. When the nauseous smoke filled her lungs, her head spun deliriously and she dropped onto the footpath, her feet in the gutter and her head between her knees.

"Emma? What are you doing?" She recognised the voice.

"John?" she said looking up.

"You don't smoke. What's wrong Emma?"

"I didn't know what else to do." She was sobbing now.

"What's happened Emma?"

"Oh God, John, I didn't want anyone to see me."

"Is it Brad?"

"Yeah."

"What? Tell me."

"I went to his place and she was there." Another long drag on the cigarette brought on a fit of coughing.

"Bit of a surprise, eh Babe?"

"I thought it would be just us and everything would be all right."

"I'm sorry Emm." He stroked her back and tenderly took the cigarette from her and stubbed it out.

"I want to go home."

"Hang on for a bit Emm. Don't get up. Can I get you something?"

"No. I'm all right, honestly. It was just the shock. I've got Dad's car and I need to get it back."

"Whoah, don't think you should be driving."

"I'm okay now, really I am. I think the cigarette helped."

She leaned her hand on his shoulder and pushed herself into a standing position. Her legs were weak but she held her head high and with John supporting her arm, made her way to the car.

"You sure about this?" he asked. "Your Mum will be there?"

"Yes, she's there. I just want to go, sorry."

He paced beside the car as she backed out onto the road then waved as she turned to go.

When she got to the end of the beach road Emma pulled over and lit up again. She dragged long and hard on the cigarette and waited for the euphoric head spin. The rings were loose on her finger and came off easily. The wedding band she tossed as far as she could, but faltered and held onto her engagement ring. It had taken so long to save the hundred dollars, she just couldn't throw that much money away. Her mother had never had an engagement ring – merely a gold wedding band that was now worn to wafer thin. Emma decided to have her ring reset for her mother.

A second cigarette hung from her lips as she put the car into gear and pushed the accelerator flat to the floor. It had been many years since her parents' Holden had done a wheelie, if ever, but they did when Emma drove off, leaving behind a trail of loose gravel.

Twenty minutes later, her mother looked through the lounge room window, as Emma shuffled towards the house, her handbag dragging on the ground, and knew things didn't go as planned.

"Can I do anything, Darling?" she whispered softly as Emma passed by.

"No Mum. Just need to lie down." As she turned to close the door to her bedroom, she glimpsed her mother standing in the hallway, hands crossed in front of her heart and her brow furrowed as she bit hard into her bottom lip.

"It's okay Mum. I'll be all right,"

She lay on top of her single bed, pulled the floral cover across her legs, turned to the wall and buried her face in the pillow. If by any chance she were mistaken and if there was a God, this would be a good time for him to show himself, to help her out just a little. It couldn't be all that hard for him to do this one thing if he could make the whole world in seven days.

22

Don't Tell a Bloody Soul

WHEN HAD HER FAMILY LAST EATEN *together*, Lee wondered? Probably the Christmas before Paul left when he was still normal. Any pleasurable anticipation of tonight's reunion, however, was tainted by the knowledge that Paul intended at some time to tell his father and he might choose tonight.

Lee reassured herself that Sam would be delighted to have Carol's company for the evening, if not his son-in-law's. Sam could never understand his daughter's attraction to Warwick but, as was rare for Sam, he managed to keep his opinions to himself.

She recalled Jewel's advice that bad news was best delivered on a full stomach. If Paul was going to do it tonight, she hoped he would at least wait until Sam was well fed. Tonight's menu, as well as being Sam's favourite, was mostly pre-prepared to allow Lee maximum time at the table, to protect her son, if needs be.

Now to the seating plan. Sam of course was at the head of the table. Carol was a settling influence on her father so she placed her on Sam's left side. Her daughter's husband she generally regarded as useless, but tonight Warwick would be gainfully deployed as a buffer, seated on Sam's right, between Paul and his father. She placed herself next to Carol, opposite Paul so she could keep an eye on him and be out of Sam's direct line of sight.

The red wine was opened and decanted and the crystal goblets set in place, a water glass beside her own. A final check that her husband had the large, and not the small knife and fork from the Hampton Court setting. Getting it wrong could set him off.

As she headed back to the kitchen Lee remembered to check the beef and ale casserole. It was rescued just before boiling dry on top of the stove. As the evening drew closer, she found it increasingly difficult to concentrate. Her chocolate and orange cake had never failed before but a perfect second attempt was coming out of the oven just as Carol arrived.

"Hi, we're here. Mum, where are you?" Carol called as she came through the front door.

"In the kitchen honey, where do you think." Lee undid her apron then hung it on the hook behind the door. She squared her shoulders and waited. She would talk to Carol first. Find out what she knew. Her daughter and son-in-law kissed her in turn.

"Smells good," Carol said, as she lifted the lid of the pot simmering on the stove to which Lee had hastily added a pint of beef stock. "Did you make your chocolate orange number Mum?" she said spying the cake on the cooling rack.

"Yes Darling, of course. It's Paul's and your father's favourite and we'll all enjoy a slice."

"Or two," Warwick added.

"He doesn't need fattening up you know. Paul looks good."

"You've already seen him?"

"We had drinkies on Thursday."

"Oh." Lee pursed her lips.

"Mum, you're not still upset he wouldn't stay with you are you?"

"No, I understand."

"Well, what's wrong then?"

"Did he tell you his news?"

"About the new job?"

THE TEACHER, THE PUPIL AND THE WIFE

"I didn't know he had a new job. About his friend and everything."

"Yes Mum."

"Then you know."

"Mum, we've known for years."

"What do you mean?"

"It's obvious."

"Stands out like dog's balls," said Warwick, licking leftover cake mixture from the beaters.

"Do you have to be so crude?" Carol chided. "We guessed Mum. And he told us just before he went away."

Lee pulled out a kitchen stool for support and perched on one edge. "Oh dear. All this time you've known."

"What about Dad? Should be interesting."

"Wouldn't miss it for quids," Warwick said, slurping a spoonful of casserole gravy.

"Carol, oh dear, do you think he is going to tell him tonight?"

"I don't know. But it's nothing to be ashamed of Mum."

"You do know your father has strong opinions about this sort of thing."

"Well, what he wants to think about is his son, not himself for a change. What about you. Are you all right about it?"

"I'm okay, sort of, as long as I don't think about what they do."

"Shirt lifters, eh," Warwick chimed in.

"Shut up, will you. Go and find Dad," Carol said.

"He's in his den I suppose?"

"Where else," Lee shrugged.

"You go too Cas, then haul them both upstairs. Dinner isn't far off."

"Don't worry." Carol stroked her mother's back. "It'll be all right."

But Lee wasn't reassured.

"Sixty percent sold already, off the plan and they're going like hotcakes." Sam was updating Warwick on the flats on The Promenade as Carol negotiated the stairs.

"Hi Dadda," she called.

"Hi Sweetheart. Here, give your favourite Dad a big hug." Sam surveyed his daughter admiringly. "You look well, honey."

"Thanks, Dadda."

"Actually, you're glowing, Darling. Obviously, this man is looking after you."

"She's easy to look after." Warwick put his arm around his wife and resisted the urge to pat her tummy, where their first child lay. There was more than one announcement to be made this evening.

"Mum wants us all upstairs and I think I just heard the door-knocker. Pauly is here."

"Don't call him that Carol," Sam snapped. "His name is Paul. Come on. Let's go greet the prodigal."

Sam opened the door with a flourish. "Good to see you son. You're looking well." He punched Paul's shoulder after giving his hand a hearty shake.

Paul looked over his father's shoulder. "Hi Mum."

"Come on, give me a big hug," Lee walked towards her son. "I've missed you so much."

Paul's relief was tangible as he wrapped his arms around his mother and lifted her off her feet.

"Don't drop her," Carol joked. "She's the cook."

"And I've got to put the veggies on. Be back in a minute."

"Come on Son, let's have a beer downstairs before dinner." Sam placed his hand on Paul's shoulder. It seemed to Lee he was dragging his prey to his den.

"Five minutes, okay?" She resisted the urge to follow. *Surely Paul wouldn't say it now?*

Sam remarked favourably on Paul's appearance as they descended the stairs. He had beefed up as a result of regular weight training and the few days' stopover in Singapore, soaking up the sun, had disguised the London pallor. His hair was shorter and he wore a well-cut pair of blue trousers with a white collarless shirt. Lee wished he had left the chain at home and maybe the fancy shoes. Then again, Sam's friends from the Gold Coast wore white shoes and gold chains, so maybe his clothes wouldn't give him away.

"Well son, have you realised that there's no better place in the world than where you are right now?" Sam tore the ring off a beer can and handed it to Paul.

"Sure Dad. Australia is an amazing place. It's just the UK is so close to Europe and all that."

"Mmm. So, you're not on your way home yet."

"Well no Dad, actually I've just got a new job. I've been promoted to Function Head, I've got twenty-five staff under me now."

"Uh-ha. Pretty settled then?"

"Yeah. I like hospitality and obviously I'm doing okay at it."

"Thought you might be coming home, Son. Had a few ideas that'd make you a motza. More than you can working over there."

"Thanks for thinking of me, Dad. But I'm okay for the moment. What was it anyway?"

"The development company. It's a veritable gold mine. We're thinking expansion." Sam stood with his legs astride, hands in pockets, and rocked back and forth on the balls of his feet. "We need some young blood. Great opportunity Son."

Paul hesitated. "Well, thanks Dad, that's a great offer. Maybe it will still be on the table when I come home."

"Think about it Son. We should talk some more." He slapped Paul on the back and turned him towards the yard. "What do you think of the pool?"

"It's great, Dad. Mum sent me photos but they don't do it justice. Do you use it much?"

"No, not really, but your mother likes the look of it. Better get up to dinner."

"Good timing you two." Carol walked out of the kitchen with a dish of mashed potatoes in hand. "Take a seat gentlemen. Mum wants you here Paul. Dad, you're in your usual spot."

Sam spread his serviette over his thick thighs and turned to Paul. "I hear those English girls are a bit of all right Son."

"Not as nice as the Aussies though I'll bet," Lee said passing Sam the decanter. "Can you pour Cas some claret?"

"Not for me Mum," she said, adjusting her serviette to hide her tummy.

"Darling, it's a good drop, best money can buy, you should try it," Sam insisted.

"No thanks Dad. I said I'd drive home today."

"Paul?"

"Sure Dad. Will be good to taste a decent red again."

"There's a cellar full when you're ready to share it Son."

When Warwick's glass was filled, Sam proposed the toast. "To the Queen."

"Which one?" mumbled Warwick and winced as Carol's shoe connected with his shin.

Carol was aware of an audible intake of breath from her mother followed by a sigh of relief when it became apparent that Sam hadn't heard.

"The one and only Elizabeth II, the Queen of England and Australia and she always will be," he answered.

Lee continued, "Did you go to the palace, Son?"

"No Mum, but I saw the changing of the guards a couple of times. I walk down the Mall a bit. Been to the Houses of Parliament."

"And that big clock?"

"Big Ben Mum."

"It sounds so exciting."

"Well, I'm pretty excited about having some home cooking, this is great Mum."

"What's for dessert Lee?" Sam asked.

"Dad, you haven't finished your first course," Carol chided.

"Maybe we should have a barbie next time. I bet you don't get many of those, with all the rain."

"Not in the flat anyway. Mum this is delicious."

Lee was relieved when Paul got up to help clear away the dishes.

"Sit down Son. Let the girls do that."

"It's good to see he hasn't forgotten his manners Sam, Lee said, spiriting him out of the dining room and into the kitchen. "Let Carol have today off. You can help me carry out the dessert Paul, love.

As Paul sat down, Sam enquired again about the quality of English girls, at which point Lee managed to let an oversized slice of orange and chocolate cake slip into Sam's lap.

"Jesus, Lee, be careful!"

"There's plenty more," she said, rather pleased with herself. Perhaps she could begin to relax, as the meal was coming to an end.

"What about coffee in the lounge room?" she said, a suggestion that she later came to regret. It was while she was sorting out the cups from the china cabinet in the hallway that Paul did it.

Carol explained later that Sam asked specifically about a girlfriend. Maybe Dad had twigged, she thought, because he wouldn't let up. Paul replied something about not dating girls. Dad tried to pass it off, inferred that Paul must be too busy with work. Without Lee to intervene, there was a tense silence. Carol was looking from Paul to her father whose face was turning bright red.

"Well son, I deserve an answer."

"Dad," Paul began.

"Don't Paul," Carol interrupted, but he insisted.

"Dad, it's not that I'm too busy. I don't date girls because I'm gay."

"No, you're not Son." Sam shook his head violently. "You're not gay."

"Dad, I'm sorry. I've known for a long time."

"The poofters have got hold of you over there, that's what happened." Sam raised his voice. "You need to come home. Right now." His fist thumped the table. "Get yourself straightened out."

"Dad, it won't make any difference. I can't change who I am."

Sam looked from Carol to Warwick then to Lee coming through the door with cups in her hand. "Jesus Christ, you all bloody knew." He knocked over his chair as he leapt to his feet and turned to Paul. "Well I can tell you one thing, you'd bloody well better sort yourself out if you expect to set foot in this house again." The flyscreen door slammed as he shot out the back.

Lee knew then that Paul had tried to spare her the moment by doing it when she was gone.

"I'll take Sam a beer," Warwick said, keen to get away.

Lee laid the cups on the table and turned to Carol who was standing with her hands on Paul's shoulders. His head was bowed and his face ashen.

"He'll calm down," Carol said.

"No. He won't. Not today," Lee sounded surprisingly calm. "I'm sorry Son. Maybe if you give him time." She tried to sound convincing as she eased herself into a chair. "He didn't mean what he said."

"It's okay Mum. I expected it." Paul's bottom lip trembled as he spoke. "I'm glad it's done."

Heads turned as Sam strode through the back door. Warwick was trying to hold him back but he pushed his son-in-law's hand away, as if he was swatting a fly.

"I mean what I said, you all hear me? I don't want any poofters around here. Now get out Paul! Get out of my house!"

Paul side-stepped his father's pointed finger and moved towards the door.

"No!" Lee screamed at her husband as she ran to Paul. "Our Son belongs in this house as much as any of us."

Sam's voice was hushed and his top lip curled back in a snarl. "Not any more he doesn't. Believe me." His hand sliced through the air like a knife blade. "He's finished."

"Then if he isn't welcome, you've seen the last of me." Heads turned to Carol.

"Cas, don't. I'll go," Paul pleaded.

"If he makes you go Paul, I'm going too and I'm taking my baby with me." Carol placed her the palm of her hand on her stomach and faced her father. "And you'll never see your grandchild."

No one spoke. Not even Sam.

"That's right. I'm having a baby and if this child turns out to be like Paul, I'd be proud."

Lee noticed Warwick wince but he was silenced by a death stare from his wife.

Carol strode into the kitchen and picked up her bag. Lee tried to hug her on the way out.

"Darling, you shouldn't get stressed. A baby Cas, how wonderful."

"Not now Mum. I'll call you later. I don't know how you live with him." She cast a backward glance at her father.

"Come on Warwick. We're going."

"Bye Sam, Lee," Warwick said. "Great meal." He picked up an after-dinner mint on the way out the door.

Lee peered through a square of the colonial windows, hoping Carol would turn around. She waited until the cars drove away and then retreated to the bedroom. The dishes were still unwashed and the table wasn't cleared but she couldn't face the mess.

It had been a while since she had taken a headache powder but she found an old packet of Bex in the corner of the bathroom cabinet. The dusty pink particles stuck in her throat and made her gag. She wanted to vomit, so she sat on the edge of the bath and breathed through her nose until the urge receded. The house was silent, Sam was in his den. She lay back on the bed, allowed her eyelids to shut out the evening and waited for the powder to take effect.

The alarm clock showed 2.35 am when she felt Sam's bulk rock the bed. His feet were bare, but otherwise he was fully dressed. He threw off the blankets, fell onto the bed and the snoring began almost immediately. Lee waited for his breathing to slow then reached down to pull up the blankets. She stifled a scream as his hand grabbed her arm.

"Don't you tell a bloody soul. Lee, do you hear me? No one, and I mean no one, is to know about this."

There was no holding it back this time. She ran for the bathroom and spewed her dinner into the toilet.

23

A Flash of Clarity

Two weeks after her return to the family home, and to her mother's relief, Emma started work as Private Secretary to the Leasing Manager of Skylark Holdings, in a modern building, smack bang in the middle of the busiest part of town.

As a bonus, she could occasionally have lunch with Sandy. They were sitting on a bench in Hyde park, under a giant Moreton Bay fig tree when Sandy reminded her of Rob's birthday.

"It's in two weeks Emm," she said, "and we're having a party. I know it won't be easy but we would both love you to come."

If it hadn't been Rob, Emma would have responded with an emphatic 'no', then she would never have gone to the party, and she would have been none the wiser. In some ways, however, the knowing made it easier.

She arrived early to help Sandy prepare, with the intention of laying low for as long as possible. But the kitchen was the wrong place to hide. One by one Bernadette, Michelle and then Ros came by and offered their sympathy before following their husbands into the yard. As the party wore on the women sought her out once again, but their interest waned when she was not forthcoming with the details of the breakup, and they moved on. The frivolity was part of the foreign landscape of the evening. She decided to leave after the birthday cake was shared around.

"Someone get a fire extinguisher," Barney called when Sandy finished lighting the candles.

"No need," replied Rob as he stepped forward.

Emma joined in a raucous rendition of *Happy Birthday*, listened to half a dozen unscripted speeches and was handing out generous slices of strawberry sponge, when she looked up to see Sandy striding towards the house dragging Michelle along by the hand. That girl had always been trouble, Emma recalled, and had offended most people in their group at some time over the years.

Emma picked up the sound of raised voices as they disappeared into the lounge room, but couldn't make out what they were saying. It was clear, however, that Sandy was going for it, wagging her finger at Michelle who by now had her arms firmly crossed, her head tilted to one side and her lips pursed.

"What's that about?" Emma asked Rob as he came towards her carrying his empty plate.

He shrugged his shoulders. "Stuffed if I know. Probably they bought the same dress or something. Don't worry about it."

Emma saw Michelle look towards her then turn abruptly away when she caught Emma's eye. Brad's name was mentioned, she was sure of it, a muffled word that filtered through the closed doors.

"Come on Emm, leave the clearing up." Rob stepped in to block her line of sight. "Let me get you another drink." He was ushering her to the bar at the rear of the yard when Michelle flew out the back-door, tripped and landed on the lawn.

"You all right?" Emma called as she ran towards her, but Sandy appeared, grabbed Emma's arm and steered her away.

"Control freak." Michelle called as she stood up.

"Well someone has to control you," Sandy hissed over her shoulder. Michelle threw her wine at her but missed by at least a foot.

"Jesus Michelle, you're a piece of work," Sandy screamed as Tony dragged her away.

"What on earth are you two on about?" Emma asked, shaking her arm free.

"Don't worry about it. She's just a stupid bitch. Please, leave her be."

"Then tell me, what were you talking about? I heard my name mentioned, and Brad's, when you were inside."

"Then you heard wrong."

"You sure this isn't about me?"

"I'm going to get myself a wine. Come with me."

"No, I've had enough and I need to pee. I'm going inside."

"Stay away from her. Okay?" Sandy rubbed Emma's arm."

"If you say so."

Emma was still on the toilet when she heard a knock at the door.

"Emm, it's me, Michelle. You nearly finished? I'm desperate."

"Yeah, hang on. Just got to wash my hands, won't be a minute."

"Sorry, can't wait." The door opened as the toilet flushed and Michelle pushed past Emma, unzipped her slacks and sat down. "Oh, I needed that."

Emma finished drying her hands and was about to leave.

"Emm, don't go. Look, I'm sorry about before. Don't know if you heard anything."

"Not really."

"It's just that Sandy and I have a difference of opinion about something that affects you," Michelle said as she zipped up her slacks.

"What do you mean?"

Michelle made eye contact in the mirror as she washed her hands.

"Well, if I was you, I'd want to know but Sandy says that I should shut up."

"Know what?" Emma stared back.

"That's just it. I can't tell you. But don't say I didn't try. Just remember that." She flicked her hair over her shoulders and walked away.

Emma spoke to her reflection in the mirror. "I shouldn't have come."

As she walked outside, Michelle grabbed her by the arm. "Come here lovey. Tell her," she said twisting Emma around to face Sandy, "that I didn't say anything to you. Did I?"

"That's enough Michelle." Sandy made a stop sign with her right hand. "Just get out of here!" she added, pointing in the direction of the street. "Go on. Go home. Before I slap your stupid face."

"How dare you." Michelle's head jerked forward, her chin held high and her eyes narrowed. "And don't try telling me what to do."

"What's going on here ladies?" Rob positioned himself between the two women who were by now providing quality entertainment.

"She threatened to hit me," Michelle yelled as she took a glass of moselle from the table and raised her arm in a second attempt to drench Sandy. Rob caught hold of her wrist in mid-flight.

"You want to be careful Michelle, you nearly spilled that really nice wine."

Sandy turned to Michelle's husband who was standing open-mouthed behind Rob. "Just get her out of here."

"I wouldn't be in the same room as you anyway," Michelle screamed as she was hauled towards the gate.

"Great stuff," Barney chimed in. His wife pulled him away by the back of his shirt collar. "Take it easy Bernadette, you'll rip me best shirt," he hollered.

Emma laid her empty glass on the fencepost then turned to Sandy. "Come upstairs with me. Please."

They sat on the bed.

"Sorry Emm. Didn't want a scene but there was no stopping her."

"You've got to tell me Sand. What was she on about?"

"Emma, I think it's all rubbish. I don't think you need to hear it."

"That's up to me isn't it. Sand, if you don't tell me, I'll have to ask her and I'd rather it came from you."

"I don't know Emm." Sandy looked at the hands clasped in her lap then raised her eyes and inclined her head. "It's just that I don't think it's going to do you any good. It's all in the past."

"Then there's no reason why I shouldn't know, is there?"

"I'm only trying to protect you, you know that."

"From what? If you won't tell me, I'll find out one way or another. Seems like everyone else knows."

"You're sure Emm?"

"Go on. Tell me."

"Well," Sandy took Emma's hand, "you know when Kerry was married to Martin?"

"Yeah, course I do."

"Well, Kerry never wanted to have sex, bloody cold fish that she is, and after they broke up Martin told her that he couldn't stand not getting a root when they were married so he used to go up the cross to prostitutes."

"Go on."

"You sure?"

"Yes, go on."

"Well, he reckons Brad used to go with him. Martin said Brad used to play up anyway so he didn't think he was leading him astray but Emm, I don't believe her."

"Really, is that what she said?"

"Yeah. See it's all bullshit."

Emma straightened up and let out a long slow breath. "I'm not so sure."

"Sandy, where are you?" Rob was calling from the foot of the stairs.

"I'm up here. What do you want?" She shrugged. "Sorry, Emm."

"Where's the port bottle?" Rob went on.

"In the cupboard above the stove, Sandy called with an apologetic look at her friend. "Go on, Emm, keep talking."

"Brad stopped having sex with me. And he used to come home late. Often. Really late."

"But that doesn't mean he was screwing around."

"His excuse was that he fell asleep in the car or it broke down. Maybe that's the bullshit?"

"I don't know Emm. Does it really matter? Like I said, it's in the past."

"I don't know what matters anymore."

"Sandy love, I can't find it." Rob's voice came up the stairs. "A bloke could die of thirst down here."

"Just hang on Rob." With two hands she brushed Emma's hair away from her face. "Can you put this in the past Emm? You're doing so well, got yourself a new job…"

"Two actually," Emma interrupted. "I'm going to waitress at the Leagues Club as well."

"God, never imagined you as a waitress. You'll be rolling in it."

"I'm saving up."

"What for?"

"Well it was for a trip but now I think it's for a divorce."

"I think that would be money well spent."

"I need the name of someone."

"I'll find out who Kerry used."

"Thanks Sandy. I'm going to go now. Can you get Rob to call me a taxi please?"

"Sure. Stay here. I'll come and get you when it arrives."

Emma looked down at her hands that were clasped in her lap. The suntan mark from her wedding ring was fading. It would be gone soon. She wished it was as easy to make the hurt disappear.

"Ready Emm?" Sandy called, "taxi's here."

Rob was waiting at the bottom of the stairs to escort her out via the laundry and up the driveway.

"Where to, missy?" the driver asked as Rob closed the taxi door.

She mumbled the address and let her head rest against the seat.

"Not feeling too well lovey?"

"Had a bit too much to drink."

"Not good for you, that drink," he said as he pulled out of the driveway.

"Problem is, I don't drink much. Need a bit more practice."

"I get drunk once on ouzo. I get so sick my cousin have to drive my cab for two days. I no drink anymore."

"I think you're very sensible," Emma said.

"Taxi driver advice. Very free and very good value." He chuckled.

Emma let a few miles go by then leaned forward. "Can I ask your advice on something else?"

"Of course. It is good to talk when I drive."

"Why do men to go prostitutes?"

The driver reached for the volume control and turned down the radio. "You want me to tell you what I think? I think they do it because they stupid."

"Well I think you're right about that," she said settling back into her seat.

"I go once to prostitute. Only once when I very young before I marry my wife. Go with friends. My friends and I go when we drinking too much. One friend, he got the disease and have to go to the hospital. Big needles. It scare me, so I never go to brothel again. I have good wife now. I happy with her. You need find good man and be happy together."

"Easier said than done," Emma mumbled as her head lolled to one side. Through the slits in her eyes, she could see two yellow lines in the middle of the road. She could make them converge into one if she tried really hard. But as her concentration waned, they would diverge again to become a parallel pair. She took several gulps of fresh air that was streaming through the open window and succumbed to the weight of her eyelids.

"Time to wake up lovey." The taxi pulled into the curb.

"Oh, I'm sorry. I fell asleep. Thank you. Here. Please keep the change…for the good advice."

"Thank you lovey, and you be looking after yourself."

Emma took off her shoes as she negotiated the front stairs.

Bed had never looked quite so inviting. She let her clothes fall to the floor and climbed under the blankets in her underwear. Sleep came blissfully and immediately but only for a short time.

One friend get a disease and have to go to the hospital. The taxi driver's voice continued to echo in her sub-conscious. Forty five minutes after she lay her head on the pillow, her body lurched forward into a sitting position and a blinding flash of clarity caused her eyes to snap open as she woke up to significance of the words.

"The injections," she moaned, "I'm so stupid!"

24

Kodaks and Car Windows

THE SOLICITOR'S APPOINTMENT WAS FOR twelve o'clock.
"You sure it's okay for you to miss work?"

"Positive," Sandy said as she took Emma's arm. "They owe me heaps of time and I wouldn't miss it for the world. It's been nearly five months since that dickhead set you free. Now we'll do it properly."

The entrance to the building was flanked by towering granite columns with the number 75 highlighted in polished brass. Emma's high heels click clacked over the marble foyer. Sandy pressed the elevator button for the third floor and they waited. Two suited men pushed past them as the doors opened.

"S'cuse me!" Sandy said out loud, but they took no notice.

Emma tidied her hair in the mirror, tucking it behind her ears and flicking up the ends.

"Gorgeous," Sandy said with a wink.

Together they pushed open a heavy timber door and stood at the desk of the bespectacled receptionist who kept her head bowed. Sandy cleared her throat and Emma elbowed her in the ribs.

The woman raised her eyes and smiled unconvincingly. "Mrs Emery?"

"Yes. I have an appointment at twelve o'clock with Mr Goodsir."

"I'm aware of that my dear." She gestured to the chairs lined up against the wall. "Please take a seat."

"Bit of a dragon," Sandy whispered. She grabbed a handful of magazines and sat down. "Hmmph. All about ten years old." She tossed them back onto the coffee table. The receptionist glared over the top of her glasses and Emma attempted a conciliatory grin.

"What you been up to anyway Emm?" Sandy stretched her legs, sliding her feet along the polished floor, leaned back in the chair and crossed her arms.

"John rang me at work this morning."

"What was that about?"

"Not sure. He's been up the coast for a while. The last time he saw me I was in a bit of a mess."

"If I remember rightly, he picked you up out of the gutter."

"God, don't remind me."

"How'd he get your number?"

"He rang home. Mum told him."

"That was nice of him. I always thought he liked you Emm."

"He asked me to catch up for a drink."

"What did you say?"

"I said I'd see him at the Riley's Bar. We go there on Friday nights."

"Who's we?"

"The girls from work."

Sandy raised her eyebrows. "Be careful Emm. You know what people are saying about him and you told me about the way he treated that girl at his party."

"Yes, I know. But I don't remember him like that and he was so kind to me that day out front of Jo's."

They looked up as the door to their right opened.

"Mrs Emery?" A stout middle-aged man walked towards them looking from one to the other.

"Yes, that's me. This is my friend, Sandy. Is it okay if she comes in?"

"Yes, certainly, you're both welcome. This way please." He ushered them into an office lined with volumes of impressively bound books. It made the room seem small and cramped.

"Please take a seat." There were two straight-back chairs that encouraged good posture but provided little comfort. Mr Goodsir sat across the desk in a swivel chair that squeaked as it moved. The scalloped leather trim on his oak desk looked tatty and worn, a little like Mr Goodsir himself.

To one side was a photo of five children, two boys, two girls and a baby, held by a woman of miniature proportions. The woman herself could have been a child, if her face had not laid bare the years of hard work that would have been required to raise a brood of fine looking offspring. In the background was an imposing two storey house. Anne of Green Gables would have felt quite at home in that Tudor mansion. Mr Goodsir's marriage, Emma concluded, was in good shape. It was other people's failed unions that supported the perfect family who beamed back at her from within the polished silver picture frame.

Mr Goodsir laid his clasped hands on the desk and leaned forward. "How can I help you on this beautiful sunny day?" he had a broad smile that plumped up his cheeks.

"She wants a divorce," Sandy said looking at Emma.

Mr Goodsir raised his eyebrows towards his receding hairline and sat upright.

"Is that correct, Mrs Emery."

"Yes, it is."

"This is of course not something that you have discussed with your husband, Mrs Emery?"

Emma began her reply but Mr Goodsir's hand rose up like a stop sign. "Because that would be collusion Mrs Emery and we don't want any of that do we dear?" He paused and with assumed agreement continued on. "May I get a few particulars from you?"

Emma nodded as he unscrewed the cap of his Sheaffer fountain pen and placed the nib onto a clean sheet of foolscap paper that had been laid out in readiness. As she responded to each of his questions, he nodded three times slowly then captured her answers in a fine cursive longhand. The story of her marriage began to fill the page, the black ink at first moist and shiny then drying into a steel grey. When Emma confirmed she had been married for three and a half years, he paused and looked up.

"That's important dear. You see, by law you cannot commence any divorce proceedings unless you have been married for at least three years."

Emma and Sandy looked at each other and shrugged.

"Now Emma, we need to establish the grounds on which you wish to apply for dissolution of your marriage."

Sandy answered. "Well, he's been having it off with another woman, a girl actually. That should be enough grounds shouldn't it?"

Emma blushed. "Sandy, we don't know that for sure."

"They've been at it for months."

"Well, we can't prove it." Emma glared at Sandy and wondered if it was such a good idea to bring her along.

"And she's a pupil at the school where he teaches," Sandy added.

Mr Goodsir looked directly at Emma. "Well, you have had a difficult time of it, haven't you my dear!"

She managed a half-hearted smile.

Mr Goodsir screwed the top onto his pen. "Please understand, unless the young lady in question is sixteen years or under, the fact that she was his pupil is not relevant as far as these proceedings are concerned."

"That's not fair," Sandy said.

"May I continue?" he asked.

"Yes, sorry," she replied, sitting back in her chair.

Mr Goodsir once more addressed the foolscap page. "I presume you are separated from Mr Emery?"

"Yes, I am."

"And when did that occur?"

"Five and a half months ago."

"Hmm." A hand moved to his chin and thumb and forefinger massaged it gently. "A bit o a way to go then. You see, there are certain requirements by law if you wish to be divorced on the grounds of separation. The first you have satisfied – you have been married for three years. However you do not satisfy the second, in that you will have to wait until you have been separated for five years to meet the legal requirements of divorce by separation.

"Five years!" Sandy burst out, glaring at him.

"That's an eternity," Emma pleaded. "Please, I don't want to wait that long."

"To expedite matters you could sue on the grounds of your husband's adultery."

"Sure could," Sandy said, "the pupil's not the only one he's been having it off with."

"There have been other parties?"

Emma glared at Sandy, she was going too far now. "We don't know any details about that Mr Goodsir."

He turned away from Sandy, who slouched into the chair, legs crossed. "Mrs Emery, would you therefore consider gathering evidence – of this current relationship?"

"You mean hire someone to take photos, a detective?"

"That's correct."

"No, I wouldn't do that."

Sandy threw up her hands. "Why not for goodness sake?"

"I just don't want to, okay?"

Sandy shook her head and rolled her eyes as if to say *you're hopeless*.

"Well, my dear. That doesn't leave you with many options. But there are a few worth considering."

Emma listened intently as he explained that ninety-four per cent of divorces were granted on the grounds of desertion, adultery, separation and cruelty. Sandy uncrossed her legs and leaned her hands on the antique desk while Mr Goodsir explained the grounds on which the other six percent were granted.

"The last one you mentioned, Mr Goodsir, drunkenness," Sandy said, "what does that mean?"

"Would you like me to elaborate, Mrs Emery?" he said turning once again to Emma.

"Yes please."

"Divorce may be granted on the grounds of habitual drunkenness should there be evidence that the spouse engaged in regular and excessive drinking causing the irretrievable breakdown of the marriage."

"Well, he sure hit the bottle. Spent most of his money on drink, went to the club every other day." Sandy sounded like a bounty hunter who had just picked up a trail.

"Is this the case Mrs. Emery?"

"Well yes, I suppose it is but I think he did that because he was unhappy."

"You're not his psychiatrist my dear, just his wife."

"He might go along with it Emm, if he wants out quick," Sandy pointed out.

"Mrs Emery, I know you wouldn't collude with him in this instance, or any other for that matter. That's so, isn't it?"

"Yes, of course," she answered, nodding her head vigorously.

"It would be the most efficient and least costly way to bring the matter to a timely close my dear. If he would not oppose the petition, of course."

"I need to think about this Mr Goodsir. Is that all right?"

They were out of his office two minutes later, Emma convinced she was going to be Mrs Emery for quite some time.

St James Station was ten minutes' walk. They wove their way past David Jones, through the crowd of shoppers. The red-light indicators told them that the next train on platform five was theirs. As they took off down the steps they heard its thunderous approach from inside the tunnel. The smell of overhead electrical wires intensified as they reached the platform, then came the squeal of brakes as the train came to a halt. Together they swung a seat to face the front of the carriage and plonked themselves down.

"Phew. Just made it," Emma said.

As the train picked up speed, Sandy turned to Emma. "What are you thinking?"

"I'm thinking that it's hopeless. What a stupid system. People should be able to get divorced if they want to."

"Well I agree with that, but I don't believe it's hopeless."

"What do you know that I don't?"

"Emma, he won't want to stay married for five years. I reckon he wants to shack up with his floozie. And Miss Goody Two Shoes won't do it unless they're married. He's looking for a quick exit."

"And you think he'll agree to adultery? No way. He'll want to protect her."

"Listen to me. I reckon he'll go for the drunkenness thingy." Sandy was excited and turned to Emma, perched on the edge of the seat. "You've got to be smart about this. You've got to let him think it was his idea."

"I don't know." She was biting the cuticle of her thumb nail.

"Well you work it out. It's his only option. Otherwise he's stuck for the next five years. I think he'll go for it and the bastard won't even have to perjure himself." Sandy slapped Emma's knee. "Not that he has a problem telling fucking great lies."

"Sandy, quiet, everyone is looking at us."

The two women diagonally opposite rolled their eyes at each other. Emma flashed them an apologetic grin. After a pause she leaned towards Sandy. "You know, I've thought about it a lot before and I honestly think he did have a problem with the booze."

"About bloody time!" Sandy yelled.

The two matrons stood, placed their handbags over their arm and with heads held high, shuffled their way further down the carriage.

"Look, this is what you do," Sandy continued in a stage whisper. "You tell him that you're going to have to be separated for another four and a half years before you can get divorced. You're not upset, really calm like. In fact, you sound a bit chuffed. He'll start freaking out I reckon. Then you nonchalantly mention that the only other options are adultery, insanity – and I reckon he qualifies for that …"

"Ha ha, stick to the point."

"You pause here and casually say 'There is the option that is used quite a lot that would sort everything out straight away.' He'll be all ears. Then you say 'The solicitor says that it is quite common these days'. And you stop and wait for him to ask for more."

"What if he doesn't go for it."

"Well you've lost nothing. I'll get my Kodak out and start looking through some car windows."

"Don't be ridiculous."

"I'm serious. But look, give this a go first. Will you?"

"I guess so. S'pose I've got nothing to lose – except a husband. Sand, can I ask you something?"

"Yeah, of course."

"You said he'd want to marry her. You know that for sure?"

"Oh honey. Don't tell me you still care?"

"Do you know? Tell me if you do."

"Only that Rob has seen them a couple of times and they've been looking pretty smoochy."

"I guess that's it then."

"I thought you knew that a long time ago. Tell me you weren't still holding out hope."

Emma shrugged and looked out of the window. The train chugged on, rocking the passengers back and forth, like the thoughts in her head. One minute she knew that she was better off without him and was excited about the future, the next she would be longing for her old life back again.

"Then all I've got to say is I'm thankful that the bit of fluff turned up when she did and thank God she's still around, because otherwise you'd still be in that rotten marriage." Sandy rummaged in her bag. "Because now I'm hearing that you'd be running back to him."

"I know. You're right." Emma accepted a Minty and patted Sandy's hand.

"Did you ever hear from the floosie's oldies again?"

"No, nothing. I guess they got what they wanted."

"I still can't believe you did that. Met up with them I mean." Sandy picked at a bit of Minty wedged between her front teeth.

"Well, it was their idea."

"And I can't believe you told them you wouldn't go to the school. I can still see your halo glowing."

Emma laughed.

"Well, all I can say is Mr. W. owes you big time. Your stop coming up Emm. Promise me you'll make that phone call. Ring the shithead."

"Promise."

Emma picked up her bag and stared out of the window.

"So what made you think he was a boozer?"

"Just before we got engaged, I sort of panicked. Thought Brad might be like my father, an alcoholic, so I sent him to Dad's doctor."

"And?"

"Well, he told Brad to have one beer every day for a month. If he could do that he wasn't an alcoholic."

"And he passed the test I bet."

"Yeah, said he was the best doctor he'd ever been to."

"A drongo you mean. But you had your suspicions back then?"

"I must have."

"Well, then you should have no qualms about doing this, okay?"

The station came into view and the train slowed.

"Thanks for coming with me and for the advice Sand." Emma kissed her cheek.

"See ya kiddo. Go and do it. Get rid of the bastard."

25

Jekyll and Hyde

IN RESPONSE TO THE GROWING popularity of wine bars in Sydney, a row of sandstone brick terraces on the corner of Campbell and Riley Streets had been converted into what was now a popular bar called 'Riley's'. Wide archways opened up the rabbit warren of tiny rooms and the expanded space looked even bigger when the mirrored bar was installed. It was late when Emma spotted John's reflection across the room.

"What you staring at?" Shahna yelled. "You know that guy?" The noise level was already at a point where it was impossible to be heard without shouting.

"Yeah, for years," Emma replied as he sauntered towards them.

"Evening, beautiful girls." As cool as ever, John kissed Emma's cheek then wrapped his arms around her for an embarrassingly long time. "Emmy, hey, good to see you Babe."

"John, this is Shahna and Irene from work," Emma explained. While he was chatting with the girls, Emma took a moment to reconcile the rumours about John, the boy who had returned from Vietnam, with her memories of the one who had left. Even now, so many people were incapable of being friends with both her and

Brad but John had done what they couldn't and she admired him for that. He smiled at her as he walked to the bar and returned carrying a tray full of drinks along with an extra bottle of wine. As generous as ever.

"Thank you and cheers," Shahna and Irene raised their glasses.

John passed a drink to Emma. "Excuse me ladies," he said as he took her by the elbow. She shrugged an apology as he guided her to a corner of the room.

"Cheers to you too, Emma."

"Thanks John. How are things?"

"You know me, Emm. It's all cool. Had a good time up the coast."

"Sounds like fun."

"What about you. Your Mum tells me you moved out."

"Yes, it was too hard going back to live with them. And Mum worries about me less when she can't see me."

"So where are you now?"

"Rose Bay."

"Oh, eastern suburbs bird. Very posh."

"Well it's actually a bit of a dump. Above a shop. Really old but cheap. My room has a wonderful view of a brick wall and there's a lounge room and a kitchen. There's one other girl who's never there and a couple who come scurrying out to eat then disappear again."

"Top up the energy levels, eh?"

"Probably. So I don't really see anyone."

"Not much fun then?"

"Not much fun, no. I thought living in Rose Bay with other people would be great."

"Why don't you give it the flick, move out?"

"I should but it's just so much hassle."

"Let me know if you want a hand."

"Thanks John. That's kind of you."

A comfortable silence settled on them. Here was the John of old. Being with him was like opening a familiar door and knowing what you will find on the other side.

"I've been to see a solicitor."

"Oh Yeah? You buying a house?"

"Ha! About a divorce."

"Far out. I mean, I'm sorry, really."

"Anyway, let's not talk about it." Emma gazed into her wineglass then smiled back at him, "You've still got a good tan going."

"Yeah, spend most of my life in the sun. You still a beach babe?" he asked.

"Not much opportunity, John. I have a night job waitressing and I'm pretty tired by the weekend. I do miss it though," she said, looking directly into his ice blue eyes.

"We'll go tomorrow then. We leave at seven."

"You're joking."

"We'll pick up your stuff tonight. You can stay at my place. I'll sleep on the couch."

Impulsiveness was one of John's more endearing traits, a childish enthusiasm for whatever was happening in the moment.

"I don't think I can John."

"Why not?"

"Well, I don't know really. Except I have to be back for work tomorrow night."

"Then let's go." He held her hand and guided her through the crowd towards the exit. The stairwell was covered with graffiti and someone had scribbled *Francesca and I have known each other for so long that we're on our second bottle of tabasco.*

"Hang on a minute." She retrieved a stick of chalk from the tin on the floor and replaced *Francesca* with *John*.

It was six forty-five when the clatter of crockery woke her. She stretched her arms above her head and breathed in the sea air. Slow deep breaths. A frown crinkled her brow as she tried to recall when she had last slept so well. Spying the terry towelling robe behind the door, Emma slipped it on and made her way to the bathroom. John was standing at the kitchen bench making tea, his board shorts perched on his hips. The muscles of his back were defined by the morning sunlight seeping in from the verandah.

When he heard the bathroom door open, he called to her to come fetch her mug, the teabag still immersed and the string dangling.

"Thanks John. Weather seems good," she said tilting her head towards the verandah.

"North-easterly swell coming in, offshore wind. Pretty bloody perfect if you ask me. We're leaving in ten. Okay Babe? Toast's in."

She touched her cheek where he kissed her as he left the kitchen. Above the sound of the flushing toilet he directed her to the Vegemite at the back of the fridge. She handed him his breakfast on the way to her bedroom and while munching on her toast, shimmied into her shorts, over her bikini, threw on a t-shirt and was standing on the balcony finishing the last of her tea when he came up behind.

"Let's split Babe." A touch on her shoulder and a nonchalant toss of his car keys.

By seven twenty-five the Triumph was making its way south through the city, past Sutherland where the rows of red brick houses began to thin out.

"This was a great idea John. So good to get out of that grotty flat. Can I put the radio on?"

"It's your day Emm."

They crossed the boundary into the National Park with John tapping out the beat to the current Bee Gees hit song *Staying Alive*. Emma joined in singing along to the chorus at the top of her voice – *Ah ha ha ha stayin' alive,* because at that moment, she decided it was well worth doing.

"Where are we headed?" she asked, adjusting the radio's volume.

"Garie," he replied. "Thought you'd be more comfortable away from, you know, where we used to hang out."

"Thank you." Emma looked out of the window to hide the tears welling up and felt a rush of gratitude for John's thoughtfulness.

It was another fifty-five minutes before he pulled over onto the shoulder of the road. Emma grabbed the plastic bag with the sandwiches and Coke and threw her towel around her shoulders. Had she known their destination was Garie, she would have worn jeans. The bush track was seldom used and the overgrown scrub clawed at exposed arms and legs.

John balanced his surfboard on his head. "Let's go!" he called and set off down the track. They walked single file through the milky white glare of morning light, John lead the way and Emma followed. The soft squelch of slightly damp leaves was interspersed with the flip-flop of their thongs. Bush smells swirled around as they brushed away the gossamer webs of last nights' weavings. A kookaburra laughed from a distance, then a little closer in came a magpie's welcoming warble. "One for sorrow, two for joy," Emma whispered to herself, then on cue, two magpies appeared from behind a curtain of tree branches and flew off like a pair of airborne spats. She knew that the cicadas were there, hidden away and waiting for the sun to appear like a conductor's baton, signalling their time to contribute to the symphony of bush sounds.

John's arms were already covered with beads of sweat that glistened in the dappled light. He glanced back occasionally to make sure Emma was still with him. After about half an hour the foliage thinned and the beach lay ahead. The bush sounds were replaced by the thump of waves, the sucking back of the sea and squawking seagulls.

They continued along the warm sand, their feet breaking through the crusty top layer, until they were opposite the best break at the northern end. As they turned to face the sea, a wall of translucent water rose up, and in the momentary pause before the wave collapsed, a school of fish were visible, swimming parallel to the shoreline.

"Beach salmon," John said as he stood in homage with outstretched arms. Emma noticed his untamed hair and the sleep that still rested in the corner of one eye as he turned to her and asked, "You be all right here? This okay?"

"This is better than okay John and yes, I'm cool. It's not the first time I've been a beach widow you know. And I brought a book if I get bored."

He surveyed the shoreline for a moment longer, choosing his point of entry.

Emma lay on her belly and was dozing in the same position when she heard the squeak of his footsteps on the sand.

"You're so predictable!" she laughed aloud as he shook the droplets of water from his hair onto her sun-warmed back. "Good surf?" she asked as she rolled over.

"Stoked. Going in?"

"Maybe later," she replied as she stretched her arms above her head. He sat on his board, his hands spread out behind his arched back and turned his face to the blue of the sky.

"You want my towel?" Emma asked.

"Nah, dry off soon enough."

"There's a midden over there." He pointed to the southern headland. "The aborigines were here way before we came along and fucked it for them."

"S'pose. I read a book about when Captain Cook discovered Australia. I mean they didn't even think of the aboriginals as people then. They were more interested in the animals and plants."

"Maybe it was just more convenient not to notice them so that they could say the land was uninhabited. Fucks you up thinking about what people do to people."

"I guess you saw a lot of that in the war."

He slid silently onto the sand, arms folded above his head. Emma noticed that the hair in his armpits and the fuzz line that ran from his belly button and into his board shorts was spun from the same golden thread. He closed his eyes as if to shut out the world.

The beach hadn't always been a place of calm and solitude. She had spent too many hours watching Brad in the surf, consumed by the problems in their relationship and oblivious to the beauty around her. *No more.* She nearly said it aloud then remembered John dozing by her side.

As she stood up she paused to look out across the ocean and felt the insignificance of her life in the history of this land. It was like a cosmic kick in the bum to get up and get on with a privileged existence that was being wasted. The sand was warm under her feet as she made her way to the waterline and dipped her toe into the rim of cool white froth.

She stood for a moment, giving her body time to accustom itself to the change in temperature. Nevertheless, she winced as the spray from the breakers hit the surface of her skin. She pushed through the foaming edge of the surf and made an arrow tip with her hands to pierce the glistening wall of water rising up in front of her. The sounds of the bush disappeared as the gurgle and rush of the sea filled her ears, then she broke through the surface of the water, her face held up to the sun and began to swim out beyond the break.

Her chest rose and fell with the rhythm of the swell as she lay on her back to rest, eyes closed to the glare. The sea lifted her effortlessly then laid her gently back down. When she broke away from the hypnotic effect of the motion and turned to make her way back to shore, she found that she had drifted further out than she intended.

Once, she had been a strong swimmer. Had even got her Bronze Medallion at school. Eight lengths of the pool had been no trouble at all but that was long ago and she had done little swimming since. Her overarm stroke was making no headway so she decided to turn and swim towards the breaking waves to catch a ride in to shore. During a pause to conserve her energy while treading water, she felt at first a caress of her toes, then a more turgid force swirling around her legs.

"Oh God, I'm in a rip," she said aloud and snatched her feet away. But in the same way that a spider quickly wraps its prey in its web, the rip had taken hold and she was trapped. She recognised the signs of panic as her breath shortened and her body stiffened. *Swim parallel to the shoreline*, she remembered, but she was no match for the sucking, gulping water and there was no choice but to go with it. The headland to her left was retreating quickly and to her right, in the direction that she was being carried, was a never-ending blueness. The emptiness of that space made her heart beat faster and fingers of fear clawed at her throat. She called for help but the sounds of the breaking surf were a barrier to her cries and with a whimper she surrendered to the will of the water.

A change in temperature roused John. The wind had picked up and clouds were moving in. He jumped up and with his hands cupped called to Emma. When there was no answer, he studied the bush at the edge of the beach then looked to the ground. The hairs on the back of his neck rose as his eyes followed her footprints into the sea. Leaping over rocks, he ran to the top of the headland and scanned the horizon until his gaze stopped short on a speck of whiteness in the sapphire blue, moving out to sea.

His first instinct was to dive in and swim for her but he knew that he would be quicker on his board, so he willed himself to turn away, agonising over the time it took to get in the water. In fact, it took only seconds, although it seemed much longer, and then he paddled with a strength that he didn't know he had until he could see her. With rising panic he called her name again and again. He knew she was still alive because she was floating but he saw her disappear every now and then and couldn't tell if she had been hidden by the rise and fall of the swell or if she had gone under. He called out each time he saw her come up, willing her to hang on.

Emma knew that she couldn't go on for much longer. She had often wondered if she would ever be desperate enough to pray and now seemed like a sensible time to indulge herself just in case she had got it wrong about God. But she couldn't bring herself to do it. If by chance he would decide her fate that day, and if his decision was that she should die, then she figured she had no control anyway.

She felt cramping in her legs and knew she would soon be unable to stay afloat. It was with this thought in mind that she raised her head to look around at the world that she might be leaving and heard a voice. John was only about twenty feet away, close enough for her to hold his gaze and see that his eyes had taken on a deeper blue, the colour of the water. He paddled close enough to grab hold then hauled her onto his board.

It felt good being pulled and pushed – like a mother cat rearranges her kittens.

Only then, when she was safely settled, did he speak.

"It's okay Emma. You're okay now, I'm here."

She lay limp and cool on the rough, waxy surface as John kneeled above her and with delicate small strokes, began their journey to the beach. A little way from shore, her left arm slipped into the water. She didn't stir as John retrieved it and gently tucked it under her thigh. The warmth of the sun had evaporated her fear, leaving a residue of relief like the salty crust forming on her soft skin.

They reached the shallows and stood up. With one hand either side of her, he guided the board towards the shoreline. Emma's arm slipped once more into the water and she left it there enjoying the reassuring chafe of the sand on her fingertips.

"Emma, are you okay. Can you walk?" He was kneeling beside her, stroking her hair.

"Yeah, course I can." But she found the strength had gone out of her legs, and so he lifted her and carried her up the beach.

"I'm all right. Really," she assured him as he laid her on her towel. She noticed the pages of her book had blown open and were parched and puckered from exposure to the sun.

"Jesus Emma, that was close," John said as he stood up.

"I knew you'd come for me," she said dreamily. It was half true.

"Well, you were bloody lucky, I can tell you." John ran his fingers through his hair.

"You saved my life."

He crouched down next to her and gently brushed the wet hair away from her ears. Then he turned to face the sea and put his head in his hands. They sat in silence, while the pace of their breathing slowed.

After a while, Emma wondered if he was asleep and touched his arm. Instantly, his face contorted. He grabbed her wrist and held it with such force that she cried out.

Then he hurled her arm back at her and snarled, "What the fuck do you think you were doing?"

"Just seeing if you were all right," she moved back from him and held her wrist against her chest.

"I mean out there. Risking your life." His stare was intense and his eyes were glaring at her.

"I didn't do it on purpose," she whimpered.

"You know better Emma." He thumped the ground and Emma felt the vibrations through the sand. "What the fuck were you playing at?"

"John, it was an accident, I got caught in a rip." She pushed herself into a sitting position and turned to face him straight on.

"Don't shit me Emma. You can't fool me. That's a dangerous game you're playing." His hair had fallen over his face again and she wanted to push it back so she could see his eyes and be sure he wasn't just pretending to be angry.

"It wasn't a game John, and you're wrong. I didn't mean it," she said standing her ground.

"Don't lie. You said you knew I would rescue you." His hair swung violently from side to side as he shook his head.

"I just meant that I had faith, in something." She bit her bottom lip.

His fist began to thump the sand. "Why would you set me up like that?" He spat out the words like gunfire.

"I told you, it was an accident. I got caught in the rip."

"Bullshit. You know the water Emma."

"Yes, I do but accidents are things you don't plan to happen and I didn't plan this." She was on her knees now, staring at his clenched jaw. She stretched her hand out towards his but pulled it back when he ignored her.

"Well you couldn't have planned it better, could you?"

He was standing at full height now, his fingers curled into fists. His muscular torso that only hours ago had been so attractive, was now a threatening presence. If there had been a door or a wall close by, he would surely have punched a hole in it. His breathing was laboured and his eyes were staring, unblinking.

"John, please, I'm so tired. Can't you just leave it? Please?"

"Leave it. Ha! You think you can play those games and get away with it," he shouted, thumping the sand over and over.

"John, for goodness sake. This is ridiculous. I just went for a swim and got carried out in the rip while you were sleeping." Emma began to twist the ends of the towel in her fingers. She looked up at him. "Can we go home now, please?"

"Don't try and make out it was my fault."

"John, stop it. Stop it." She stood up and took two steps back from him. "I didn't say it was your fault." He turned his back to her and after a moment she moved towards him. "Look, I'm incredibly grateful for what you did." Emma touched his shoulder but he shrugged her hand away then turned to face her, a snarl on his lips.

"I'm sorry I spoilt your little game."

"John, you're not listening to me. What's wrong with you?"

"What if you fucking died?"

"But I didn't." Emma raised her voice in an attempt to get him to understand better. "And if I had, not one person in the world would have blamed you."

"Jesus Christ, you're wrong about that. Get your stuff. We're going." He jumped up, grabbed his board and took off towards the bush track.

"John, wait!" Emma picked up her clothes ran to catch up with him as he tore through the scrub, pushing aside any branch that dared to stand in his way, one arm a machete and the other holding onto his surfboard as it teetered on his head.

Who was this person, Emma wondered? *John one minute and God knows who the next. Like Jekyll and Hyde.*

John threw the surfboard into the back seat before the top was completely lowered. Emma threw the towels on top and barely had time to put her seatbelt on before he swung the car onto the road in front of a truck coming the other way. Its horn blared as it accelerated past to avoid a collision.

There was no getting through to him. Knuckles were white on the steering wheel, eyes fixed on the road. He had gone to some place Emma wasn't invited so she shut up and clutched her seatbelt as he threw the car around corners, screeching the tyres, burning brakes, and pushing the tachometer into angry red with each gear change.

By the time they passed the boundary of the park she noticed his grip had relaxed on the steering wheel. From the corner of her eye she could see his jaw was no longer clenched shut. Gradually, the needle on the speedometer began to swing back towards her as the pace of the car slowed. Then she heard a voice she recognised from early that morning.

"Want to stop for an ice cream at Heathcote?"

"What? Did you say something?"

"Do you feel like an ice cream or maybe a drink at the pub."

"You're kidding, aren't you? I just want to go home."

"What's wrong Babe?" His voice was calm. "I thought you'd want to celebrate being alive."

"Hang on John, what just happened back there?"

"Wha'd you mean?"

"You completely lost it. I mean you were someone I didn't know."

"Well, you frightened me no end." He patted her leg. "And I got a bit upset." He gave her a toothy grin.

"A bit upset! You were a madman John, you terrified me. I've never seen you like that."

"Like what?"

"Don't do this John."

"Don't do what?"

"Pretend you don't know what I'm talking about. That nothing happened back there."

"Apart from the fact that you nearly drowned."

"There's no point in talking to you is there?" She crossed her arms and looked out the side window.

"Look, sure I got upset, but wouldn't you? If I hadn't found you, you'd be drinking sea water by now." His seductive drawl was back. "I got a real shock Emmy. You can understand that can't you Babe?"

"That's not the point," she snapped. Although, she thought he did have a point. But damn, he wasn't going to make her complicit in this ruse, a party to his game of pretence that his actions were normal.

"Look John, it's okay to get upset, I'm not saying it isn't. It's just the way you went into anger overdrive, you freaked out, I didn't know who you were."

"I think you're overreacting Emm. Look, you've just had a big fright, you're not rational. Now, do you want an ice cream or a drink?"

Maybe it *was* her, maybe she did overreact. "One drink," she said, "and then I need to get home to get ready for work."

"Done," he said as he turned the radio on and began tapping out the beat on the steering wheel. She slipped her t-shirt and shorts over her costume.

John leapt out of the car to open her door. "Here, take my arm," he said. "You feeling all right?" he asked. She ignored his request and his arm moved to her waist as they walked to the beer garden. Sprawling gum trees shaded the mismatched tables and chairs and Emma could detect the fatty odour of the sausage sizzle.

"Hungry?"

"Nup. Just a drink."

John pushed a glass of Asti Spumante across the pinewood table. "Here's to 'Stayin' Alive' Emm. Sorry about the cheap grog. The best they've got in this joint. Cheers." He held up his schooner, his free arm draped over the back of the chair, his legs spread, looking relaxed and carefree, as if nothing had happened.

Did she imagine it? Was it as bad as she thought? Maybe she was overwrought? Had she caused it, by arguing with him? Around and around in her head the doubts swirled, like the bubbles in the glass of the cheap champagne she was holding.

The alcohol was taking effect. Always did on an empty stomach. She felt more confident. "You were horrible John. Promise you'll never do that again."

"But I thought we had a nice day Emmy."

She crossed her legs and turned away.

"What's wrong?" He leaned towards her and put his hand on her knee.

"Nothing John. Let's just go home."

"Only if you promise we can do this again next week – but not the drowning. I couldn't stand to lose you Emm."

26

Drawing a Line

"Hi. It's me. Can you talk."
"Sure Sand. Boss is in a meeting."
"What you been up to?"
"Usual stuff. Went to the beach with Johnno last weekend."
"So, you finally got together. How did it go?"
"Well it started really well."
"What happened?"
"Sandy, he's got an incredible temper. I had no idea."
"Was he pissed? That can make them stroppy."
"No. We were at the beach like I said."
"What happened then, to make him go off?"
"I nearly drowned."
"Can't think why that would upset him," Sandy chuckled.
"Sure, but it was really weird."
"Like how?"
"I got caught in a rip and he had to come and get me on his board. He was really worried, really nice. Then the next minute he just lost it. Honestly, I was frightened of him."
"So you don't think he had reason to be upset?"

"I know where you're coming from, but no is the answer. It was obvious I was all right. He wasn't worried about me anymore, he just snapped, was out of his tree. Started yelling at me. I was frightened Sandy."

"Not good. I did hear he went off at some secretaries at work."

"I feel for them."

"It's probably Vietnam. They're all mad you know, the vets, they're nutters."

"Then it's not his fault."

"Emm, if he's like that, give him a big miss. You're not the Red Cross and he's not what you need right now. You don't want to get mixed up with a psycho."

"Suppose you're right."

"Anyway, you know that's not why I rang."

"Guessed as much."

"Have you sorted it yet, with Shithead?"

"I will, just give me time. It's hard Sand, it's so final."

"It will be good for you Emm. Draw a line under that crappy part of your life."

"And now it's the good part?"

"It will be, but you've got to move on. Then I'll stop nagging you."

"Okay. I'll call him, promise. Boss's coming back. Got to go."

Emma rummaged in her purse for fifty cents as she negotiated the stairs from the office. "Damn!" Her left foot missed a step and a jolt of pain shot up the side of her leg as her ankle twisted. She grasped the railing and limped the rest of the way to the phone outside the nearby cafe. Miracle. It was empty and there was actually a dial tone.

While massaging her ankle with one hand, she slid the fifty cents into the coin slot with the other then dialled the number that she knew by heart. It rang twice. The shock of hearing his voice made her draw breath. She hadn't expected him to answer. With her eyes closed she breathed deeply and swallowed hard.

"Senior staff room," he said for a second time.

"Hi, it's me. Can you speak for a minute?"

"Sure."

She had been to see the solicitor, she said. He grunted. "It's for the best, isn't it?"

"Yeah. Fair enough."

"Hang on a minute." The pain in her heart caused her to wince.

"What'd he say Emma, the legal eagle?"

She shook her head twice and breathed deeply. "He said it will take five years if we get a divorce." There was a pause and a noise in the background.

"Someone's coming into the staff room," he said.

"Is that okay with you?" It wasn't going to script and she tried to remember what Sandy had said.

"Not now Emma," he interrupted

"Sorry."

"Let's meet up. Can't really do this at work."

"Sure," she said, gripping the receiver with both hands. Could the finality of this last step, the undoing of the vows that bound them, cause him to have second thoughts?

"After school tomorrow," he told her.

"I work tomorrow night. I won't have time to come your way. It will have to be at my place." The inside of the phone booth smelt sour and the sun was shining on her back. She was beginning to feel queasy.

"At your Mum's?"

"No. I've moved out."

"Where to?"

She gave him the address and they agreed to meet at five forty-five. She would need to leave work early. Tidy up the flat. It wouldn't make a lot of difference but she'd do it anyway.

At 4.30 she began by picking up stray articles of clothing, sticky coffee cups and crusty plates. She plumped up the bean bags and dusted the coffee table. The mindless repetition of the routine chores diverted her mind. Moving to the bathroom, she sprinkled

Ajax around the toilet bowl and hand basin and with a rhythmic circular motion removed some of the stains and smudges. When she was done, she stripped off and stood under the shower, letting the water wash away a little more of her anxiety. Was there still a chance? Sandy would kill her but she wouldn't be the first woman to forgive a man.

With fifteen minutes to go, she wrapped herself in a towel, walked to her room and sat on the bed. She would dress as if she had just come from work and chose a denim shirtmaker. Pale blue suited her. The top button she left undone to show just a hint of cleavage. Then did it up again. Her hair, she tied back with a white grosgrain ribbon then changed her mind and let it hang loose. The doorbell rang as she slipped into her shoes. As she walked down the stairs, she clipped on her pearl earrings.

The swollen timber door dragged across the carpet and he was there, in his shorts, his hair longer than she remembered. It took resolve and willpower not to throw her arms around his neck.

"Hi, come on in," she said. He wiped his feet on what was left of the door mat and followed her up the steep stairs. Emma sashayed her way to the top and could feel his eyes travel along her legs.

When they reached the top of the stairs they paused and he looked around. The sunlight streaming through the window had faded the back of the maroon lounge to a dusty pink and the cushion springs had long ago given up the ghost. In places, the carpet was worn through and paint was flaking from the walls where the damp had seeped in. The dilapidated furniture had been in the flat for so long no-one knew who owned it, so no one was ever going to pay to replace it. When Emma first moved in, she had toyed with the idea of making scatter cushions for the lounge and contributing a throw rug to hide the discolouration. She thought it polite to wait before making any changes, but as time went on even she couldn't see the point.

"What'd you move here for?" he asked.

"I like the Eastern Suburbs," she replied. "Good nightclubs, bars, restaurants. It's all happening here. My flatmates are great.

There's never a dull moment in this place." Had she overdone it? Sounded too enthusiastic?

They would sit at the dining table, she decided. At least it provided evidence of good times rather than sheer neglect. The wooden top was scarred by molten candle wax and burnt by stray cigarette butts. Overlapping ring marks were evidence that diners didn't allow the clearing of the table to delay their departure to the bedroom.

"You find your way okay? I mean, didn't get lost or anything?"

"Nup. No trouble."

"How's your Mum and Dad?"

"They've gone to Tassie for a couple of weeks."

"That's nice. You want to sit down?"

He pulled out a chair. "Bloody hell!"

"That one's got a loose spring. Try this one."

"Do yourself damage if you're not careful," he mumbled. "So, what happened at the solicitors?"

A deep breath. "Like I said on the phone, it takes five years to get a divorce."

"Bloody stupid."

"Yeah, that's what I thought."

"And?" he asked, palms upturned.

"That's on the grounds of separation, five years. She tried to remember Sandy's instructions. Not to sound too interested. "There are other ways but they probably wouldn't work."

"What, you mean like adultery?" he asked.

"That's one, I guess," she nodded in agreement.

"You're right. Wouldn't work."

She felt the muscles around her heart contract. Her nails dug deep into the palm of her hand.

"That's it?" he asked.

"Admission of cruelty and insanity. Or if you were imprisoned, we could get a divorce straight away." She attempted a light-hearted giggle.

"Sorry, but I don't intend to oblige."

"The other one is drunkenness." She was about to say that it was an option that many people choose.

"What's that about?"

"It's when the petition is granted on the grounds that one party drank too much. Evidently, it's used quite a bit because it doesn't have to be true, it just has to be uncontested."

"How long would that take?"

"I'm not sure, pretty well straight away I guess. Do you want a glass of water or something?"

"Got a beer? Since we're on the subject."

"I'll have a look in the fridge." She held the door open and breathed in the cool air. He watched her walk from the kitchen.

"Sorry, no beer but there's some wine left." She held up the flagon that had a couple of inches sloshing around in the bottom.

"That'll do. You join me?" he asked

"You do the honours?" she said handing him two empty glasses.

"So, if you petition me on the basis of drunkenness and I don't oppose it, the divorce will happen quickly." he said nodding his head.

She avoided his gaze and focused on the glasses filling up. "Well, that's what the solicitor said. Happens often, evidently."

"What do I have to do?" He passed a glass across the table.

"Nothing. I do it all. You just don't oppose it."

"It would be better for us both to do it quickly. Wouldn't it?"

"If that's what you think." Her hands shook so much she had to lay the glass on the table.

"Then cheers. Go for it." He tapped her glass then drank the contents of his in one go. "I don't want to hurt you anymore, Emma," he said, pouring himself the last drop. "I never intended to, you know, hurt you," he repeated.

"You've got no idea, have you?" And all the hurt came hurtling back, the pain nearly unbearable as she looked at this man who seemed able to leave their love behind without a backward glance.

"Emm." He pushed his chair back and walked around the table. He stood behind her chair, placing a hand onto each of her shoulders. "I didn't tell you about her because I didn't know where it was going."

"I don't believe you."

"Try to see it my way Emm. I was confused, didn't know if maybe, well you know, we could have worked it out." He paused.

"Don't Brad. This isn't fair. You made a choice."

"I didn't really."

"What do you mean?"

"Her oldies found out before I had time to get my head straight."

"So, you just went along with it because it had gone too far? Is that it?"

"You and I weren't getting on anyway."

"You might have thought that, but I didn't."

His hands moved along her shoulders, slid down her arms then he leaned forward and kissed her neck.

"Stop it Brad. Don't. Please. It's not fair."

"Stand up." She did as she was told. "Now turn around."

He guided her head to his chest and stroked her hair, wrapping it around his index finger and letting it run through his fingers, as he used to, in the beginning. She looked up at him, licking away the salty tears. Slowly he bent down and kissed her mouth and sucked the sobs out of her.

As he led her along the hallway, she tried to pull back.

"Emma, come on. I've missed you so much."

"You've missed me? How do you think I feel?"

"Then come here. Is this your room?"

She nodded as he pulled her through the doorway. "You're still so beautiful you know."

They stood and held each other, then he began to undo the buttons on her dress and she let him, for one last time. He took her arms and wrapped them around his waist. The touch of him was a homecoming.

When he sat her on the bed, she waited, hands in lap as he undressed her.

"Lie down Emm. You're shaking. I'll cover you up."

She did as he asked then shut her eyes and allowed herself to go back to the time when his presence to her was as critical as breath, when his touch and the sound of his voice were vital to her being. And she knew he had felt the same.

When he finished with her he reached for his cigarettes, then lay on his back. She turned on her side and faced the wall. The smoke drifted past and out the window.

"Got to go Emm." He dropped the cigarette into an empty water glass, got up and left the room. The toilet flushed. When he came back, he didn't get in beside her. He finished dressing and she felt his weight on the bed as he leaned towards her and his lips touched the back of her head.

"Go ahead Emm. I won't oppose it." Then the door closed.

Muffled conversation came from the next room, then laughter in the corridor. Her eyes opened and adjusted to the receding daylight. How long had she been lying there? She checked her watch. Forty-five minutes until she was due to start work, on her feet for five hours and her ankle was aching.

From a sitting position, she swivelled around to face the dressing table. There was an image of a girl in the mirror and she willed it to stand up. As she stared at her likeness, she felt a moist warmth escape onto her thighs. Her fingers touched the wetness then they went to her tongue and she tasted his bitterness. Her head began to clear and a thought flashed into her mind. If she had been walking along a street, the realisation would have stopped her in her tracks but standing as she was, naked and trembling, she cried out, and with unsteady hands began to count on her fingers.

Five, six, seven, maybe eight months, since she had last taken the pill.

27

'It's Time'

IT WAS MORE DIFFICULT THAN expected for Jewel to follow her own advice and allow Brad access to Sally. Although Derek had reluctantly conceded to the arrangement, he eventually agreed that he was hard-pressed to find evidence of Brad's intentions being other than genuine. But he was still looking. An uneasy peace had settled over the household. By the beginning of December, with exams finished and the school year over, Sally and Brad became a public couple.

"Sal, don't forget we've got Sam and Lee coming for dinner tonight," Jewel called up the stairs.

"Again?"

"I know, your Dad's idea this time."

"Are you coming home after the beach?"

"No. We're all going for a Chinese, then straight there."

"And there is?"

"The pictures." Sally bounded down the stairs, licking toothpaste from her upper lip.

"Don't be late then."

A groan from Sally.

"He's given a lot over the last few months, you know."

"Mum, don't tell him but he had no choice," Sally said as she did up her sandals. "What you *can* tell him is that Brad's divorce is coming through, probably by Christmas. That should make him happy."

"Oh, so soon."

"Yeah, cool isn't it?

Jewel paused and turned to face her daughter, who had grown up too quickly in the last few months. Summer sun had bleached her hair whiter than the beach sands. It was pulled back into a pony tail that brushed her shoulders as she walked by, head held high.

"Sal, you won't do anything silly will you?"

"What do you mean Mum?" She had moved to the bay window, watching for the V-Dub.

"You'll give yourself time? We agreed Sal. Sally, you hear me?"

The noisy rumble of the air-cooled motor interrupted the silence. "He's here Mum. Got to go. Love you."

Jewel walked towards the kitchen to finish preparations for the evening's meal and paused at a photo on the wall of the three of them on the beach the year before Brad arrived. It captured the simplicity and joy of those times, in stark contrast to their life today.

At 7pm sharp Sam and Lee pulled into the driveway.

"Don't know why you need an esky," Lee said as Sam hauled it out of the boot. "It's only a ten minute drive."

"Beer can get hot in five Lee."

She balanced a plate of homemade rum balls in one hand and bunch of camellias in the other.

"A bit like taking coal to Newcastle." Sam observed as they walked through Jewel's flourishing garden and along the path to the front door.

"Not a word about Paul," Sam said as he pressed the door bell and chimes rang out from inside the hallway. "Do you hear me?"

Lee knew that the cat was already out of the bag, but she could trust Jewel, couldn't she?

"Evening all. Come on in." Derek kissed Lee's cheek and accepted a hearty handshake from Sam. Perry Como could be heard crooning in the background.

"What smells so good?" A piquant aroma had replaced the fragrance of the garden.

"You'll have to ask Jewel, I wouldn't have a clue."

"Spicy chicken legs," was the reply as she emerged from the kitchen, oven glove in hand.

"Hello gorgeous." Sam greeted her with a kiss on the mouth, as he did most women, and Lee handed over the camellias.

"My favourite. So clever of you Lee."

"Or just bloody lucky," Sam chimed in, looking straight ahead to avoid the stare of disapproval that he knew would be coming his way.

Derek seated his guests in the lounge room.

"Beer mate?" Sam asked, opening the esky and tossing a can to Derek.

"Thanks Sam. What about you Lee? Soft drink, or would you like me to make you a lemon, lime and bitters?"

"I'd like a red wine please Derek. If that's all right?" she said, her hands clasped in her lap.

"Oh really? Good-oh." For as long as he could remember, Lee had been teetotal. Sam gave him a *stuffed if I know* shrug.

"I've decanted a bottle of red, a 1965 Lindemans. How's a glass of that sound?"

"She wouldn't know mate. Might be a bit of a waste," Sam sniped.

Jewel finished passing around Jatz biscuits, some topped with smoked oysters, others with cheese and pickled onions, then retreated to the kitchen. Derek headed for the dining room. He took an extra wineglass from the cabinet and filled it to halfway for Lee.

Left on their own, Lee shot back. "What did you say that for?" she hissed.

"Well it's true. You wouldn't know one red wine from another. What's got into you anyway?" He leaned to his left, crossed his legs, and passed wind.

"I just feel like a drink."

"Be my guest. Derek's guest, to be precise." He finished his beer and belched into the back of his hand.

"You're disgusting," she said

"I covered my mouth."

"You think that's all it takes?"

Jewel paused in the doorway waiting for the exchange to finish as Derek stood alongside, carrying the glass of wine.

"Who's that for?" she whispered.

"Lee," he said with raised eyebrows.

"Really?"

"Don't ask me. Come on, don't leave me on my own." He ushered Jewel into the edgy silence of the lounge room.

"Dinner in five minutes," she chirped. "Hope you're hungry."

"Could eat the arse out of a fly-blown horse," Sam replied.

"Well I think it will taste a lot better than that," Jewel reassured him, perching on the far end of the couch.

"Cheers." Lee proposed the toast. "To good friends."

"Hope you enjoy it, my dear," Derek said.

"Yeah, we'd hate to waste it on the unappreciative," Sam chimed in.

All eyes were on Lee as they waited for her to take a first sip.

She swirled the deep red liquid inside the raised glass then brought it to her nose "A good bouquet Derek." She took a sip. "And it's nicely full bodied. A shiraz?"

"Well done, Lee," said Derek.

Sam harrumphed as he reached into the esky for another beer.

"You seem quite the connoisseur Lee," Jewel commented over the clatter of cans. "I can't stand red wine myself."

"Developed a taste for it recently."

Sam was damned if he was going to ask how that came about and they were back to a strained silence.

"Yes, well," Jewel continued "I remember I couldn't stand oysters a couple of years ago and now I love them. Tastes change."

Perry Como had run his course and Derek got up to change records. Jewel excused herself and returned to the kitchen.

THE TEACHER, THE PUPIL AND THE WIFE

"What you playing at?" Sam asked

Lee inclined her head. "What do you mean?"

"When did you start drinking?"

"I've been having lunch with my daughter and son-in-law when you're at golf. Carol can't have any alcohol because of the bubby, so I've been having a glass of wine with Warwick if you really must know. They don't want to have anything to do with you – or would you rather I tell all that to the Watsons."

"Tell them whatever you want." He was about to add he couldn't give a stuff when Jewel walked past carrying the first course.

"Dinner's served," she called, arranging the hot dish on the mats in the centre of the table. "Sam, Lee, your usual seats please when you're ready."

Lee cast daggers at Sam when he picked up the chicken wings with his fingers. She bristled when he sucked noisily at the bones, then clenched her jaw and sucked air in through her nostrils when he licked his fingers.

"Sorry Sam, I should have put out finger bowls," Jewel tried to disguise her distaste with a smile.

Derek managed a change of topic as the table was cleared and a discussion ensued about Sam's new investment scheme. The Beef Wellington was a hit with everyone. Sam managed to use his knife and fork and they polished off the first bottle of Lindemans and were well into a bottle of Woodleys before knives and forks were laid to rest. Lee emptied her third glass and Sam was in full flight, berating the interference of the unions and boasting about his contacts in the council. As he droned on, Lee's head fell forward onto her chin.

When Sam paused to take another mouthful of red, Lee straightened her back, leaned into the table and out of the blue said, "So what do you think Derek. Do you reckon that..." she paused for emphasis, her hands rising to form quotation marks, "it's time!"

Derek knew that Lee was referring to the Labor Government's catchy new advertising slogan but politics was a sensitive topic for dinner parties – even when the guests were sober and getting on with each other.

"Time for dessert, you mean Lee?" Derek signalled to his wife.

"Funny, Ha ha. You know what I mean D'rek, time for a change in gov'ment, for Christ's sake." Lee never swore.

"Oh, I think we'll know that on 2nd December," he replied light-heartedly.

"But what Glough Whitmam says is right. Don't you think?"

"I am sure he talks a lot of sense Lee." Derek would generally have offered to fill Lee's glass as a ploy to change the topic but on this occasion he judged it would be adding fuel to the fire. He looked to his wife for assistance.

"I'll get some water," Jewel said and left the table with a sense of urgency.

"Anyway, how are the family, Lee?" Derek thought he was on safe ground.

"We don't see much of them these days," she drawled, holding onto her chair for support.

"Oh, everyone busy I suppose?"

"No, they avoid us."

"That's bullshit Lee," Sam said, crossing his arms and legs.

"Sorry, I didn't mean to intrude." Derek tried to backtrack.

"It's okay Derek. For once he's right. Well nearly. They don't avoid us." Lee's finger moved around the room until it found her husband. "They avoid *him*."

Jewel handed Lee a glass of water but it was declined with a flick of her wrist that would have sent it flying over the carpet if Jewel hadn't reacted quickly.

"And if you want to know where my taste for red wine came from, it was from having lunch with my daughter and her husband on my own, because she's having a baby so that's the end of it for her. So, it's Warwick and me. He's teaching me. He's very know...," she cleared her throat. "Very clever. He's ed-u-cating me in the finer points. So there."

There was an awkward silence while everyone worked out what she meant and Sam's face continued to flush magenta red.

"Oh, yes, he's very knowledgeable about red wine." Derek recalled that Warwick was a member of a cellar club.

"Lee, that's wonderful," Jewel chirped, "that Carol's' pregnant, I mean. Congratulations, your first grandchild. When is the baby due?"

"Fevruary."

"Congratulations buddy." A pat on the back from Derek to Sam.

"Hmph. Thanks mate."

"You both must be very proud," Jewel said.

"And what about Paul? Has he gone back to the UK?" asked Derek, looking once again for safer, unfurrowed ground.

"As quick as he could." Lee attempted to snap her fingers. "Since he wasn't welcome here. His father told him to go," Lee paused and waved her arms back and forth as if she were shooing away a flock of seagulls. "Told him to get – out – of – the – house." She was enjoying centre stage.

"That's enough Lee," Sam said. "Enough drink and enough talk." He stood up in an attempt to exert some authority. "I must apologise for my wife, I have no idea what's gotten into her apart from too much wine."

"You, apologise for me? Well, that's a laugh." Lee's eyes were now half closed and she had to tilt her head back to see through the slits.

"Let's go into the lounge room, shall we?" said Jewel, in an attempt to give purpose to Sam's hovering. "We can have dessert in there where it's more comfortable." Derek didn't want to revive Lee but he was concerned for her safety. The next time she leaned back, she might keep on going and break either the back of their Chiswell dining chair or her own spine.

"Here let me help you dear." He took hold of both sides of the chair and edged it out ever so slowly and guided her away from the table

"Thank you Derek, you were always a furrer gentleman and you know I'm right, don't you?" She leaned into him as he guided her past the side tables – a hand around her waist – and in a stage whisper told him, "You should vote Labor, D'rek, because they aren't like the other mob who hate the homosexuals. Like my Pauly."

Derek was puzzled, did Paul hate homosexuals or was Lee referring to something else? Sam answered his question.

"That's it Lee. We're going. You were told to keep your mouth shut about Paul. Where's the esky?"

"I'm not going anywhere." The short walk had revived her. "I want my dessert."

"Lee, if you say another word!" His right hand was curled into a fist with trembling forefinger pointing at his wife's temple.

"There's nothing you can do to me that would hurt me as much as what you've done already." Her diction had improved. "When you hurt my children, you rip out my heart." To illustrate her point, she grabbed at the front of her cardigan with such force that three of the pearl buttons popped off exposing her Playtex Cross Your Heart brassiere.

"Jesus Christ Lee, what are you doing," Sam cried.

Derek immediately let go of Lee, uncomfortable to be so close to a bare-chested woman who wasn't his wife, and she toppled towards the couch. Jewel caught her on the way down, guided her into a sitting position and passed a cushion for modesty which Lee held tightly to her chest. She began to rock back and forth.

Jewel broke the silence. "Sam, don't go now." She stood up and began to pass the dessert plates and cake forks. "How long have we known you guys, twenty years or more? We know that families go through difficult times."

"Well, you would, wouldn't you, the stress your daughter and that predator's caused all year. And he's still a married man."

The plates clattered and two forks fell to the floor. Jewel turned to her husband.

"He knows about Sally?"

"I sought some legal advice Darling. For her sake."

"From him?"

"And why not?" Lee piped up. "My husband was a very successful lawyer."

"I'm sorry Sam, I didn't mean that." Jewel stammered as she retrieved the cutlery. "It's just that, well, we weren't going to tell anyone. But school's finished now and he'll be divorced soon, he won't be a married man."

Sam and Derek exchanged puzzled glances.

"What was that look for?" Jewel said, turning to her husband. "You should be pleased."

"Jewel, are you sure? They'll be divorced that quickly?" Sam said authoritatively. "This is important."

"Well, yes, that's what Sally said." Jewel turned to Derek. "I only found out this afternoon. I'm sure she said around Christmas."

Sam took the floor, pocketing both hands, rocking back and forth on his size twelve feet. He was tall, about six feet two and stocky with it so that his presence conferred a superiority, if only because of its physicality. Jewel had always thought men's shoes a symbol of dominance. How could a woman in teetering high heels, with strappy bits keeping them together, ever hold sway over someone who walked around in these tokens of power and authority? The practicality of the footwear reminded her that people expect men to get things done while women are supposed to sit around looking pretty.

"Jewel, are you with me? We need to get this right, because if it's that soon, the grounds are clearly not separation. It means his wife could be going him for adultery." Sam avoided stating the obvious but Derek managed to fill in the gaps.

"Jesus Christ." He jumped to his feet as if ready for a fight. "She could be naming Sally as the co-respondent."

"Jewel?" Sam looked to her for confirmation. "Did she definitely say around Christmas?"

"Yes, I think so. I didn't take much notice of the timing. Didn't realise it was so important. You two having your little parleys without me, as if I'm just here to make the tea. She's my daughter too you know."

Lee sighed. "Poor Sally. At least she wasn't seduced by someone of the same sex."

"Lee, you've got a big mouth, keep it zipped," Sam snapped over his shoulder as he waddled towards the bathroom.

Derek stepped in. "Look, let's wait until we talk to her, get our facts straight, okay?"

Jewel agreed, then went to tend Lee who had begun to sob into the cushion. She put her arm around her friend's shoulder and passed over a lace-edged handkerchief.

"Children aren't easy honey. Here, blow your nose."

"Ta." Lee blew forcefully, then wiped the black mascara that was running down her blotched cheeks onto the newly laundered white linen.

"Sam means well Lee," Derek said as he patted her shoulder in a fatherly way.

"He's disowned Paul, and Carol won't even come home anymore." Her nose exploded once more into Jewel's hanky.

Jewel saw Sam striding along the hallway. She stood up and turned towards him.

"Homosexuality is nothing to be ashamed of Sam. I told Lee before and I'll say it again, it makes no difference to our feelings for Paul."

"She bloody told you? Jesus, can't anyone keep a secret around here?"

"Attitudes are changing Sam," Jewel continued, "the thing that hasn't changed is Paul. He's still the same fine young man he's always been."

"How can he be the same. He's got the hots for other blokes!"

"You know Dunstan legalised it in South Australia? It can't be long here." Derek added in an attempt to depersonalise the topic.

"You mean the poofter in pink shorts," Sam snorted.

Jewel moved to the coffee table and single-mindedly began cutting slices of cake. "Here, have some Sachertorte." She passed the first slice to Lee.

"Port anyone?" enquired Derek from force of habit and immediately regretted the offer.

"Yes please," Lee replied, through a mouth full of chocolate sponge.

Sam slumped on the armchair. "Son's a poofter and my wife's an alcoholic. The only one that's normal is Carol and she won't talk to me. Cheers everyone." He downed his port and passed the glass back to Derek for a refill.

"Loverley cake Jewel." Lee returned the empty plate for seconds and slumped back into the lounge, caressing her cushion. They watched her head loll back until it was supported by the back of the couch. Her eyes closed and a gentle rumble rolled along her tongue to escape from her open mouth.

Jewel, Sam and Derek sat in silence and were startled when the phone rang. Lee didn't stir.

"I'll get it," Jewel and Derek said simultaneously but Jewel was first on her feet and Derek deferred to her agility.

"That was Sal love. She's staying at Mazza's. I spoke to Susan, she confirmed they're there."

Derek nodded. Either way, his girl wasn't coming home.

"It's the bloody kids." Sam said standing to attention. "They stuff up your life. You know Steve Thompson?"

"Yeah. Haven't seen him at the club lately."

"He's got a problem with his son."

"The one who went to Vietnam? John, I think."

"Yeah, that's him, Johnno." Sam placed one hand in his trouser pocket and studied his port glass. "Well, the kid went off the rails. Family's distraught. Don't know what to do with him." He took a sip. "Used to be pretty steady, a good kid. A worker. And no problem doing his bit protecting the country from the reds. Saw a bit of action I believe." He drained his glass, laid it on the coffee table.

"Yeah, well I can understand him having troubles," Derek said, "fighting in that war."

"But our kids, they had nothing but an easy life. Too easy probably." Sam the lawyer was working his closing argument and began to sway back and forth, toe to heel, both hands now in his pockets. "Paul should have a wife and two kids by now. That's what he needs. That'd straighten him out." He began to vigorously nod his head. "Yep, that's what he needs, no ifs or buts."

"Sam, you really think it's that easy for Paul? Maybe he doesn't have a choice," Derek said.

"Yes, he does. Why you'd prefer a bloke's arse when you can have pussy. Sorry Jewel," he said without a hint of sincerity.

"I don't get it either," Derek replied. "But it doesn't mean we're right and they're wrong."

"They were just made differently," Jewel added.

"It makes me sick." Sam shook his head.

They sat with their own thoughts while Andy Williams crooned through the last track on the LP and all was quiet apart from the sound of Lee's snoring. The wall clock struck 11.30pm.

"Mate, you never know what's going to happen in life, but you can bet it's not the happy ending you imagined," Sam said.

Lee let out an enormous snort and her eyes blinked open. She looked around the room as if it were the first time she had seen it and then reached for her untouched port and downed it in one.

"Come on Lee, we're going." Sam helped her up before she could ask for a refill and hoisted her into a standing position. "Home to bed," he said as he supported his wife from the room.

"Nite Sam." Jewel kissed him on the cheek. "What about your esky?"

"I'll drop it around tomorrow," Derek said, thankful for a chance to follow up on the night's disclosures. "You're sure you're okay to drive? We can call a cab."

"No, I'm good mate. Thanks again."

Derek closed the door and left the porch light on. He went to collect the empty bottles and Jewel leaned across the table to blow out the candles just as Lee vomited into the garden.

"It's the cold night air," Derek said as they listened to the retching. "Does it every time. Let's leave this till the morning."

he said as he laid the bottles back on the table. "I'm beat. Come to bed." He offered his hand.

Jewel couldn't remember the last time she'd left the mess from a dinner party, nor could she remember feeling this tired.

""I just hope she missed my camellias," she said as they walked up the stairs.

"No chance."

"Darling, what about Sal and the divorce? Is it going to be all right?" she asked anxiously as she took Derek's hand.

"We need to get our facts straight. Let's not think about it tonight."

He sat on the edge of the bed and took off his shoes. "You're not mad about me talking to Sam, are you."

"No, I know you were looking out for Sal."

"Yes honey and I still am." Derek watched Jewel pull back the bed covers. "Aren't you going to take your make-up off and put that gunk on your face?"

"Nope. May as well be completely slack."

"God, I don't know what the world's coming to. But you really are okay about Paul, aren't you?" He lay down and encircled Jewel in his arm. She snuggled up to him, her head on his chest.

"As long as I don't think about what they do. That's what Lee said and I feel the same way."

"Well, that's honest."

"And if we expect Sam to accept Paul's choice in life, shouldn't we accept Sally's?"

"There is a difference Jewel."

"And what might that be?" she asked, propping on an elbow.

"Paul is an adult, he can make up his own mind. Sally's not, she's still an adolescent and we have a duty of care to her. That's what every school teacher has to each of their pupils and that's what Brad Emery chose to ignore."

"But it's gone past that, Darling. You'll have to accept him now, for her sake. I mean these things can break families apart. Look what's happening to the Thurgood's."

"Come here." He tucked her under his arm. "I promise I won't break up our family. Now, go to sleep. It's late and I love you."

28

Ripened Fruit and Umbrellas

It was after five when Emma folded her shorthand notebook, sharpened her pencils and put her typewriter to bed. The doctor's appointment was for five thirty, a ten minutes' walk, so she needed to get a move on.

He would want to know when she had her last period. To pinpoint the date, she tried to think back to where she was when she started to bleed. It was at work, she was sure because she borrowed a tampon from Shahna. That was all she could remember. As she replayed the scene in her mind she realised it was pointless, because one work day was much the same as the next.

The receptionist asked her to fill out a new patient form. She didn't have to lie about her marital status, she still was Mrs Emery. She ticked 'No' to a list of illnesses then hesitated. 'Number of Previous Pregnancies'. No-one need to know that it was before she married. She wrote '1' in the box.

The doctor was young and she thought he probably wasn't long out of medical school. He sent her to the bathroom to take a urine sample and on her return, she handed him the warm container.

She thanked him, paid the bill and left the surgery. As she walked back to work, she was surprised at how calm she felt considering that the direction of her life was once more out of her control. Three days later she went back for the results. Clutching her handbag, she sat on the edge of the chair while the doctor opened the manila folder.

"The results are negative Mrs Emery." He adjusted his glasses. "I note you have no other symptoms which might indicate a pregnancy. Therefore, I wouldn't make any assumptions at the moment. There are many things that can cause irregular menstrual cycles."

She conceded that there had been some tension in her life of late, thanked him and settled down to wait for the mild cramping that preceded her period.

After a few weeks, Emma noticed a subtle and unpleasant nausea wash over her when she woke. She dismissed the sensation as an increased aversion to mornings, but the symptoms persisted and she began to keep a dry biscuit on the bedside table to nibble before she got out of bed. As the urge to urinate intensified, she wore a track to and from the ladies' room, checking each time for a discoloured discharge, the first sign of her period. But there was nothing.

Then one evening towards the end of the following week, she stepped out of the bath and saw herself from the waist up in the mirror that doubled as the door to the bathroom cabinet. At first, she thought the image was a distortion from the steam so she moved closer to clear away the condensation with a circular rub of the towel. She had to stand on her toes to see more clearly but there was no doubt that her nipples were bigger. Not just enlarged, they were dark and plump, like ripening fruit. Her hand went to her mouth and she stifled a cry.

When she began to bring water to her desk each morning, she thought back to a conversation with Mrs O'Toole, as she was pouring her tea, just a few weeks before they were all retrenched. Mrs O'Toole's stories were like a set of Russian dolls, one hidden inside the other.

"My hubby and I tried for years to have a baby and we'd just about given up so I never put two and two together when it happened. I was a teller in the bank at the time and began to get really thirsty, so I plonked a glass of water on the counter before I opened my window in the mornings. One day I was in the lunch room and the young man who worked next to me asked when the baby was due. I told him he didn't know what he was talking about but he pointed out that an insatiable thirst was the first sign his wife had when she fell. He said, 'Mary, you're up the duff', and he was right. It was my Patsy that was causing me to drink up all that water. So that's how I knew the secretary before you, Robyn was her name, that's how I knew she was pregnant. It was the glass of water she had perched right here on this same desk. Six months later Robyn left and you came along. A lovely baby girl Robyn had."

So it was the clear life-giving liquid that confirmed for Emma what the doctor couldn't. She greeted the realisation with a mixture of elation and dread.

When Saturday morning arrived, Emma rose early, in time to let the nausea settle before she met Sandy.

"You're looking good Emm." She was waiting at the station entrance as agreed.

"I like the suede boots. New?"

"No, not new, I'm saving remember."

"You been eating the leftovers at the club?"

"You're observant. A couple of pounds, that's all."

"About time, I was sick of you being the skinny bitch."

As they were walking down the stairs the train arrived, so they quickened their pace. Sandy noticed Emma holding onto the railing and decided that it must be the boots. They talked over where they would go to find the perfect dress for Sandy to wear on her date with Rob to celebrate their fourth anniversary.

"Something that will knock his socks off," Emma said.

"And I'll the get the rest off when we get home," Sandy added with a smirk.

When the train pulled into St James Station, Emma decided to get it over and done with."

"Sand, come and have a cup of tea first, will you? I've got something to tell you."

"Oh no. You're not going back to him?"

"No, I'm not. Come on, let's go up to the tea rooms. It's quiet there."

Sandy ordered coffee and a cream horn, and Emma a pot of tea.

"Well go on, what's the big secret?"

"I think I might be pregnant."

"Jesus Emma." Sandy lurched back in her seat. "You're kidding."

"No, I'm serious."

Sandy leaned forward and whispered, "You sure?"

"It's not confirmed, but I know I am." Emma went through the list of symptoms and Sandy listened with unusual attentiveness.

"Whose is it Emma?"

"No idea," she lied. "Had a couple of one-night stands."

"Really? More than one?" Sandy asked.

"Got sick of being good."

"God Emma, this is all a bit to take in."

"Sorry Sandy. But I needed to tell someone."

"Sure. You need some advice?"

"Sandy, I'm going to have it."

"You can't," Sandy shouted, stopping the waitress in her tracks. "Sorry. Yeah, the cream horn for me, thanks and the coffee." When Sandy glared at her she took off like a shot. "Bloody hell Emma. How far on are you?"

"Not sure. I had a urine test but it must have been too early."

"Then it's not too late to have something done."

"Sandy. I can't go through another abortion," Emma whispered.

"But Emm. Without a father? You're nuts."

"I'm not you know. I've thought this through. Really, I've got it worked out." Her eyes filled with tears. "I want this baby."

"Oh Emm, sorry, I didn't mean to give you a hard time." Her hand reached across the table. There was cream on her fingers. "Was it Johnno?"

"God no. He rang me again by the way, asked me out."

"Maybe you should go. At least he's got money."

"Sandy, you said yourself, he's a psycho and I think you're right. You should have heard him go off the deep end when I said I wouldn't be much company, working nights, I get tired. He swore and hung up on me."

"Yep, I was right the first time." Sandy finished her coffee. "So you really don't know then?"

"Nope. No idea." Emma stared at the teaspoon circling her tea cup.

"How are you going to do this on your own? Have you really thought it through?"

"I've been saving, for a trip to England. So I've got enough to live on for a year and I'll keep working till I'm seven months."

"Great, and what then? Where do you think you're going to live? You going back home?"

"I'm going to live on my own."

"Oh fantastic. Then it's all settled, we can get on with the shopping."

"Sand, don't be like that. I thought you'd be pleased. You'll be the godmother."

"Oh, Emma, honey, it's you I'm worried about. I think this has all been too much for you. You're not thinking straight."

"I feel more settled about the future than I ever have," she said.

"Emm, this isn't going to work. You need a husband to support you."

"Sandy, I'm really happy on my own now. I don't want a man any more. I think they're all too much hard work, and anyway no one's going to be interested in me if I'm preggers."

"You're right about that."

"I can do this." Her head was bowed and tears dropped into her teacup. "On my own."

"Oh, Emmy, you won't be on your own. Rob and I will be there for you, every minute. Give me your hand." She held it tightly and with a sigh, kissed it tenderly.

"People are looking Sandy. Hurry up and finish your coffee and that revolting cake. It's nearly twelve o'clock. We need to get your dress before the shops shut."

An expanse of clothing confronted them as they stepped off the clunky timber escalator to the third floor of David Jones. Sandy dashed from one rack to another, piling her arms high with dresses, skirts and blouses.

"That's gorgeous," Emma exclaimed as Sandy emerged from the fitting room wearing outfit number four, a sheer black Georgette mini with pockets strategically placed over each breast.

"I wouldn't have thought this style would work in a sheer, but it does. Would look great with my sequinned belt, what do you think?"

"Perfect, need a black bra," Emma said. "Can we get out of here? I'm feeling a bit queasy."

"Sorry kiddo. Gonna take time for me to get used to this. But it will be good."

"Yeah, I know it will."

"We've left a bit of a mess I'm afraid," Sandy said apologetically to the sales lady as they left the counter. She turned to Emma. "I want to get a shirt for Rob too. Can you handle that? The men's section is across the road. We can grab some fresh air. You all right to walk and everything?"

"I'm not an invalid."

"Here take my arm anyway, dearie."

"Get lost."

As they walked up the marble steps into the men's store, Emma noticed the profile of a man which had a sense of the familiar. As he turned in their direction, she said out loud, "Couldn't be."

"What?"

"I think that's Greg who used to drive me to work, but he looks different."

"You reckon? Thought you said he was a dork?"

"Maybe it's his good-looking brother."

"Wow, Emma. Hi." Greg smiled in recognition and walked towards her, ignoring Sandy.

"Hi Greg. I wasn't sure it was you." She couldn't help but stare. "Sorry, this is my friend, Sandy."

"Hiya," Sandy said.

"We haven't seen each other since Jackson's folded, have we Greg?"

"No, we haven't. How are you, Emma?"

"Good. What you been up to?"

"I work in the city now. And you?"

"I do too, work in the city." She was surprised and distracted by Greg's changed appearance. His skin had cleared up and his tangle of hair had been shaped into a stylish cut. *Why was he wearing a suit on a Saturday*, she wondered?

"I just finished a meeting with a client, that's why I've got my bag of fruit on." He must have read her mind.

"What are you doing then, for work I mean?"

"I'm qualified now. "

"In?"

"Accountancy. That's what I was studying at night while I was at Thompsons."

"Congratulations. That's amazing."

"What about you Emma."

"Same old, same old. A secretary at Skylark near the Quay. But I'm living at Rose Bay, near the chocolate shop. Not too good for the figure I'm afraid."

"You look really great. So, did everything work out, you know with the....?"

"The marriage? Sort of. It's over. New start for me."

"Oh, sorry, I guess." Greg raised his eyebrows, and stuck out his bottom lip in an attempt to hide a wide grin.

"Thanks Greg," Emma replied with a smile.

"For the best I reckon," he replied, a little too enthusiastically. "Anyway, we've got shopping to do. Good seeing you."

"Yeah, and really great seeing you. Bye Mandy."

Greg stood his ground clutching his DJ's bag as they walked in the direction of the shirt department.

"Why did you shut him down?"

"I didn't mean to. He's just so different."

"And cute. Not good with names, but cute," Sandy said.

"You wouldn't believe how much he's changed."

"He fancies you."

"Rubbish. Anyway, he won't when I start to show."

Emma turned around in time to see Greg duck behind a rack of ties.

"You're interested, aren't you?"

"No, intrigued." She pulled Sandy towards the display of shirts. "What colour do you want?"

"Something to match his baby blues. Emma, can I tell Rob.?"

"Yes, sure, he'll know the colour when he opens the parcel anyway."

"You know what I mean."

"Of course. But ask him to keep it quiet. I'm not going to tell my oldies yet. I'll give them another few weeks of blissful ignorance."

"I wonder what your Mum will say."

"When she recovers from the shock? Divorcee, single mother."

"Promise me you'll have a proper test? Then we'll talk some more."

"I promise, but it's a waste of time."

"In a week, Emm."

"Why a week?"

"Before Greg rings."

"Don't be ridiculous. I'll never hear from him again," she said holding up a blue and white checked shirt for inspection.

They were both wrong. It didn't take a week. On Monday morning, he called at Skylark.

"An umbrella," he said. "You left it in the boot, the day we got the boot." They both laughed at Greg's attempt at a joke and she agreed to meet up after work. To collect the umbrella.

29

Silent and Still

FOR WEEKS JOHN CHEWED OVER the phone call to Emma. Too tired to go out and have fun? No wonder if she's working two jobs. That's not the life she deserves. Brad had never looked after her and working nights was dangerous. She didn't understand the risks. No wonder she was exhausted. Over and over, he gnawed at it like a hungry dog at a bone until he saw clearly what needed to be done. He'd look after her, make her quit the job, buy her a car. Then she could visit her Mum and Dad after work and they'd have weekends free, to spend together.

He let three days pass, then on the afternoon of the fourth dialled the number for Skylark.

"Hello." A voice he didn't recognise answered.

"Emma?"

"No, this is Irene."

"Is Emma there?"

"Is that you Greg? She's just left. Should be waiting for you outside. Have fun you two, she…"

The phone bounced off the side table as John slammed the receiver into the cradle. His anger simmered during a sleepless night and at first light he headed for the beach.

"Bitch, lying bitch," he cursed as he ran along the sand then threw himself into the surf, desperate to have the pounding of the waves drown out the sound of the voice. *Have fun you two.* As he tried to negotiate the churned-up breakers it was obvious he should have chosen his point of entry more carefully. Even now it would make sense to move along the beach but he wanted to pick a fight with something and the sea would do. He rolled onto his back and held onto his board to by-pass a wave that looked okay to start but would end up crap, a bit like his life.

It was a mixture of skill and belligerence that got him into a crouching position for his first ride but the wave was a dumper. It dropped away, slapping the sand before being sucked back into the sea. It threw him against the ocean floor and corkscrewed his shoulder into the sand. He wanted to open his mouth to scream but there was no air, only water. "You bastard," he shouted as he surfaced wasting the little oxygen left in his lungs. He'd come off second best in round one and the pain that he felt when he moved his left arm told him that he wouldn't be going back for another bout.

His feet found the bottom and he waded to shore, his anger seething like the sea that had just beaten him up. *Everything's full of shit* he decided. When he got back from Nam, he could see it, this empty life, for what it really was.

A shower washed away the salt but not the pain in his shoulder. He adjusted the nozzle so that the jet of water massaged the ache. He dried off then chucked a pair of jeans and a shirt into a duffle bag, grabbed a couple of cans and his car keys and headed out the door, determined to get away from her, from his old man, his mother, from everyone. Leave all the crap behind.

John heard the scrape of the passenger wing mirror against the concrete wall as the Triumph lurched out of the driveway. *Stuff it.* He took another swig of his beer and accelerated towards the highway. *Should'a called Pete.* Had the number somewhere but he figured his mate'd be home. He had nowhere else to go, did he?

Emma'd led him on, that's for sure. Chicks do that. Prick teasers. He thought she was different, maybe the only one who was, but he got that wrong too. She was the same as all the rest. He'd never thought he'd get a chance with her, and then he had had it. It was a gift, a dream come true, but like everything else he touched, he stuffed it up. She felt the same, he was sure of it, in the beginning. The way she looked at him. It had been going really well right up until the fake drowning. How did she expect him to react? She should have understood why he lost it. She would have, if she knew how he felt. He should have told her earlier, then it would have made sense to her. Another thing he got wrong. Thought he'd give her time. No point trying now. Couldn't do a bloody thing right. Couldn't keep a job or a chick. Couldn't even catch a bloody wave.

Parramatta Road was chockers with peak hour traffic and lines of semis heading west over the mountains. He turned up the radio and sat with his head leaning on the headrest, eyes closed, waiting for the lights to change. They were all red, one after another. You think they'd share the shit around, but it doesn't work like that. Some people get all the luck, others none. Occasionally a horn would sound when he was slow off the mark, distracted by the throbbing in his shoulder and he'd give them the finger then move off with a wheelspin. *Pricks.*

The traffic started to thin out and he finally nudged the car into third gear. An hour later he was cruising on the open road. It was after seven by the time he got past Orange and the dark was coming in quickly.

Got to watch out for the 'roos. John recalled Pete's warning. Dusk was the worst time. "Stupid bastards see the headlights and do a death run, straight into them."

He crossed his arms and leaned on the wheel, eyes peeled, focused on the road. Around eight, he pulled over to buy a hamburger. The stodgy food felt good, and he wished he'd brought more beers.

It would be shit hot to be with Pete again. You never had to explain to Pete because he understood, never had to answer questions.

Tomorrow, they'd just take off, like when they got back from 'Nam.

He wouldn't have to shoot anything, just go along with his mate into the silence of the bush where no one's on your back trying to make you be something you can't be any more.

No stopping now, have to keep going. He wound down the window and the blast of fresh air felt good but it was too bloody cold so he wound it back up and turned up the heater. The last thing he remembered was his head rolling onto his chest, then the resounding wail of a horn.

Instinctively he slammed on the brakes and swung the wheel away from the blinding headlights. He smelt the pungent burning of rubber, heard the screech of metal on metal, a whiplash noise, a high-pitched whine, then nothing. Like two beady eyes, a pair of tail lights stared at him from the rear vision mirror as the truck accelerated over the hill and into the night.

"Fucking hell. Jesus fucking Christ." John's hands shook as he turned off the motor and sat listening to his heart pump blood and his lungs suck air. He desperately wanted to pee so he threw open the door but as he stood up, his legs struggled to hold his weight and he had to lean against the car for support. His pupils were still contracted from the glare of headlights and the bush was an inky black hole in front of his face. With his good arm he unzipped his pants and the steam of his urine glowed in the light from the car door. He kicked it shut with his foot.

"Got to lie down." To his left, there was a field of tall grass shimmering in the moonlight.

"Cold," He said to himself as he reefed a travel rug from the boot.

The smell of dried dust filled his nostrils as he tried to shimmy under the wire fence on his belly, his nose to the ground like a bloodhound. His left shoulder was pretty useless now, stiff from driving and throbbing like the rotors on an Iroquois chopper. But there was no rescue underway, no safe ground waiting for him. After several attempts, he realised there was no chance he'd get under the fence, so he gave up, rolled onto his back and lay where he was.

"Fucking hell," he said again, and yanked the blanket further around his chilled body that continued to shudder spasmodically. He would need to rest if he was going to make it early to Pete's but when he closed his eyes the headlights were still there, imprinted on the back of his eyelids, like exploded shells. He rolled onto his right side and stared at where he knew the dirt was. He held his gaze until the flashing images faded and the mosaics of broken light retreated into blackness, into nothingness, and he slept.

At first, he thought that the seagulls had gone mad. The bastards woke him up at dawn every time he slept on the beach. But through half-closed eyelids, he registered they weren't gulls. His arm shielded his eyes from the morning sun and he watched a flock of frigging galahs breakfasting on what he'd thought last night was grass.

"Stupid prick,' he scolded himself, "sleeping next to a field of oats."

In an effort to turn away from the squawking, he rolled onto his side, but a jolt of pain from the damaged shoulder threw him back to where he was. He didn't want to get up yet, just wanted to lie there and go back to sleep but the noisy, ravenous horde wasn't going to let him.

"Piss off you bastards!" he screamed but they kept on munching, squealing like a gaggle of women at a morning tea. He pulled the blanket over his head and looked at his watch. Another two hours to Pete's, if he didn't get lost. Better get going. Gear changes would be a bitch with this shoulder, but there wouldn't be many of them on the open road. He tried to brush off the dust as he stood up and, holding onto the fence, made his way to the car.

Would have been bloody ironic to survive Vietnam and then get killed now, he chuckled to himself as he drove up the hill. *Would have solved everything really. Shouldn't have yanked that wheel. Just instinct, eh?*

"Christ, I stink." He had got used to it on patrol, the smell of sweat and urine. But since he'd been back, he'd showered three or four times a day if he wasn't in the water. He didn't want that stench to come back, ever. Would clean up first thing at Pete's.

He made it in two hours and twelve minutes flat. Straight there, as if he'd done it a dozen times. The Bellett was parked well away from the house and he pulled alongside. There was no-one about so he walked towards the sound of the whistling kettle. The screen door objected to being opened. He knocked on the timber frame and waited.

"Bloody hell, who's that at this time of mornin'?" John heard a chair being pushed back and the scraping of heavy boots on timber. Pete's father looked out at him vacantly.

"Yeah, mate?"

"I'm John. Pete's mate." He was about to apologise for being so early but the door was flung open and Pete stepped up. Mr Barker turned away and shuffled back to the table without a word.

"Come in mate. Jeez. Bloody good to see you." Pete's calloused hands held John's.

Mrs Barker was standing by the stove. "Good morning John," she said looking over her shoulder, "some breakfast? You look like you need a good feed."

"Thanks Mrs. B." John removed his hat and hung it on the back of a chair. "Could do with a clean-up first."

"Good to see you mate, good to see you." Pete repeated the words as he walked John to a tap suspended over a chipped terrazzo tub. A few plants were growing in the moisture from the water that spilled onto the red brown soil. John bent down to douse his chest and face and picked up the scent of wild mint. As he straightened up and dried himself on his shirt, the minty smell was replaced by the aroma of fried bacon and hot toast. He was hungrier than he'd been in years.

Mr Barker was engrossed in his newspaper when John walked back in. His gnarled fingers held a pencil that had been sharpened to within an inch of its life. He was either doing a crossword or working out his bets. The source of the yellowing around Mr Barkers fingers lay smouldering in the ashtray. On the dresser was a speckled Bakelite radio that crackled a tune John didn't recognise. Bacon and eggs sizzled in the cast iron frypan.

Pete handed John a piece of one-inch thick white toast dripping butter.

"Here mate, get started on that."

John bit into it greedily.

"Tea?"

"Thanks Pete."

"Still three sugars?"

John nodded, wiping the grease from his chin.

"And to what do we owe the pleasure of your company, eh?" Pete tore his slice of toast apart with his teeth.

"Oh, just thought I'd see what was happening out west for a bit."

"Not much. Still as dry as a witch's tit." John looked for a reaction from Pete's mum, but she remained engrossed in splashing fat onto the egg yolks that were as yellow as the fields of sunflowers he'd passed on the way up.

"What you got in mind?"

"Not sure mate, wondered if you wanted to do a bit of shooting."

Pete looked to his Dad who raised only an eyebrow. "Jobs needin' doing around here first," he said with a grunt.

They sat back as Mrs Barker passed the plates around and shared out the contents of the frypan. Everything came thick around here, the toast, the bacon and the flies. They were already buzzing outside the windows, attracted by the heat and kitchen smells.

"Don't let me stop you though. Take the ute. Been a couple of days since the dogs had fresh meat."

"Sure. No problems." John sipped his tea and they ate in silence. Mr Barker stood up, stretched, then ran his fingers up and down his braces. He put his folded newspaper on the dresser and turned to Pete.

"Shed in five minutes." He nodded to John and left.

Mrs Barker untied her apron. "I'll make up the bed in the lean-to love." She handed him a spongy parcel of sandwiches, held together by brown paper and string. "Take this with you. You get hungry shooting, I know."

"Thanks Mrs B. Much appreciated."

"No trouble love."

Pete came in holding his twelve-gauge under and over.

"Here. mate. And some ammo. A dozen cartridges, still in the box. Barrel open when you're on the move, remember?"

"You'll be wiping my arse next."

"Can I help it if you look like a dumb bastard." Pete playfully punched John's shoulder as he walked past. John winced.

"What's wrong with you?"

"Nothing that won't mend."

"Head north. Then walk in from the bridge. See ya t'nite. Maybe come with you tomorrow," he said as he walked towards the shed.

Mrs Barker was engrossed in the washing up and her radio. She hadn't missed an episode of Blue Hills since December 1952 and cursed herself for not tuning in three years earlier. She didn't notice John leave the kitchen and slide into the seat of the trusty FJ Forty. The gear shift was stiff and the clutch took up with a jolt. He reversed past his Triumph and sent up a cloud of dust as he took off up the drive. For a moment John imagined himself back in 'Nam, in one of those shonky Land Rovers. At least now he was the only one with a gun. The empty passenger seat was another reminder that life never went the way you planned.

It took fifty minutes to find the timber bridge and it rattled its objections as he passed over. Tyre prints in the dried mud guided him onto flat ground where he pulled over, turned off the motor and sat in the silence. There was nothing beautiful about this part of the country. Everything here would struggle to survive and often it didn't. Skeletons of trees that had given up the ghost were dotted amongst the brown stubble that crackled as he passed over.

Down by the creek, if you could call it that, was the odd patch of green on the banks. He'd follow the water course in the hope of catching a 'roo feeding.

For over three hours John walked without stopping and the sun was high when he found flowing water and crouched down to drink. He stood up and wiped his mouth with the back of his hand. With one arm blocking out the sunlight, he surveyed the land around him. The country had improved as the creek grew in size, spreading its life force out into the land. About one hundred feet away he saw a buck, big bastard about five feet tall, eating the tender grass close to the water's edge. John took a round out of his jacket and loaded.

The noise of the gun cocking startled the animal but John held his position behind a tree stump and the 'roo went back to its feeding. He waited a moment and let his breathing steady, then checked to see if the buck was still there. It seemed oblivious to the world but John knew they were always on alert. Slowly, he raised the gun and pointed the barrels at the buck's head. He would want a clean shot, didn't want to injure it and have a chase on his hands. The image of an injured animal distracted him and the roo, a primal alarm ringing in its head, sensed his hesitation. Its ears twitched urgently, like antennae, instinctively searching out the sound that would confirm the presence of danger.

That's right mate. You can be eating the good grass one day and the next minute you're blown out of existence. John felt powerful. He had the ability to control a life with a movement of his finger.

The 'roo sprang forward even before the gun went off as its ears picked up the sound of John readjusting the position of the gun. A flock of galahs exploded from the tree tops as it discharged and the sound rippled across the countryside. There were no mountains or hills to stand in the way or to allow it to return as an echo. It kept going, unimpeded, into the void. As if in shock, the land became silent and still.

30

A Man of My Word

ALTHOUGH DEREK'S EYES REMAINED CLOSED against the morning light, he lay wide awake, regurgitating the words that had stolen his night's sleep, the words that denied him any chance of nodding off again – *divorced around Christmas.*

Jewel stirred as he climbed out of bed. "What are you up to getting up so early?"

"Nothing Jewel. Go back to sleep."

"You're going to Sam's, aren't you?"

"Might be."

"Don't think Lee will be up to making you breakfast," Jewel murmured as she rolled onto her side, arms wrapped around her duck-down pillow.

"Be back soon." Derek kissed the soft curls that had fallen over her cheek.

Two hours later she was in the kitchen, enjoying her second cup of Darjeeling, when Derek's car drove into the garage.

"Tea?" she asked as he walked into the kitchen.

"No thanks," he said, hanging up his keys. "Managed to make myself some at Sam's. But I could do with a coffee."

The Nescafe was spooned into a mug, the hot water, then the milk added. Jewel slid the brew along the kitchen bench. "How long do I have to wait Derek?"

"Sorry Honey," he blew on the hot liquid, "It's not clear cut. Sam agrees, we have to make sure of the facts before we can decide what to do. It's all hearsay at the moment."

"And what if I'm right, what if it is Christmas?"

"Then I'm afraid it looks like adultery."

"Oh God no. And Sally?"

"She could be named co-respondent. If she isn't named, then the logical conclusion is that she's not the only one."

Jewel's fingers moved to her lips as she stifled a distressed cry. "Oh, Derek. What a mess."

He gave his wife's back a gentle rub. "When's Sal home?"

"She didn't say exactly. Sometime today, after the beach."

The Sunday rituals went on as usual although Derek had trouble concentrating on the crossword and Jewel burnt the roast. They agreed to forgo the bottle of red and were seated in the lounge room with the curtains open when the V-Dub pulled up.

Derek jumped to his feet and Jewel reached forward to pull him back down.

"Darling, wait. He's not coming in. Let Sal get inside and settle for a moment."

"I suppose so," he agreed, setting off for the kitchen with Jewel close behind.

"Hi Mum. Hi Dad," Sally called, coming in to join them.

"Good movie honey? What'd you see?" Jewel asked.

"Love Story."

Derek rolled his eyes.

"Don't be like that Dad," she said, peering into the open fridge.

"Sally, sit down. We need to talk." Derek patted the stool opposite.

"Now?"

"Sit down Sal." The fridge door slammed shut.

"Tea anyone?" Jewel had hold of the kettle.

Sally shook her head no and looked down at her clasped hands.

"Sally this is important. Look at me," Derek said, placing his finger under her chin and raising it so that their eyes met.

"I want you to think clearly. Did you say that Brad would be divorced around Christmas?"

"Yep," she said. She looked from her father to her mother and back. "Thought you'd be pleased."

"You're sure?"

"That's what he said."

Derek's hands gripped the sides of the bench top and he drew air into his lungs. "Sally have you got any idea what this means?"

"Well it means he's not married anymore."

Derek caught Jewel's eye and realised it would be best to let the remark pass. "What it means, Sally, is he's being petitioned for adultery." There was a measured pace to his words. "You, young lady, could be named in that petition."

"No, you're wrong. It's not adultery."

"You don't know what you're talking about Sally. That's how you get a quick divorce."

"Well I can only tell you what I was told." She crossed her arms. "And don't shout at me Dad. Please."

"What were you told?" he said, his voice restrained but his eyes wide.

"It's habitual drunkenness."

"What!" A simultaneous outcry from each parent.

"Look, don't go off the deep end. It's just a quick way, like you said, to get out of his marriage."

The kettle was spitting water onto the stove and Jewel reached across to turn it off.

"We want it this way, Dad. Otherwise it'll take years."

"So he's a drunk as well as a liar."

"You never give up do you, Dad." She stood at full height then added, "Anyway, Mrs Emery wants it too, but I don't suppose you believe me about that either." Then she stomped out of the kitchen.

A moment later they heard her bedroom door slam shut.

Derek turned to his wife. "Sally wants to get married straight away Jewel. I'll lay odds on it. I bet that's why she wants this to go through quickly."

"She promised she wouldn't do anything silly, Darling."

"I don't believe she has any idea what silly is any more. What she needs is time to come to her senses. Waiting years sounds good to me. She certainly won't get our blessing."

"Oh my God. This is what I was frightened of."

"What?"

"Can't you see? If you mess this up, if we're the cause of them being kept apart – we'll lose her! Can't you see what's happening?"

Derek took his wife in his arms, breathing deeply, in an effort to slow his heart rate. "Darling, what's happening is we're frightened for Sally. Just let me sort this out properly and then we'll talk."

Jewel reached for the paper towel dispenser and tore off a sheet. She blew her nose. "You can't stand in her way."

"You're presuming she's got her facts straight. Although I doubt it. Sam didn't mention habitual drunkenness. But what if Sally's got it right – does that mean he's a drunkard? The wife would know the truth, wouldn't she?"

"You're going to contact her again aren't you?"

"Well, you can't trust him."

"Oh God. I prayed nothing like this would happen."

"I don't see any other way. She can confirm everything Sally said, about the divorce and his drinking."

"You can't involve Sally this time. She'd never talk to you again. So how are you going to find the wife? The place she worked closed down, didn't it?" Jewel could sense Derek's mind working through the problem.

"Not the constructions side, Darling, it's still going. They'd still have all the personnel records. They'd have her next of kin contact details. Shouldn't be too difficult."

"Really?" Jewel paused. "Oh… of course, Sam. Good old Sam" Jewel slapped her knee, "He probably plays golf with the owner."

"I think he knows him."

"And what then, what if Sally is right?"

"Let's cross that bridge when we come to it."

"Derek, if this drunkenness thing is only a way to get this done quickly, then you must promise to let it go. You can't expect Brad to wait years. He's a mature man who's been married. Think about it."

"I'd rather not," he replied sharply and left the room.

Two days later, Sam came up with the goods. Derek considered telling Emma's mother the whole story but decided God would forgive him another white lie. He rang the family phone number and a very obliging Mrs Saunders willingly passed on her daughter's new work number to an old friend from Jacksons. Getting a meeting with Emma however, proved more difficult and Derek believed it was the combination of her good nature and his heartfelt pleas that eventually got her across the line.

"There's a milk bar next door," she said reluctantly, "I'll meet you there tomorrow at ten but I only have fifteen minutes for morning tea." This was home territory for Emma, where she would often meet Greg for lunch.

Derek was sitting in a booth at the back and stood up as she approached. "Hello Emma, thank you for coming."

"Hello Mr. Watson. Would you like something to drink?" She beckoned to Effy, the daughter of the owner, who took his order. "The usual for me, please Effy," she said as she slid across the padded booth seat opposite and waited for him to begin.

"Thank you for again seeing me Emma."

She looked directly at him. "What can I do for you, Mr Watson?"

He cleared his throat, then began, "Sally tells me the divorce is going through quickly. Would you be able to tell me on what grounds?"

"Habitual drunkenness," she said, clasping her hands and resting them on the Laminex table top.

"Then she was right." He slumped into the hard timber seat as the ginger beer and tea was being delivered.

"Thanks Effie," Emma poured the pale amber liquid into her cup and added milk,

Derek leaned in towards her. "He's a drunkard then?"

"No, not really. I don't want to be married anymore and neither does he. This is a quick way out."

Derek lowered his voice. "What do you mean, 'not really'?"

"He drank a bit but I think it was because he was unhappy in our marriage."

"Chicken and egg, isn't it Emma?"

"Maybe." She shrugged and watched Effie lingering in the adjacent booth, topping up the salt and pepper shakers.

Derek waited until she moved away. "Emma, I don't want this to happen quickly. I want Sally to wait."

"Well, they don't want to wait and neither do I. With all respect Mr. Watson, it's really not your decision."

He paused to avoid reacting, to regroup his thoughts. "Sally needs time Emma. She's too young to marry."

She looked him in the eye. "Mr Watson, I have my own reasons for not wanting to be married to Brad for the next four and a half years." Her left hand rested on her belly. "And I have to be honest with you. They don't include what Sally needs."

Derek managed to disguise his surprise at the change in Emma. He cleared his throat. "This could be construed – correct me if I am wrong, but isn't it collusion?

Emma's right hand formed a stop sign. "You once asked me if there was anything you could do for me. I'm asking you now, don't interfere in this."

Derek poured the last of his ginger beer into his glass.

"You could ask her to wait to get married," Emma suggested.

"It's not that easy I'm afraid."

"Nothing is." Emma said firmly.

"Emma, it meant a lot to us, Sally being able to finish school. She's been accepted into Uni you know, she'll do really well."

He caught a look of antipathy from Emma and silenced himself.

"That's good Mr Watson," she held his gaze, "but you haven't answered me."

"Ah, yes." Derek stroked his chin. "He was stupid to leave you Emma."

"But he did," Emma lowered her eyes, stirred her tea then looked directly back up at him. "You won't stand in the way then." Her monotone made it clear she wasn't asking a question.

He patted her hand then cleared his throat. "I am a man of my word."

Emma slipped her handbag over her arm. "I have to go now Mr Watson."

"Of course. Thank you for coming."

Emma returned Effie's broad grin with a nod, as she passed through the café doors.

31

A Botticelli Angel

With a thud, Pete pushed his chair back from the table, stood up and stared out the window. His father's eyes remained focused on the form guide while Mrs Barker stood with her back to the men, drying the dishes. As she hung up the tea towel she said what they were all thinking, "John's late."

"Yeh. Dogs still starvin'," Mr Barker said, wetting the tip of his pencil. "City blokes. Reliable as a second-hand chainsaw."

"I'll leave John's tea in the oven Pete." She nodded to her son, with a shared look of concern.

"May as well feed it to the dogs," Mr Barker mumbled, a damp rolly hanging from the corner of his mouth.

"I'm going for my bath." Mrs Barker squeezed Pete's shoulder as she left the room.

When he heard the water running, Pete reached for the keys to the Falcon. "Goin' for a drive."

His father grunted from behind the newspaper.

The directions were straightforward. No way Johnno could get lost. Pete ran through other possibilities in his head. The FJ was in good nick, plenty of petrol so he didn't expect to see it by the side of the road. Anyway, someone would have picked his mate up by now and dropped him back. Pete switched on the spotlights and scanned both sides of the road in case the stupid bastard had rolled it into a ditch. An hour later a bumper bar glinted back at him, just past the bridge. John had got this far.

"Johnno. Mate. Cooee." The black night swallowed his call. He waited. The silenced frogs started up again then he tried a second time. "Johnno," he hollered, "cooee." A quick recce of a hundred-yard perimeter revealed nothing. Pete kicked the soil as he made his way back to the truck to wait for sun-up. He was good, but no one could track in the dark.

Couldn't sleep. The dogs had chewed up the back seat and the front seat wasn't much better. He kept knocking his shins against the steering wheel as he rolled around trying to find a comfortable position. Besides, a knot in his gut kept him in a semi-conscious daze. When at last the stars began to fade, he kicked open the door, stood up, stretched, then rolled his first cigarette of the day. Dawn arrived as he took a last drag then ground the butt into the dirt with the heel of his boot. When he reached the creek, he crouched down, took off his Akubra and scooped up a hat-full of night-chilled water, quenched his thirst then washed the tiredness out of his eyes.

Pete picked up Johnno's trail straight off. It followed the meandering curves of the bank and Pete upped his pace. Around the next bend, a big 'roo was feeding. It took off as soon as he heard Pete's boot crunch in the grass. *Jumpier than usual. They wouldn't normally leave a good patch so quickly.* The trail was leading to the first waterhole and he followed reluctantly. Over the last two and a half hours, there had been no response to his calling. Then he spotted Johnno up ahead, in the grass, a hand over his eyes as if shielding his face from the impending daylight.

Pete cupped his cold fingers around his lips. "Johnno, mate." His breath froze in the air. So bloody cold. No reply. The only reason you'd stay out in this weather was because you couldn't make it back. Maybe Johnno's broken something. Maybe his leg.

That'd slow him down, for sure. As he got closer he saw John's other arm, bent back in a way that wasn't natural. No one would lie like that unless they had no choice. He stopped where he was, right there, because until he saw different, there was a chance John could be alive. If he was wrong, it was the only way he knew to prolong his mate's life.

"Garn, piss off you bastards." Mournful black crows were hovering in the tree nearby.

Pete took one hesitant step, then another, until he could no longer deny what he feared. "Oh Jesus, no. What've you gone and done? Oh Jesus, mate." He laid his gun on the ground and when he moved John's arm away from his face, he could see bone, splattered amongst a congealed mass of blood that had gone black and hard. Pete knew his mate wouldn't like the way his hair was sticking up, like he'd seen a ghost, and his first instinct was to flatten it down, put it back into place. But he let it be. It didn't seem that important now.

The liquid blue eyes had faded into lifelessness and Pete's hands trembled as he placed his fingers onto John's eyelids and folded them towards the colourless cheeks. Ants were already crawling in the mess and he used his sleeve to gently wipe them away.

It was the heat of the sun on his back that made Pete sense the passing of time and he knew he needed to leave. Pete had never kissed a man before and looked around make sure no-one was about. He bent forward and placed his mouth onto his friend's bloodless lips. Then he put John's arm back over his head where he found it and took off his jacket, laid it over John's face and tucked it in so the birds wouldn't get at him.

Mrs Barker was standing in the yard, washing basket on her hip. He saw her raise her head and look further up the road, to see if the FJ was following. When she met his gaze, he knew that he wouldn't need to explain what had happened.

"Come on Son, I'll make you a cuppa." She waited until he was by her side, laid the washing on the ground and together they walked towards the house.

"I should'a gone with him."

"No, you shouldn't. Your place was here. You had nothing to do with it."

"But I gave him the gun."

"It was what he wanted. You weren't to know."

Pete weighed up the meaning of his mother's words, she had a sixth sense for things like this. It didn't matter now. It was too late to help him and maybe she was wrong. It had happened before, blokes who knew their way around guns, get sloppy and blow their heads off.

"Here son. Drink this." She added a dram of brandy to the thick black tea that had been stewing on the stove. The Blue Hills theme song was playing. She turned off the radio.

"Been to the police station yet?"

"Yeh, went there first. Ben was on. Took him back out with me. Showed him where. He called in the head coppers. Said they'd want to talk to me, being first there and all that."

"Do you know John's family?"

"Nope." He struggled to hold the mug steady.

"Leave it to the coppers then. I'll get you a change of clothes."

Pete pushed the chair back and stood tall, pulling up through his body the strength to go on with the day as if nothing had happened, because that was the way it was for them. A moan escaped from his throat that spoke to the sorrow and loss that was deep in his gut but couldn't be put into words. He was glad his mother was out of the room.

"Your father could do with a hand Son" Mrs Barker said as she handed Pete a clean pair of jeans and shirt. "Got to get the sheep down before Friday."

He buttoned his fly, pulled on his boots and walked onto the verandah. The Triumph stood like a red sore on the landscape. Pete drove it into the shed and closed the doors.

It took about five weeks for the coroner to issue his findings. Death by accident.

"You going to the funeral love?" his mother asked when Pete told her.

"I'll be away the whole day. Dad'll have to manage."
She nodded her approval.

If he left at 2 am, figured he'd make it to the crematorium in time. Parking outside the main gate and walking in seemed to be the best way to get his bearings. He thought about borrowing a suit but decided Johnno wouldn't recognise him, looking down from above, and he wanted his mate to know he'd come.

The gravel crunched under his feet and there was a bank of rain clouds moving in from the south. A gardener directed him to the chapel and he turned along the pebbled pathway. *Johnno wouldn't be at home here*, he thought to himself as he walked past the 'Keep off the Grass' sign. Beyond a bed of flowers, planted in rows of colour in a way that they would never grow naturally, he looked up to see a girl staring at him and slowed as he approached.

"Pete?" she called way before he knew who she was.

"Yeah?"

"Jane, Jane from Gilgarra."

"The school teacher. Yeah. Hi Jane."

"I'm back in Sydney. Obvious, I guess," she smiled.

"Johnno said you were coming back."

She began to walk briskly towards him, a broad smile on her face, her ponytail swaying to the rhythm of her steps.

"So, he's back, too, is he?"

"That's not why you're here Jane? For John?"

She stopped short. "No, my fiancé's buried here Pete."

"I'm sorry Jane. I didn't know." Pete mumbled then stood silently, his hat in hand.

"Oh my God, you mean you're here because...." her hands covered her mouth because not saying it would stop it being real.

He regretted that he told her then while he was too far away to reach her in time to stop her falling. He managed to get her to one of those benches with a plaque on it, then he explained about the accident because she wanted to know the details. He was sorry, he said, apologised to her because it seemed the right thing to say. When finally she finished blowing her nose and wiping her eyes, he stood up.

"I have to go Jane," he bowed his head, his fingers gripping the brim of his Akubra.

"Of course." She touched his hand. "I would have come for him, you know that, if I had known."

"Sure. Anyway, look after yourself Jane." A few steps on, he turned back and gave her his number, in case she needed anything, he said. As he walked on, he wondered what happened to her fiancé.

As Pete approached the chapel, he could see a crowd milling around outside. He stayed back, watched and waited. At the entrance a man stood with his arm around a woman. She sobbed continuously into a hanky as they accepted condolences from a line of mourners. *Probably Johnno's parents* Pete thought. His Dad had called their house a couple of weeks after Johnno died. Mr Thompson knew that Pete had been the last person to see his son alive, wanted to know that Johnno was okay that day, before it happened. So Pete obliged, as best he could. The bloke was raving a bit, didn't have it all together, which was understandable. Kept going on about how he should have looked after his son better. Shouldn't have been so hard on him. Seemed like he was doing a big guilt trip down the phone line. In the end Pete just let him talk and eventually Mr Thompson ran out of puff.

Pete continued to watch as two cars pulled up. Some blokes on their own got out and some with girls. Most of them looked like they spent a fair bit of time in the sun and reminded him of the way Johnno looked when they first met. Last time he'd opened the door to his mate, he'd looked nothing like that. The mischievous spark in his eyes had been replaced by a gnawing emptiness. Felt like you could see right into his skull. It could have been a premonition, a momentary vision of Johnno stalked by death, if Pete believed in that stuff.

He scanned the crowd from under the brim of his hat. The girls were all pretty, and dolled up a bit too much for a funeral Pete thought. But none of them matched the image of the girl John spoke of during their two years in 'Nam. A brush stroke here, another there, a *Botticelli Angel* he called her, an angel with no name, the one who slipped through his fingers. Pete told him he was soppy bastard, going on about her, but since then Pete had put the pieces together. Her name was Emma and she wasn't gone, she was still around, married to his mate.

He waited a good five minutes after the last person had gone inside before he made his way to the door. It was a full house and he had to squeeze into an already packed aisle near the back. A bloke tapped him on the shoulder and he turned around to accept the booklet handed to him. It was then he saw her coming through the door. Johnno had got the description down pat. A newborn complexion, hair that caught the light as it wove around itself and lips, full and soft like a ripened fruit. Then he knew what those angels looked like.

'Order of Service' it said on the front page of the booklet and a photo of Johnno was staring at him. But not a Johnno he remembered, a much younger version, with an innocence yet to be snatched away by the ravages of war. The priest up front tapped his microphone. Didn't know Johnno was a Mick, not that it would have made any difference. Religion wasn't something they talked about, even when things were looking bad. God seemed a long way away in 'Nam and Pete preferred to think he had nothing to do with the fighting. It was humans that got themselves into that shit and they had to get themselves out of it. God, if he existed, wouldn't be rushing to save any of them.

The words of the hymns were on the second page, which was lucky because nobody seemed to know them. He tried to follow the prayers but lost his place with all the standing up and sitting down. People started crying when Mr Thompson broke down, couldn't get through his speech and a mate had to take over, read the words he had written.

The coffin was already up the front. Polished wood, big shiny handles. There was no way he could imagine his mate in that box. He had never met any of Johnno's friends or family and he meant to keep it that way. Most of them never even knew he existed but he'd bet his bottom dollar he knew Johnno better than any of them. It sounded like the priest was finishing up. *Don't need to see the last bit*, Pete decided, so he stood up and as delicately as his bulk would allow, edged his way to the end of the pew. He took one last look at Emma as he walked past and the girl sitting next to her gave him a proper going over.

By taking the long way around to the car, Pete figured he'd avoid running into Jane again. The rumbling of an empty stomach reminded him that he hadn't eaten since four am. The pub just over the mountains did good hamburgers. He'd stop there and toast his friend with a nice cold schooner.

32

What a Mess

"Did you see that?" Sandy whispered.

"What?"

"The guy wearing the big hat. He stared right at you. You think he's the bloke from the country, the one who found Johnno?"

"I've no idea. That was his mate from Vietnam, wasn't it?" Emma asked.

"Yep. Another nutter."

"Brad's here Sandy," Emma said softly.

"So are all our friends. Your point?"

"He's on his own."

"For God's sake! Don't you read anything into it, hear me. Why should his floosie come? She didn't know Johnno."

A woman in the pew behind tapped them both on the shoulder, "Hush you two." Sandy nudged Emma in the ribs and rolled her eyes.

While heads were bowed during a final prayer, Emma took another quick glance to her left. Brad's hair was longer and he was tanned. The divorce would be through by the time their child was born. She placed a hand on her belly. *Was it the right decision not to tell him? Would it have changed anything, or everything?* She shifted in her seat to relieve the dull ache in her lower back that had been troubling her since early morning. *Even if he works it out, he can never own up.*

As they raised their heads, Greg patted her arm. "You okay?" She felt his reassuring warmth as he leaned towards her. "Your back still troubling you?"

"Just a little."

"Be over soon." He squeezed her hand.

A loud gasp from the mourners brought Emma's attention to the front of the room. The coffin started to move along a conveyor belt into the cremation chamber. Mr. Thompson leapt out of his seat and for a moment it looked as if he was going after it. A big burly man jumped up, grabbed Mr Thompson by the arms and held him back before he collapsed, sobbing into his mate's shoulder.

"Oh, the poor man," Emma gasped.

As the heavy velvet curtains closed, a Beach Boys song played over the sound system. The quietened mourners sat in silence. *God only knows what I'll do without you, John.* Emma sobbed silently.

As they rose and made their way along the pew into the aisle, Emma tapped Sandy on the shoulder, "I want to go to the wake."

"Forget it. We all agreed no wake and anyway, Greg said he's got to get back to work."

As they emerged from the chapel, Emma noticed dark clouds like an ink blot spread across the sky. Drops of rain dotted the footpath. She felt a reassuring hand on her shoulder.

"I'll get some umbrellas," Greg said then took off in a jog towards his car.

"Over here, Emma," Sandy called and pulled her to the side of the building.

"What is it?" Emma demanded.

"Why do you need to go to the wake?"

"For Johnno."

"You've done your bit. You're here."

"It's because of the last time that I spoke to him."

"What about it?"

"He wanted to go to the beach. I knocked him back. He got really angry and hung up." Emma's voice broke. "And a week later he was dead."

"You think you're responsible?"

"What if I'd gone? What if I talked to him?"

"Emm, you should have been a nun, wanting to save everybody. Seriously, don't even go there, you dumbo."

"I can't help but wonder, if I had, would he be alive?"

"Emma, it was an accident. You know something the Coroner doesn't?

"I still want to go to the wake."

"Tell me this isn't about Brad, Emma. I saw you staring at him."

"Sandy, please try and understand, you can't just stop loving someone because they've stopped loving you. It's not a switch you can turn off. Believe me, I've tried so hard."

"It's all those hormones running around your body. You're not thinking straight."

"Probably."

"Good then let's agree, no more stupid thoughts." Sandy looked around, "Greg's here, come on." They linked arms and disappeared into the crowd of mourners.

"Don't blow this with him, Emma," Sandy whispered, "he's such a good guy. God, he'll even meet you in a milk bar where they don't serve beer. He walks you to the station." Sandy turned to face Greg with a broad grin, "and here he is with umbrellas." She looked over his shoulder to see Roslyn walking their way.

"Thanks so much. You must be Greg," Roslyn said, "you were smart bringing umbrellas."

"You're welcome to share one, and you're?"

"Roslyn, and this is my husband Darren, Rob's brother.

Sandy kissed Roslyn's cheek. "Sad day, eh," she said and heads nodded in general agreement.

"You going to the wake?" Darren asked.

"No we're not," Sandy got in quickly. "Greg and Rob have to get back to work."

"We'll probably skip it too. Stuff to do," Darren agreed.

"Poor Johnno," Roslyn dabbed her eyes with a handkerchief, "I feel so sorry for his Dad."

"At least he can be proud of his son." Darren put his arm around his wife. "Did his bit keeping us safe from the Commos,"

"You really think they were a threat?" Greg asked.

"No point in taking any chances. Better dead than red, mate."

"Not the best choice of words today Dazza," Rob chimed in.

Heads turned as Brad strode from the chapel towards the parking lot, his head bowed and hands in his pockets.

"Good riddance to bad rubbish," Roslyn mumbled. A few pursed lips, a few sniggers. "Guess what?"

"I think you're going to tell us, Ros," Bernadette replied as she ducked under Sandy's umbrella. "Hi everyone."

"Where's Barney?" Sandy asked.

"Gone to get the car and probably have a smoke. I think Tony's with him, Michelle should be here somewhere. Sorry Ros, I interrupted. What's your news?"

"I'm going to go to Uni."

"What for?" Bernadette and Sandy said in unison.

"To do an arts degree."

"I'm really envious," Emma said. "I always wanted to go to Uni."

"Yeah, well we couldn't have afforded it before but looks like the Labor party will abolish fees."

"Really? That's great." Emma said. "And I hear Kerry's got her own business."

"God, isn't anyone happy just doing ordinary stuff?" Sandy quipped.

Michelle tapped her on the shoulder. "Who's ordinary?"

"Oh, hi. No-one. That's the point. How are you anyway, Michelle?"

"Wonderful actually. Tony got a promotion."

"Congratulations to him," said Sandy.

"And," she waited until all eyes turned to her, "we're selling the house to buy something bigger," she feigned a whisper "on the water."

"See what I mean?." Sandy replied. "Michelle's going to be filthy rich. Roslyn's going to be a genius and Kerry's going to be a tycoon."

Michelle moved closer to Emma. "What about you sweetie?" she whined softly, "coping all right on your own?"

"Oh, we haven't introduced you to Greg, have we Michelle?" Sandy interrupted. "Michelle, meet Greg, Emma's boyfriend."

He was smiling broadly as he extended his hand. "Hi Michelle."

"Nice to meet you Greg." she said.

"Sorry Michelle, but we have to get going," Sandy added, "Boys got to get back to work."

"Hope to catch up again," Greg said, taking hold of Emma's hand as they walked to the car.

Michelle grabbed Sandy by the shoulder. "We're all so glad that you-know-who's gone. Her new bloke looks lovely."

"He is," Sandy replied, "better catch up to them. See you guys."

"Not the best way to spend an afternoon." Rob said as they reached the parking lot. "Thanks for coming Greg,"

"No problems. Thanks for dropping Emma home." He turned to Emma. "Same time, same place tomorrow, eh?"

Sandy watched as they kissed then she squeezed into the front of Rob's ute, Emma by her side.

"You look like shit. Did Michelle upset you?" Sandy said.

"No, it's not that. I've still got that back pain."

"Come home with us then. You don't want to be in the grotty flat tonight. Sleep in tomorrow. If there has to be a funeral it's better on a Friday, I say."

Rob treated them to take-away Chinese, eaten on their laps in front of TV, watching an episode of Homicide. Emma carried the empty plates to the kitchen.

"Good chow mein. Thanks Rob. You want to keep the leftovers?"

"Nup. Chuck them out." Sandy yawned. "I'm going to bed if you guys don't mind?"

"I'm with you." Emma stood up, arched her spine and pressed flattened palms into her lower back.

"Here Emm." Sandy opened the kitchen draw and took out a packet of Aspros. "Take two, help you sleep."

The Aspros worked for the first couple of hours but for the remainder of the night Emma's sleep was fitful. As the painkillers wore off, the backache intensified and by dawn she was experiencing sharp abdominal cramping. When Sandy knocked at the door she had been wide awake for well over an hour.

"Wakey, wakey. Brought you a cuppa."

"Thanks," she said wrapping her fingers around the warm mug. "Lovely."

"Move your legs," Sandy propped on the edge of the bed. "Sleep okay?"

"Had better."

"Your back?"

"Yeah. Still aching. And Sand, I've had pains most of the night. There's another one." Sandy grabbed the mug of tea as Emma doubled over.

"Lie on your side and pull your legs up," Sandy said. She lifted the blankets so Emma could turn over. Her eyes moved to the white sheets. "Emm, there's blood on the sheet."

"Oh, no. I'm sorry."

"Don't! Don't get up. Stay there." Sandy ran to the bathroom. "Can you get this under you?" She slid a towel along the bed. "You got another pain?"

Emma's face contorted.

"Breathe, Emm. Slowly."

"I'm trying, but they're getting worse, Sand."

"I'm going to call a doctor, okay. Just in case. Don't move. Stay where you are."

Sandy tore down the stairs. "Rob! Rob!" A moment later, she was back. "The doctor's on his way. Rob's waiting up top for him. Just relax, okay."

The perspiration was trickling down Emma's temples. "This shouldn't be happening, should it?" she said in a small voice.

"I've put the kettle on."

"I don't want more tea, for God's sake."

"For a hot water bottle!" Sandy yelled as the whistling of the kettle sent her racing down the stairs for a second time.

Emma moaned as the pain clawed at her belly.

Sandy burst into the room. "Here Emm, the hot water bottle." She pulled back the sheets.

"Oh no. There's more blood – look!" Emma cried.

"Oh God!" Sandy raced back down to the kitchen. Emma could hear her shouting into the phone, then her footfall as she double paced the stairs again.

"Ambulance is coming Emma. You'll be fine. Don't worry. I'll be with you."

Seven minutes later they heard the siren as it turned off the highway.

"Be careful," Sandy said as the men negotiated the stairs with Emma tucked into the stretcher.

"We've done this before love. Just give us some room."

Rob apologised for the steepness of the driveway.

"Can I come with her?" Sandy said. "I'm her sister."

The trip to the hospital took twelve minutes and Emma went straight through the emergency waiting room and into a cubicle. Sandy complained when the doctor told her to wait outside. "I'll be right here," she whispered as she let go of Emma's hand and began to pace the floor.

Fifteen minutes later, the murmuring behind the curtain ceased and the doctor emerged, followed by the nurse. Sandy pulled a plastic chair alongside the bed. She didn't have to ask. She took hold of Emma's hand and began to stroke the back of her palm.

"I've lost my baby."

Sandy nodded and bit into her lip. When Emma cradled her belly and began to sway as a mother might, consoling a child, Sandy pitched forward, her arms encircling Emma, holding her until she stilled.

"Oh Sand. I really wanted to be a mother."

"I know you did." She wiped Emma's eyes then her own on the sleeve of her blouse.

"I had it all worked out."

"And you would have been brilliant." Sandy fastened the pearl buttons on Emma's nightie.

"Do you think it's punishment? For the abortion?" Emma asked.

Sandy slumped into the chair. "That's the second stupid idea you've had today. Should I buy you a hair shirt?"

"A what?"

"Religious fanatics used to wear them to punish themselves."

"No thanks."

"Then get that idea right out of your head."

"They're going to do it this afternoon. A curette."

"Sooner the better, eh?"

"I can probably go home tomorrow."

"Only if you feel strong enough."

"I don't want Mum to know. Can I come to your place?"

"Where else do you think you're going? I'll call work and the club. Make something up."

They heard the march of footsteps and the nurse reappeared. "We need to get Mrs Emery prepped. You'll have to leave dear."

"See you kiddo. Chin up." Sandy kissed Emma's brow.

"See you Sand."

"Love you Emm."

"Love you too."

The nurse cleared her throat. Sandy paused. "I'll be back tonight, okay? I'll bring some clothes." She turned to go then inclined her head and added as an afterthought, "Some Darrel Lea?"

"Swiss caramels?" Emma attempted a smile.

"Of course."

Rob was waiting at the front entrance and put his arm around his wife as they walked to the car in lockstep. "You know she's better off, don't you?"

"Doesn't stop me feeling sad Rob."

As he unlocked her door, Sandy rummaged in her handbag. "God, where are my tissues?"

"Here, you'll never find them in there." Sandy blew into the man-sized handkerchief.

"Come here Babe," he said, leaning his broad back against the side of the car, his arms stretched wide. She burrowed into his chest and he stroked her hair.

"She's pretty tough you know. She'll be fine."

"Yep. She'll be fine. Eventually." She touched her lips to his.

"Home?" He held the door open.

"Yes please."

Sandy adjusted the rear-view mirror. "Oh God, I'm a mess." She wiped the mascara from under her eyes with Rob's handkerchief. "Know what," she said as he righted the mirror, "I think it was Brad's baby."

"You said she didn't know whose it was."

"I can tell when she's trying to cover something up. She's hopeless, her voice gets really high pitched."

"Wouldn't she tell you?"

"And I'd tell you and then she'd have to manage both of us. I mean we'd want to have a piece of him. No, she needed to keep it quiet, for the baby's sake."

"Bloody hell. What a mess. Definitely better this way."

33

Just You and Me Again

ALL MORNING, JEWEL STAYED IN her bedroom and ignored the constant ringing of the telephone in the hallway. Giving in to hunger pangs, she made her way to the kitchen. It rang as she walked past. She grabbed the receiver with the intention of hanging up then leaving it off the hook when she heard the unmistakeable sound of Lee's voice.

"Jewel, are you there?"

"Yes, I'm here," she said with a deep sigh.

"Thank God. I was starting to get worried. Where have you been? I've been trying to call you for ages."

"Sorry, Lee."

"Busy planning the wedding I guess."

"Of course. The wedding."

"Darling, well anyway, I've got some wonderful news." Lee's high-pitched voice reverberated along the phone line. "I'll be over in half an hour, got to tell you in person."

"Half an hour?"

"I'll pick us up something scrumptious for morning tea. So excited!" she said and left Jewel listening to a dial tone.

An ugly, puffed-up face stared back at her from the hall mirror. Just like Sam's ego, she thought. *Half an hour,* she mumbled then force marched herself back up the stairs to the bedroom, slumped down onto the dressing table stool and zipped open her make-up bag. A few minutes and several layers of cover-up later, the blotches were disguised. Her eyeballs looked as if a child had taken to them with a red pen. An old bottle of Murine in the bathroom cabinet faded the scrawl to a rose pink. Would have to do, she decided as the doorbell rang.

"Hiya!" Lee bounced through the door, turned to Jewel and narrowed her eyes. "You okay?"

Jewel turned aside and set off down the hallway before Lee could continue her interrogation. Any hint of compassion would liberate a stream of tears that were banking up like floodwaters behind a dammed-up wall of emotions.

"Coffee or tea?" she asked biting her lip.

"Tea please." A quietened Lee chose a cake plate from the dresser. "Want me to do the honours?" she said, knife in hand.

"Sure. Looks delicious."

"Got it from the new shop in that centre near the drive-in."

Jewel retrieved the kettle to avoid scrutiny and began to fill the teapot. "Go on, tell me the news." It was clear that Lee was gagging.

"Well," she said with renewed vigour, "it's because of the funeral."

"The Thompson's son?"

"Yes." Lee took a bite of cake. "Terribly sad. Mmm, this is good. Freshly made this morning they said."

"The news, Lee?" Jewel said, balancing the strainer as she filled the cups. The tea was watery, but Lee wouldn't notice.

"Let me tell you," she said, leaning forward, "I thought John's father was going to take off after the casket when it started to move. Anyway," she said licking her sticky fingers, "when he lunged after it, Sam kind of jumped up and pulled the poor man back to his seat." She paused. "You're not eating your cake, Jewel?"

"Sorry." She didn't like Victoria sponge at the best of times.

"Well, Sam was really quiet on the way home in the car," Lee paused to take another bite, "told me to leave him in peace, now I come to think of it. Anyway, when he got out of the car he went straight to his den. 'Nothing unusual about that,' I hear you say."

Jewel blew on her tea and sipped it tentatively, eyes downcast.

"I took a couple of my pills, went to bed and the next morning – no Sam." Lee extended her arms, palms turned upwards and waited.

Jewel obliged. "So, where was he?"

"Still in his den. Hadn't come to bed all night. I mean usually he makes it up the stairs at some point, and yes, I also wonder how he does it when he's got a belly full." She paused to eye the cake. "Mind if I have another slice? Won't leave much for you and Derek later on."

Jewel placed a hefty portion on Lee's plate and topped up her tea.

"Well, I went downstairs and there he was, sound asleep in his rocker-recliner. I woke him up and do you know I believe he'd been crying. Sam! Can you imagine that?"

"Not in a million years."

"Anyway, the long and the short of it is, I can't remember exactly what he said, something about having an epiphany."

"Really?" Jewel's interest was aroused.

"You won't believe this but he's had a change of heart about Paul." Lee placed her cup in the saucer and allowed her wrist to go limp. "About, you know, how he is."

"Because of the funeral?"

"Well, yes. You know how they say, 'good things come from bad'? It seems when the dear man saw John's father fall apart, he realised how lucky he was to have a son, alive." Lee cleared her throat. "Even if he is how he is."

"I am happy for you Lee."

"Sam got on the phone to England that morning – do you know how much that costs? He told Paul he was welcome home any time. Of course, I called Carol straight away. Guess what? Everything's forgiven. My darling daughter and her husband are coming over next week for dinner.

Lee struck a pose that reminded Jewel of the clowns at the Easter Show, their tilted heads turning from side to side, waiting for someone to drop a ping pong ball into the gaping mouths. "Happy families!"

"That's wonderful. Really is Lee." The balls never did roll into the right number, Jewel recalled.

Lee bit into her cake and cream oozed from the side and into her lap.

Jewel handed her the dishcloth.

"What about you?" Lee said, dabbing at the stain. "What's happening with the wedding?"

"Well, Derek's agreed. You knew that." She took a deep breath. "Anyway, seems we might have to bring it forward."

Lee raised an eyebrow, "You mean Sal's..."

"Oh no!" Jewel was emphatic. "Not that!"

"Oh, just can't wait I guess. Too much in love?" Lee asked.

"They're going away." Jewel clenched her hands between her thighs to stop them shaking.

"Their honeymoon?"

"No, for good."

"Where to?"

"Canada."

"Pardon?"

"They're going to live in Canada."

"What, with polar bears and ice?"

"It's not all like that Lee."

"What on earth are they going to Canada for?"

Jewel let out a long sigh. "Brad says teachers earn about three times the money in Canada that they earn here."

"Oh yes, he wasn't a good catch money-wise, either." Lee walked to the sink and rinsed out the dishcloth. "How far away is Canada?"

"Seven thousand, seven hundred and fifty-seven miles to Vancouver."

"Oh dear. But they'll come back?"

"Not till after they save the money for a house."

"There you are. Not so bad. Paul's been away a couple of years and it's just flown."

"Lee, how would you feel if Carol was seven thousand miles away?"

"I know, Jewel, dear. It will be hard. What about Derek?"

"He'll miss Sal, of course."

"But he let them get married early?"

"Well, he'd already agreed and they have to be married for Sal to stay in Canada."

"It's all happening so fast. Have you bought your outfit?"

"No."

"I know just the place. Gorgeous little boutique in the city. And what about the florist, I've got someone who'd be perfect."

"Lee, I really don't have the energy at the moment. Can we talk about it another time?"

"Sure we can. Just thought it would be so exciting. I remember when Carol was getting married, the fun we had shop...."

"Lee, not today. Please, I've got a splitting head."

"Sorry, I'll go then, let you rest."

"And take the cake, Lee. It'll only go to waste."

"Sure? I brought it for you. You don't want me to stay, talk things over?"

"Lee, I'm sure. Please, you take the cake."

"I'll let myself out then. You have a lie down." She patted Jewel's shoulder as she passed by. "Call you tomorrow."

When she heard the door close, Jewel leaned onto the kitchen bench and rested her head on her arms. She felt so tired. Her eyes closed and she dozed. The sound of Derek's car registered in her subconscious but she dismissed it. Much too early for him to be home. The rumble of the garage door made her straighten up.

"Morning," he said as he strode towards her, planting a kiss on her cheek.

The jauntiness of his entry was confusing. "What's going on? How come you're home?"

"No reason. Can't a fellow call in for a cuppa without getting the third degree?"

"Derek you've never called in for a cuppa. If nothing's wrong, why are you here?"

"That tea still hot?"

"No, I'll make you another while you tell me what this is about."

"I've been worried about you Jewel."

"I'm all right. You know I'll perk up."

"Darling, I can't abide seeing you like this."

"I can't help but think, if I hadn't gone along with them, if I'd been strong like you wanted and stood up to them, maybe they would never have got this far."

"We can't change it Sweetheart. We did what we thought best at the time."

"I suppose."

"Time to take a different tack. Agreed?"

"What does that mean? Since we're not in a sailing boat."

"It means, I'm going to find a positive in this."

"Good luck."

"You know we've been married twenty years next year?"

"That long!"

"Put that teapot down and come here." Derek stood up, wrapped his arms around his wife and kissed her brow. "Doesn't seem long to me."

"This last year has been the longest."

"But that battle's over Sweetheart. And with what this wedding is going to cost me, I think I may as well enjoy it."

"I'm having trouble getting excited about it at all."

"Then how about this for an idea. What say you and I plan a little trip?"

"Where to?"

"Canada. And then a cruise to Alaska." Derek reached into his briefcase and took out a brochure. "Called into the travel agent's this morning."

"You're kidding?"

"Brad starts in the April semester, so I thought we'd go middle of June, spend a bit of time with Sal while he's working, then maybe the four of us could take a little holiday up north together in the school holidays."

"Really?"

"Why not? Twentieth anniversary celebration. No sooner will you have recovered from the wedding than you can start preparing for the trip." Derek reached across and took Jewel's hand. "Darling, don't start crying, I thought this would make you happy."

"It does."

"Then give me a smile."

"You're such a lovely man, you know," she said stroking his cheek.

"And I get to check up on you-know-who at the same time."

"And you're also an honest man," she said, ruffling his hair.

"You agree then?"

"Hard not to." Jewel picked up the brochure. "It does sound exciting. Look, Darling, a polar bear. Lee was right after all."

"She was here this morning?" Derek glanced at the plates in the draining rack.

"Seems Sam has had a change of heart about Paul."

"Really? Well, that's good news. And unexpected."

"I'm more interested in your change of heart."

"Let's just say I'm preparing for a number of contingencies."

"Which are?"

"If Sal and Brad do make a go of it, we want to be part of their lives. You've always said that and you're right."

"Yes, what else?"

"And if by chance it doesn't work out, I want Sal to know that we support her and she can come back here anytime, where she's safe."

Jewel's shoulders relaxed and she let out a loud sigh. "So, if her marriage doesn't work, she'll be miserable, then we'll be happy because we'll have Sal back? Sad isn't it."

Derek came up behind his wife and wrapped her in his arms. He nibbled her ear lobe then whispered, "Just life Darling. What say we go and have some lunch at the beach."

"Not going to work?" she said turning to face him.

"Taking the day off to be with my wife."

"Guess I'd better get dolled up before you change your mind."

"Just you and me again Jewel." He stretched his arms to the ceiling.

"Seems so."

"Remember what that was like?" he asked, patting her bottom as she walked by.

The travel agent had been Derek's second appointment that morning. The first was to his doctor who he had been avoiding. The chest pains had changed his mind. His Doctor reprimanded him for not taking Jewel's advice to get a check-up some months before.

When he heard the tap running in the upstairs bathroom, Derek took the packet of pills from his pocket and popped one under his tongue. No need to worry her unduly. Things would work out – one way or another.

34

The Right Decision

"OKAY. I'M OFF. SOMEONE'S GOT to earn some money." Sandy placed a kiss on Emma's cheek. "You sure you're strong enough to go home tonight? You know you can stay as long as you like."

"Truly, I'm fine." Emma draped the tea towel over the oven door handle and turned to Sandy. "You and Rob have been great. I couldn't have managed without you both."

"Our pleasure Emm. Make sure you rest today. We'll be back about six." Sandy headed into the garage where Rob was waiting, engine running.

"I'll put the roast in about four-thirty so we can eat before we leave," Emma called after her.

"Perfect," Sandy shouted over the noise of the car engine.

Emma watched the ute drive away, topped up her tea and wondered what she would do with the rest of the day. She was drawn to the courtyard where shafts of morning sunlight wove their way between fluttering gum leaves. She found the block of stone that she had used as a seat while she had waited for Sandy to come home from work. Many months ago now, but it felt like years. It was the day she was retrenched. The week after Brad left her.

With a mug of tea balanced on her knee Emma rested her head against the bricks. They had not yet lost their overnight chill. Her eyes closed as she turned her face skywards to garner the warmth of the sun's rays.

She never did have to tell her mum about the baby. Sad in a way, Emma knew she really wanted a grandchild. There was a story that came back to her in that moment from years ago, about a Scotsman called Bill Black. Her mother spoke fondly of him; a lean blonde boy, of average looks who had wanted to marry her mother. 'A good, solid man', she'd said. Then Emma's father came along and swept her off her feet with his swarthy good looks and confident swagger and Bill was soon out of the picture. Her mother confessed that she had often wondered how much easier life would have been if she had married Bill Black.

Is Greg my Bill Black? Emma wondered. He is a good man, she was sure of it. Recently he had spoken about his dad. They had always been close it seems, his mum dying when he was so young. Mostly he spoke about the good times, before his father got sick and occasionally of the months leading up to his father's death, his sense of humour that never failed him. The week before he died, Greg was putting his dad to bed. Managed to get him out of his wheelchair and had him resting on his walker. Greg patted the edge of the bed and said, "Dad, put your bottom here."

"Bit hard when it's attached to me legs," he replied.

That recollection made Emma laugh as she did the first time Greg told her the story. She cringed as she recalled her past behaviour towards Greg, her ignorant criticism of his appearance and her irritation at the questions he asked. She thought he was prying when all along it was concern for her wellbeing.

Her bare legs were stretched out in an offering to the sun. She inspected her nails. The cuticles were smooth and intact. A lot had changed. Her mind was no longer consumed by fantasies about Brad and Sally. It was getting easier. With this thought in her mind she stretched her arms wide, raised her head and sighed into the sunlight.

Nearly eleven, according to her watch. A shower now, then an afternoon spent reading on the couch. Bliss. When she had finished scouring Sandy's bookshelf and found nothing of interest, she decided to make herself lunch then take a walk. It was after one when she set off along the straight, narrow footpath, which was not unlike the traditional direction she had followed in the first twenty-one years of her life. Now there were so many roads to follow.

For the first time ever, she had a healthy bank account and relished the sense of security and freedom of choice it afforded. However, working four nights a week to supplement the meagre salary of a secretary was a short-term option at best. She needed to earn more money, longer term, to retain her independence and give herself security for the future.

When she reached the end of the road, she doubled back through the bush. The house was quiet and peaceful and the walk had tired her. She lay on the lounge and must have dozed off because it was nearly four o'clock when she woke, just in time to prepare dinner. As she tied the apron around her waist she looked down at her shrunken belly and was overcome by a moment of deep regret and sorrow.

The phone rang.

"How's your day been?"

"Good, Sand."

"Everything all right?"

"Yep. Feel fine honestly. Just about to shell the peas."

"Okay, see you soon."

As Rob's car drove into the garage, Emma took the lamb and potatoes from the oven.

"God that smells good," Sandy said, as she came up the stairs. Emma was stirring flour into the pan juices. "Ten minutes, okay?"

"You want a job?" Sandy asked, breaking a piece of meat from the shank.

"I think I could get used to being a lady of leisure."

"You look nice Emm. I always liked that red dress."

"Sick of looking like a dag. How was your day?"

"Rotten. End of month invoices. I'll get changed. Rob, can you open some wine?" Sandy called as she walked to the bedroom.

At quarter past seven they cleared the table, Sandy washed and Emma wiped. "I'll get my bag," she said as she put away the last of the cutlery.

"Best dinner, Emm." Rob said as he came down the stairs. "Never ate so well."

Sandy threw a dishcloth and hit him on the side of the face. "That's why you look so underfed is it?"

"I'll put it in the car," Rob said scooping up Emma's bag. "You know I'm happy to drive you both."

"No, we're fine Darling," Sandy answered and signalled for him to throw her the car keys. "Have a little chat on the way."

"Take it slow then," Rob said.

Sandy blew him a kiss. "So, where to from here, Emm?" she asked as the car pulled onto the roadway.

"Rose Bay please driver," Emma replied, straight faced.

"You know what I mean. Things have changed."

"I know, and I've thought about it a lot."

"Okay, give it to me."

"Maybe I'll go to Uni."

"I think I said this to Ros – but, what on earth for?"

"I need qualifications, to get a better job, support myself properly."

"Right."

"Sand, you ever looked in the paper? The only jobs in the women's section are secretarial, receptionist, nursing and teaching. All the well-paid jobs are in the men's section."

"So, you're going to change the world?"

"No. Just me."

"What about Greg?"

"Why do I have to choose?"

"Holy crap." Sandy burst out laughing. "And I thought you were reading the Woman's Weekly the last couple of days and there you were planning the rest of your life ."

"Watch the road Sand."

"I am. Just don't make any hasty decisions. You've been through a lot. What about giving yourself a break from the night job?"

"I thought you said I shouldn't make any hasty decisions."

The car slowed as they approached Emma's flat. "Isn't that Greg?" Sandy asked.

"Where?"

"There, near the chocolate shop."

Emma focused on the solitary figure, hands in pockets on the other side of the road, looking towards them.

"Could be," she agreed. "Fancy that."

"What did you say to him?"

"I kept it vague. Said it was women's troubles. That shut him up."

"I never told him, you know, about the baby."

"I know. Now you don't have to."

"I was going to when we were just friends but then things changed and I didn't want to spoil it."

"It doesn't matter anymore Emma. This is a new start for you."

"I suppose so."

"Listen Emm, you've got a lot going on. Take your time to decide what you want to do."

"Sure Sand."

"But remember, he won't wait around forever. Ring me in the morning, okay."

Emma stood on the kerbside and waved as Sandy accelerated, with three sharp bursts of the horn, along Old South Head Road. She turned towards Greg and waved. He indicated she should stay where she was. They stood facing each other, waiting for the lights to change. He crossed the road in several long confident strides. His demeanour was one of self-assurance without a hint of cockiness. As he got closer, Emma saw his smile was broad. There was tenderness and warmth in his eyes.

"You don't mind me coming?"

"No, not at all."

"He brushed her cheek with the back of his hand. "Just wanted to make sure you were okay."

"Thanks, I'm good."

"I'll carry this up the stairs for you," he said taking hold of her bag.

"Greg, you know what I'd really like?"

"No, what?"

"A walk. Before it gets dark. Just put my bag inside the door."

"Yeah, sure. Whatever you want. Around the Bay?"

"Perfect."

"You okay in those shoes?"

Emma balanced on one leg and held the other out for inspection. She turned her foot to the side to show the four-inch heel and ankle strap to best advantage. "Greg, I could dance till midnight in these shoes."

"Sounds good to me, but maybe not tonight." He took her arm and tucked it through his. "Just in case," he said.

"So, what's been happening?" she asked.

"Got a new client. A big one."

"Wow, Mr Successful. Well done."

"The boss hinted at another wage rise."

"Congratulations."

At the side of the shops they cut down an alley-way that led onto the shoreline. A cool, gentle breeze greeted them as they turned the corner.

"You cold Emma? Here." He had his camel wool jacket around her shoulders before she could reply.

"Nice coat."

"This lady in David Jones helps me choose."

"She's doing a good job."

"Maybe you'd like to apply?"

"Stiff competition."

"I need a new suit. We could go shopping on Saturday morning.

Maybe you'd like something for yourself. Oh, I forgot. Bought these while I was waiting." He handed her a small white paper bag tied with a red bow.

"Remembered you like caramels."

"Thank you," she smiled. "Want one?"

"No. Bit hard to talk."

They strolled to the end of the walkway then doubled back. Emma was aware of a feeling of lightness and contentment, unique to the moments she spent with Greg.

"I think that's enough for you today. Till Saturday then?"

"Sounds fun."

They remained facing each other for longer than was comfortable.

"Bye then."

"Emma." He took hold of both of her hands. "Emma." He cleared his throat and stood up straight. "Do you think? Well do you think we could?"

"What?"

"Go out?"

"We've been doing that, haven't we?"

"I mean properly, officially. You must know I've been very fond of you for a long time." Emma began to respond but Greg touched his fingertips to her lips. "No, don't say anything. I know you don't love me and that's okay, for now."

"I guess I'm still a bit muddled." She looked at their hands, fingers entwined. "But I love being with you. That's important, don't you think?"

"Yes, it's a good start. Now come here." He held her and kissed her lips tenderly. When he pulled away Emma still had her eyes closed.

"Bye," he whispered.

Slowly, she opened her eyes and watched him walk to the kerb. He didn't wait for the lights to turn green but bounded between traffic then turned around when he reached the other side, did a little jig and waved.

Emma closed the door to the flat and picked up a bulky envelope that had been pushed through the letterbox. It was addressed to her.

She hurried up the stairs and paused in the doorway of her bedroom. A silvery shaft of moonlight was reflected from the dressing table mirror onto the opposite wall. *Not such a bad little hideaway*, she thought to herself. Holding onto the envelope, she flopped onto her bed and with her thumbnail tore open the seal. It had been months since she sent in the application and it had completely slipped her mind. Her fingers traced the gold embossing on the midnight blue front cover. Underneath the coat of arms was the word 'Passport'. She undressed hastily, threw her clothes into the corner, pulled down the blankets, jumped into bed and turned to the first page.

The Governor-General, Paul Hasluck, requested all those whom it may concern to allow her to pass freely without let or hindrance. Furthermore, he asked that she be afforded every assistance and protection of which she may stand in need. Maybe it was the reassurance that Mr. Hasluck was looking out for her that allowed her to fall asleep immediately.

She woke in the middle of the night and her hand crept under her pillow to touch the passport. It was then she remembered images from her dream.

One moment she was standing on the deck of what appeared to be an ocean liner. Her head spun as she looked over the side to a labyrinth of ancient and unfamiliar cobblestoned streets far below. The sensation of vertigo was so real, it woke her briefly. When she dropped off to sleep once more, the tableau of images returned and she saw herself, wearing a black robe and a mortarboard with a tassel. She stood alone on the stage from where she spotted a man in the front of the vast auditorium applauding, with the biggest grin on his face.

She stirred and looked at her watch. It was still too early to get up, four-twenty to be precise, so she rolled onto her side and wrapped her arms around her spare pillow. Who was the elusive man in her dream? Probably Greg, who would always be there for her, give her the devotion and security she craved. So why couldn't she see his face? She shut her eyes tightly in an attempt to recall the image that she knew was there, somewhere, but succeeded only in drifting off to sleep.

Perhaps it was the clarity that comes in the still hours of early morning, for as her consciousness resurfaced, stirred by the sound of the cockatiels in the jacaranda tree next door, the face revealed itself to Emma. Saying his name gave the image substance, "Brad."

She threw back the blankets, and in an effort to ground herself, found the floor with her feet and sat for a moment holding onto the bed. The flat was quiet and a glance at her watch confirmed that the morning was well advanced and the phone call to Sandy well overdue.

Ten minutes later, she was standing in the phone box on the corner. Sandy answered after two rings.

"Thank God, I was getting worried. You okay?"

"Yeah, sorry Sand. I'm fine. Had a few niggly pains. Nothing to worry about."

"Did you sleep all right?"

"Sort of." Emma cleared her throat. "Sand, can I ask you something?"

"Sure. You're at it early."

"Do you think dreams mean anything?"

"Well last time I looked at my psychology notes…nah, they're all crap. Why do you want to know?"

"No reason, just wondering."

"You're sure you're okay? Do you want us to come when we finish work?"

"I'm okay, and no thanks."

"Long day ahead. What are you going to do?" Sandy wondered if the line had gone dead but realised she could hear traffic noise on the end of the phone. "Emma, are you there?"

"Yes, I'm here."

"So, what have you got planned?"

"Today or the rest of my life?"

"Let's start with today?"

"I think I'll rest up, do a bit of thinking."

"Good idea, the rest up that is. Emma, I've got to get back to work. Let me know about the rest of your life when you work it out."

"Okay Sand. Give my love to Rob."

When Emma left the phone box, she decided to walk to the bay. The sky was cloudless and the blue of the water merged into the skyline. The rest of her life. There were so many possibilities. She felt the sun on her back as a physical weight, not unlike the burden of making the right decision.

A seagull landed at her feet and strutted around looking for food. It squawked in disappointment when she stood up suddenly and shooed it away along with the notion that she needed to make a choice. It had been that way for her mother but did it have to be for her? Perhaps not.

She set off to walk the length of the foreshore. As her pace quickened and her stride lengthened it became as clear to her as the crystal water lapping the seawall, that she need not choose between marriage, family, study, career or travel. As she turned to make her way back, Emma began to believe she could have them all.

www.ingramcontent.com/pod-product-compliance
Lightning Source LLC
Chambersburg PA
CBHW050259010526
44107CB00055B/2095